D1065044

The Complete Guide to Offshore Money Havens

How to Make Millions, Protect Your Privacy, and Legally Avoid Taxes— Whether Your Net Worth Is $100 or $100 Million

REVISED AND UPDATED

Jerome Schneider

PRIMA PUBLISHING

This book is about the profit, privacy, tax, and asset protection benefits available through offshore money havens. To get started, the author offers financial advice through workshops and one-on-one private consultation. For more information, Mr. Schneider invites you to contact him through his office in Vancouver, B.C. Canada at (604) 682-4000 or fax (604) 682-7700.

Investment decisions have certain inherent risks. Prima therefore disclaims any warranties or representations, whether express or implied, concerning the accuracy or completeness of the information or advice contained in this book. Any investment a reader may make based on such information is at the reader's sole risk. You should carefully research or consult a qualified financial advisor before making any particular investment. The publisher has no affiliation with or participation in any workshops or consultation provided by the author.

The names of the individuals referred to in this book have been changed in order to preserve their privacy.

Library of Congress Cataloging-in-Publication Data on file.
ISBN 0-7615-0996-8

97 98 99 00 01 HH 10 9 8 7 6 5 4 3 2 1

Printed in the United States of America

How to Order
Single copies may be ordered from Prima Publishing, P.O. Box 1260BK, Rocklin, CA 95677; telephone (916) 632-4400. Quantity discounts are also available. On your letterhead, include information concerning the intended use of the books and the number of books you wish to purchase.

Visit us online at http://www.primapublishing.com

Contents

ACKNOWLEDGMENTS

This book was written with the encouragement and constructive comments of many people. I owe a debt of gratitude to the many business associates and colleagues who suggested that it be written. The members of my personal staff have earned a special thanks. In particular, I wish to express my appreciation to Max Benavidez and Kate Vozoff, Martha Sandino, and Brenda Nichols for their editorial guidance. I must also thank Howard Fisher and William Norman for their legal insights into matters both taxing and complex. Finally, but most important, I wish to thank Jaycee Cooper for her continued support and patience.

INTRODUCTION

History repeats itself in interesting ways. . . .

Imagine, for a moment, that the year is 1912, and the entire Western world is in love with its own technological know-how. Among the most cosmopolitan and affluent sophisticates of the day, there is a new and almost irresistible sensation: a not-to-be-missed, once-in-a-lifetime opportunity to take the most luxurious sea voyage ever envisioned. A first-class ticket on the ultramodern cruise ship promises you the most fabulous trans-Atlantic journey in history. So, of course, you purchase that ticket; and from the instant you walk on board, your every need is met without delay. Your cabin is spacious and beautiful: a wood-lined haven of elegance. Your meals are exquisite and your evenings are filled with the chatter of urbane conversation and ballroom dancing. What could possibly go wrong in a world so divine?

This scenario, of course, describes the maiden voyage of the *Titanic,* just before the vessel plunged into the

Atlantic Ocean, killing more than two-thirds of the people onboard and shattering the industrial world's deep sense of infallibility.

The bittersweet image of that ill-fated cruise haunts me as I write the introduction to the fourth edition of this book. I am struck by the disturbing similarities between the *Titanic's* apparent security and America's presumed stability. As Americans, we are still utterly enamored with our own past achievements. We are still convinced that we lead the world. We still see ourselves as "the last best hope for humankind." Like the *Titanic's* complacent voyagers, who wined and dined in lush state rooms even while frigid waters flooded the decks below, we allow ourselves to be lulled into passivity by the veneer of opulence. Like them, many of us cling to the illusion of security, even as we are slowly sinking. And just as those aboard the *Titanic* were ultimately lost in the dark, unforgiving waters off the coast of Newfoundland, I suspect that many Americans will be lost in the ruins of an economic disaster that looms just ahead.

The 1996 elections made Bill Clinton the last U.S. president of the twentieth century. Like the cheery-faced captain who welcomed passengers aboard the doomed *Titanic,* Clinton greeted his constituents on the eve of his second presidential victory with happy assurances that they have nothing to fear. The economy is sound, he assured us. The deficit is down. Employment is up. The country is less divided than it has been in a very long time.

Yet as I collected my research for this edition, as I conferred with colleagues and sought input from those I admire, as I spoke at conferences and chatted with people after my presentations, one thing became unmistakably clear: There is tremendous anxiety below the surface in America. People are scared, and for good reason. They have begun to recognize Clinton's slick sleight of hand. His budgetary shell games, mass economic deception, and the country's feeble financial growth are no longer able to mask the rank inability of government to reverse more than twenty years of economic decline. The truth is clear if unnerving: Bill Clinton's *Titanic* is heading for a run-in with the tallest, sharpest, fiercest economic icebergs the financial world has ever seen. Disaster is inevitable. Passengers aboard the *Titanic* never knew what hit them. And unless you do something significant and do it quickly, you probably won't know what hit you.

But you don't have to be a victim. There are ways to save yourself and those you love. In a step-by-step plan, I will show you how to have an economic life raft ready and inflated for any disaster. Frankly, our domestic monetary system has long ago seen its heyday. Never again (at least in our lifetime) will it be able to offer the exciting and lucrative investment opportunities that already exist in any number of foreign financial centers. By following my advice, you can circumvent the limits of the U.S. market and be among the happy few who can sit back ten years from now and watch the vagaries of the domestic economy without sweating bullets. Why? Because your money will be safely protected and working for you in offshore havens that offer handsome profits,

By following my advice, you can circumvent the limits of the U.S. market and be among the happy few who can sit back ten years from now and watch the vagaries of the domestic economy without sweating bullets. Why? Because your money will be safely protected and working for you in offshore havens that offer handsome profits, genuine tax protection, and an unparalleled level of financial privacy.

genuine tax protection, and an unparalleled level of financial privacy.

And what if my dire predictions are wrong? What if the U.S. economy somehow manages to limp along for another decade or even two with erratic ups and downs? Even then, you can still be part of the game because the basic components of an international portfolio allow you to make money within the domestic market. There's nothing about offshore finance that precludes you from onshore profit-making. It's the domestic market that limits you. Legal requirements and bureaucratic red tape have so bogged down our monetary system that you can no longer make and maintain sizable profits abroad. So making a move into the global arena simply gives you a larger playing field, a chance to earn money here, there, anywhere.

My recommendation is to be ready because America's economy *is* slowing down. In the third quarter of 1996, economic growth slowed to an anemic 2.2 percent. I am convinced that the last three years of this century will be filled with grim economic news. Some economists are even predicting a "quiet" depression before the year 2000. A depression is a response of free markets to economic imbalance. A "quiet" depression is a less extreme response, but more than a recession.

In his famous book entitled *America's Great Depression,* Murray Rothbard argues that the depression of the 1930s was not caused by the stock market crash or by a cut in the money supply, but because of a foolish overexpansion of credit during the 1920s. His analysis is absolutely correct. In the years preceding the crash, individuals and businesses extended themselves far beyond their means. And I would argue that exactly the same overextension has taken place in recent years. Today's Wall Street aficionados talk about the great bull market out there, with the Dow percolating between 6,000 and 7,000. Yet they forget to mention that buying shares with borrowed money is at an all-time high.

Personal debt is soaring, too. Since 1992, when Clinton was first elected, Americans have increased their personal debt load by 50 percent. In fact, total consumer debt is now at $1.2 trillion! That is four times more money than Americans aggregately save per year. The country is in a borrowing craze. I recently spoke with one upper-income professional who has saddled himself with so much credit card debt that it will take him twenty years to pay it off! And what did he purchase with this make-believe, plastic money? Extravagant trips to the Far East? Precious gemstones for his wife? A mansion along the oceanfront? No. He spent the money to pay bills: monthly telephone, water, and power costs, even groceries. This is a guy who makes over $150,000 a year and still can't meet his most basic expenses. He's among the hardest and most unfairly hit of all Americans: the hardworking affluent who have been forced to shoulder the burden for the economic ineptitude of past policymakers and a desperate attempt by the Clinton administration to correct an intractable problem.

But let me give Clinton some credit, he's an excellent campaigner. He can smooth talk with the best of them. Nevertheless, many of the country's economic ills are exacerbated by the policies of his first term. He gave us the biggest tax increase in American history. Although President Bush had paved the way—by raising the top-bracket tax rate to 31 percent—Clinton was not happy with just a hungry tax system. He wanted a voracious one! In 1993, he demanded 39.6 percent of every income dollar earned by professional America. He thinks anyone who grosses more than $75,000 per year is rich! In 1997, the top-bracket tax rate still stands at that 40 percent mark, but who knows what will happen during Clinton's second term.

Clinton also wants to ensure that Uncle Sam collects all of the officially mandated tax on American income, so he doubled the number of IRS auditors. Currently, one out of every ten federal employees (excluding defense-related workers) has a desk within the halls of the IRS. Frightening, isn't it? From a purely bureaucratic perspective, Clinton's plan has worked. Due to the extra auditors, the government has collected record-breaking amounts of income tax—an extra $20 billion in 1995 alone.

That's not all, of course. U.S. corporate profits have headed due south. Third-quarter earnings for 1996 were the weakest in four years. During Clinton's watch income stagnation has hit American families with a vengeance. Indeed, even as his policies have led to a fall in family income, he has demanded higher and higher income taxes from everyone but the working poor.

Under the Clinton administration, we have also seen a staggering rise in Social Security and sales tax rates. According to respected economist Ravi Batra, that increase was really just a hidden and direct tax on income. The hike, he says, along with a simultaneous jump in self-employment taxes, "practically broke the back of entrepreneurs" in the 1990s. "In addition to paying a tax of 7.65 percent on the wages of workers they hired, they had to part with a self-employment tax of 15.3 percent on [their] own income. Furthermore, they were obligated to pay the regular income tax on their profit." Batra concludes that the American entrepreneur—the lifeblood of all economic growth in the U.S. economy—is literally being bled dry by a vampire tax system. And, he insists, the economic consequence will be a downturn unlike anything seen in the last twenty-five years.

I first wrote (and periodically update) this book to help readers escape the effects of this economic wreckage. I write for people like Floyd Sutcliff, a pistachio farmer originally from California's agriculturally fertile Central Valley. Floyd is a real old-fashioned American. In fact, with his ambling walk and masculine presence, he reminds me of John Wayne. One of the most interesting things about Floyd is that up until the early 1990s, he had an abiding faith in the U.S. economy. In fact, he was almost religious in his passion for the American way of

Currently, one out of every ten federal employees (excluding defense-related workers) has a desk within the halls of the IRS. Frightening, isn't it? From a purely bureaucratic perspective, Clinton's plan has worked. Due to the extra auditors, the government has collected record-breaking amounts of income tax—an extra $20 billion in 1995 alone.

life. Still, Floyd is nobody's fool, and at some point he clearly saw the writing on the wall. Floyd's profits were down. They'd been diminishing gradually over time, and all projections indicated continued decline. Maybe that's partly why he lost his faith in America. Floyd no longer believed in the federal government's ability to govern. He was dismayed by the overall failure of Washington to produce a balanced budget. The country's continued fiscal irresponsibility had thoroughly eroded the value of the dollar, and Floyd felt bankruptcy snapping at his heels. "And that's a damn shame," he barked out at our initial meeting. "Hell, I used to be rich."

It didn't take much effort to convince Floyd that he should diversify his assets and get a hefty chunk of them offshore. Shortly after we met at one of my seminars, he sold two of his three farms and, to top it all off, moved to Canada. This born and bred all-American took his money and his faith up north where he thought both would be better appreciated and protected. "This isn't the America I used to know," Floyd once told me. So rather than wait for some fantasy turnaround by trickster politicians, he chose to become what I call "an international man." That was four years ago.

Today, from his Canadian home office, Floyd manages an offshore financial portfolio that includes partnerships with two Middle Eastern pistachio farmers, a small auto parts distributorship throughout eastern Europe, and a chain of bed-and-breakfast-style hotels in British Columbia. Without outrageous taxation or government's economic bungling, he's making much more money than he ever could here in the United States.

I also write for people like my client Dan Houssman, a soft-spoken techno-whiz with the mental speed of light. When Dan was still in college on the East Coast he first developed software for downloading fine-art images off the Internet. His plan was to then collect those images on CD-ROMs and market them internationally. But he had a problem: debilitating shyness. Dan is a genius, but he has trouble putting two words together when he's forced to talk with someone face-to-face. So shortly after earning his bachelor's degree, he took half his graduation gift from his parents of $25,000 in "career seed money" and purchased an offshore bank charter. It was a brilliant move.

Dan's bank, located in the British Virgin Islands, gave him a completely anonymous base of operation. By advertising his investment concept in several international money magazines, he put together enough capital to launch the project. Within two years, his fine-art CD-ROMs had earned him roughly $1 million in profit. He successfully broadened his market to include university art departments worldwide. The last I heard from Dan, he was estimating year-end profits of nearly $3 million. Equally appealing for someone like Dan, the international marketplace protects personal privacy. Within the United States, success like Dan's would have required a full-blown public relations effort and loss of privacy. Overseas, it came with no strings attached.

And I write for people like Dr. Yves LeGrande, a cardiac surgeon living in Chicago, Illinois. His is the classic American success story. Yves was born to immigrant parents and grew up with virtually nothing—except intelligence and charm. This is a guy who can talk about open-heart surgery with an air of confidence that would calm even the most skittish patient. My sense is that Yves is more than a doctor. He is a healer—someone with a calling to care for people and help make them well.

When I first met Dr. LeGrande, he was in his early fifties. We sat in my office and chatted for nearly four hours about the international market and the economic principles that govern it. It was obvious that Yves had done his homework, and like anyone who has taken the time to learn how the U.S. tax system operates, he was disgusted. For decades, he had watched his profits get swallowed up by various forms of taxation. The concept of offshore tax protection made sense to him, but he just didn't know how to make it happen. Once informed about the available options, he never hesitated. And in the same way that he excels at everything, Yves has been enormously successful offshore. He's legally sheltering his assets from the American tax system and making piles of money at the same time. For too long Yves watched his money flow straight to Washington, D.C. Now he sees it flow in his direction.

Profit. Privacy. Tax protection. These are the three major benefits to globalizing your portfolio. Like Floyd, Dan, and Yves, perhaps you agree that America is not what it used to be. America's feeble economy, masked by a deceptively active stock market and crippled by a debt-laden government, was not providing the kind of economic security they wanted. The decision to operate offshore paid off for all three of them.

How about you? Don't be caught unawares. Unless you prepare your financial lifeboat now, you may go down with Bill Clinton's U.S.S. *Titanic.* A plethora of offshore investment opportunities is beckoning. Now is the time to explore this brave new world. Let me introduce you to an exciting new way of making money work for you.

CHAPTER 1

THE LAST DAYS OF WEALTH IN AMERICA

A man in the prime of his life is lying on an operating table, bleeding from open wounds. A team of surgeons is busily clipping his toenails.

— **HARRY E. FIGGIE JR., *BANKRUPTCY***

The United States of America is in serious trouble. Our standard of living is declining, and has been for a decade. The proportion of two-parent families in which only one parent works outside the home is dwindling. The amount of leisure time available to the average American worker is shrinking. The percentage of citizens who can afford to own a home is dropping, and those who do buy are waiting longer to take the plunge. The cost of education is beyond the means of more and more families every year. People all over the country are forced to spend more than they earn, and attempt to delay the ugly inevitable with wallets full of credit cards. Personal bankruptcies have reached an all-time high. In fact, one million bankruptcies were filed in 1996, and there's every indication that the number will continue to increase year after year. Something is very wrong. The lifestyle my parents were able to afford on $100,000 per year would now require an annual income of $700,000.

The problem has escalated far beyond a cause for concern. Literally, our country's wealth is being drained, drop by drop, by a federal government that can no longer meet even its most immediate financial obligations, much less eliminate its staggering debt. Yet, inexplicably, our representatives in Washington carry on with business as usual. Like characters in some pathetic rendition of *Alice in Wonderland,* they move from one fiscal year to the next in wide-eyed disbelief, immobilized by the seriousness of the problems and the inadequacy of resources with which to solve them. On the one hand, we are treated to the Democrats, who seek to address the spectrum of our social ills by funding programs for everybody—from teenage welfare moms to the angora goat breeders of the Southwest. On the other hand, we have the Republicans, who by the end of 1996 could muster the support of no more than 42 percent of the American people. If the truth be told, the Grand Old Party has done nothing to bring about the kind of genuine reform they were peddling so successfully only a decade ago. Let's remember that between 1980 and 1992, Republicans managed to take this nation from the status of world's largest creditor to world's biggest debtor.

When Ronald Reagan assumed the presidency, he urged fast action to address our economic crisis. "Our federal deficit is nearly $80 billion," he said. "Can we, who man the ship of state, deny that it is somewhat out of control?" Ironically, that deficit, inherited from Jimmy Carter and a Democratic Congress, was the last one ever expressed in double digits. When Reagan left office in 1988, it hung around the neck of America like a weight—more than $255 billion. And when George Bush vacated the White House in 1992, it had swelled to more than $400 billion. Just as frightening, we were in debt to almost everybody: wealthy Japanese, Germans, Englishmen, Canadians, Arabs, Dutchmen, Taiwanese, and Koreans.

At the beginning of 1997, Bill Clinton has managed to put a fairly attractive veneer on the surface of our national economy. The deficit is down (though it's difficult to get too sentimental over an annual debt that still hovers at slightly more than $107 billion). Inflation is under control. Productivity is up. The president's budget plan starting in fiscal year 1997 actually claims it will eliminate the budget deficit by the year 2002 and simultaneously provide $111 billion in tax cuts for the middle class. It looks good, but will it work? Yes, but only if all of the administration's assumptions about the economy over the next five years come true. Do you trust that the Democrats have that accurate a crystal ball? I certainly don't.

What happens if some of the president's best guesses prove to be wrong? Well, Clinton says that if the country's deficit is not at least $20 billion below the Congressional Budget Office current estimates for the year 2000, then most of his well-publicized tax cuts will be reduced or rescinded. In effect, the White House is saying that if, ultimately, Uncle Sam can't pay for your tax cuts, then you won't get them.

Hindsight, of course, makes all things easier to analyze. Even in the dreary light of the late 1990s it is possible to look back and see what went wrong, as well as when it all started heading south. But hindsight does nothing to change the present. It does not alter the circumstances that have conspired to create the predicament we face today—a predicament that, I would argue, cannot be remedied through traditional methods of government intervention.

I am not alone in this assessment. Wall Street analysts are fairly unanimous in predicting that after a six-year expansion that began in 1991, the American economy seems likely to slow down, no matter what course the government pursues. Still, the experts explain, this sort of direct talk would be considered far too crude for either political party, so we are treated to an endless series of political "promise-a-thons." The trouble is, neither side will ever be able to deliver on its pledges.

Respected economist Charles Schultze of the Brookings Institution has come to virtually the same conclusion. "The truth is that there is not a hell of a lot the government can do," he argues. The problem is that both sides of the political forum tend to oversell Uncle Sam's power to affect an economy the size of the United States'. For example, Schultze compares Clinton's financial plan to the set of GOP promises that took Bob Dole absolutely nowhere in the 1996 presidential campaign. There's nothing much to get worked up about, he says. Even if Dole's 15 percent tax cut had been carried out, it would have increased growth by only about one-tenth of 1 percent per year—hardly the stuff from which an economic turnaround is made.

We are stuck, my friend, in a mess so complex and insidious that it will ultimately destroy all who work to eradicate it. The only hope, in my view, is to circumvent the problems of modern economic America. We must stop looking for a way to repair the damage. We must get out of the mess altogether, and like Lot leaving the wicked cities of Sodom and Gomorrah we must never look back. We are now living in the economic equivalent of the morally corrupt cities of the Bible.

IMAGINE THE INEVITABLE

I want to paint you a picture of your future. Not your distant future, of course. I'm not psychic. This is a picture of your life in, let's say, four or five years. It's based on the assumption that you ignore my advice as presented in this book. That is, if you read through these pages, take it all as interesting theory but decide not to make any significant change, then I predict that . . .

You'll wake up one Saturday morning to the sound of your kids arguing with your parents about what constitutes a healthy breakfast. Your kids, mind you, are in their twenties, and your parents have been retired for quite some time. So why are they all staying with you? Is it some sort of a family reunion? No, it's what's come to be just another ordinary day.

Your parents settled into your guest room almost a year ago. They couldn't afford the city property taxes on the home they'd owned for almost forty-five years. By the same token, they couldn't afford to rent an apartment in a safe area after social security payments became their major source of income. Last year your dad's pension fund reduced its monthly payment by nearly 75 percent. The letter from the pension office explained that a big drop in real estate and stock investments had brought the fund almost to its knees. Your dad, along with all the other union retirees, would have to live on less than they had originally been promised.

Your children have been back and forth between your place and their own apartments for more than two years. Your daughter graduated from college with a degree in engineering, but government cutbacks have forced all the local defense contractors to lay off rather than hire workers. At the moment, she's working part-time as a clerk at

The short explanation centers around the country's enormous level of debt. The United States has allowed itself to run up an outrageous tab. At this point, the figure stands at about $5 trillion, and despite a number of frantic attempts to get the economy under control many experts predict that our troubles have only begun.

the nearby grocery store. She gets a 2 percent discount on all store items, but with beef prices now at $10 per pound and fresh produce priced differently each day (depending upon the foreign country from which it comes and that nation's fluctuating faith in the U.S. dollar), the discount doesn't make much of a difference in weekly food bills for six adults.

Your son was a junior in college until last spring when he couldn't get any of the classes he needed to fulfill his major. The state-funded university had been operating with a reduced budget for several years and, in the effort to stay afloat, had forced several departments to eliminate some regular courses. There was a good chance his classes would have become available eventually. But then a major shortfall hit the state this past fall, and the entire campus closed its doors. "We anticipate only a temporary closure," the chancellor said in his public statement. But now, eight months later, there's still no change in sight.

You had been planning a trip with your spouse to Baja California for this summer. But with only you working, the vacation idea has been shelved. Your wife feels horrible that you have to bring home all the bacon yourself, but there isn't much to be done about it. Out of nowhere, her thriving computer company's line of credit had been pulled and its mortgage called in without even a month's notice. All the bank had said by way of explanation was that given the current environment of financial uncertainty and lending risk, it had decided to rebuild its own capital base and reduce outstanding debt. She was one of sixty employees who got put out in the cold—overnight.

Things aren't all that secure for you, either. As a civil engineer employed by the city, you've spent over a year working on reconstruction plans for five freeway on-ramps. It used to be a busy office because, with federal allocations dramatically reduced, the city's infrastructure has needed almost constant repair. Lying in bed this morning, you remember back to when you were in your early thirties, designing nothing but new, state-of-the-art systems. Now you just try to create affordable "Band-Aids" for old ones. Everything got a lot worse at work three months ago when your entire department was put on notice that existing operational funds would be exhausted by the end of the year.

Local neighborhood groups are currently trying to get a bond measure on the next local ballot, calling for city dollars to complete the on-ramp project. But that won't come up for a vote until next April, well after your department comes up against no budget at all. So, as your supervisor said last week, "Unless somebody's fairy godmother wants to intercede, the department will have to close as of the first of the year."

At the moment, though, you have even more immediate concerns. Payday is this coming Friday, and you're anxious to cash your check as fast as you can. That may be a bit harder to accomplish than it was last time. The television news reported last night that your bank, First Capital—the third largest in the state—has merged with another bank because it was on the verge of insolvency. It could no longer meet its obligations.

It's happening everywhere. Last month one of your coworkers went to cash her check and found that her bank had closed completely. Everybody at the office kept trying to reassure her. "You know," they said, "all your money is insured by the government." But privately you wonder: With so many bank failures around the country, how will there ever be enough insurance money to go around?

So as you lie in bed this lazy Saturday morning, you wonder what happened to the life you once envisioned for yourself. You always figured that by this point everything would be getting easier, not more difficult. With your children raised and on their own, you and your spouse would be spending more time alone, doing all the big (and little) things you weren't able to do while they were small. Instead, you're living with six adults in a three-bedroom house. There's only one full-time paycheck to support the lot of you, and it's no longer looking like a sure thing. You're tired and you're worried and you're angry. You ask yourself: What the hell happened to the United States of America?

SLOUCHING TOWARD DOOMSDAY

A lot of what I've described as tomorrow's reality is already happening today. Think about it:

- With a very poor rate of return on their traditional investments, pension funds managers are worried about how to meet their current (much less future) obligations. They are being forced to take speculative risks such as investing in derivative securities.
- Crime is rampant, and an increasing number of people are being forced to choose between living in safe neighborhoods at high prices and living in crime-ridden neighborhoods at what they can truly afford. Criminals are becoming more and more resourceful. In areas that were once considered safe, people are being robbed over and over again.
- The cost of private education is so high that only the ultrarich can enjoy it. (I know one young family that spends nearly $15,000 a year on elementary school tuition for each of their two young children. That comes out to a little more than $3,200 a month so that their kindergartner can work with Play-Doh and their fourth-grader can

learn how pioneer women churned butter.) "It's strangling us," they told me. Yet public education has so deteriorated that they worry that poor schooling might limit their kids' future.

- More and more young and dynamic businesses are being shut out of the market because our banking system, tottering on the edge of disaster, is reluctant to lend the money they need during the critical first few years. These businesses are also being hurt by government constraints and endless regulation.
- Even older and once-stable employers are sacking their workforce in a desperate attempt to stay alive. *Downsizing* is the operative term, which means no more job security.
- Big government is no longer able to fund necessary improvements to our national infrastructure: bridges are in disrepair, roads are full of potholes, the national sewage system is ready for a major overhaul, public schools are in shambles.
- The cost of foreign goods continues to fluctuate between high and outrageous as offshore markets worry about the real value of a U.S. dollar.

How did it get this way? That's a simple question, but it calls for a very complex answer. The short explanation centers around the country's enormous level of debt. The United States has allowed itself to run up an outrageous tab. At this point, the figure stands at about $5 trillion, and despite a number of frantic attempts to get the economy under control many experts predict that our troubles have only begun. Former Congressman Robert Dannemayer, for example, claims that in 1980 a hefty 30 percent of the nation's income tax revenue went to pay interest on our national debt. Putting aside the debt itself, by 1992 the interest payments alone were

Make no mistake, by almost any standard of measurement, the quality of life for successful U.S. professionals and entrepreneurs continues to decline rather than improve.

demanding 60 percent of our income tax dollars. And by the end of this century, Dannemayer warns, that interest debt will drain every single cent from the government's income tax coffers. "Of course, at that point, we're broke," he maintains, because we won't be able to pay for anything else.

Sounds pretty bad, doesn't it? According to the internationally recognized economist and author Ravi Batra, it is. "Today, the economic profession is greatly bewildered," he writes. "The economy has grown slowly since 1992; both inflation and interest rates have declined to lows not seen since the early 1960s." Yet, Batra argues, the economic fundamentals are profoundly flawed. Despite a bottom line that reads well on paper, the financial reality for most Americans continues to worsen. Batra claims that for 80 percent of all U.S. workers, real purchasing power has been tumbling steadily since 1972. In a national economy that boasts a jump in total profits from $229 billion to $390 billion (a 70 percent increase!) between 1990 and 1995, we nonetheless saw the elimination of three million U.S. jobs.

You know who has it toughest in today's financial environment? Not the enormously wealthy. Their contacts and mobility make it possible for them to camouflage most of their money, protecting it from excessive government regulation. Meanwhile, the lower class is also well protected by a Democratic administration that seems deeply concerned about those who are on the brink of poverty. It's those between these two extremes who suffer most: the hardworking affluent, the 6 percent of Americans who pay more than 45 percent of their total income to Uncle Sam. People like you. If you're reading this book, chances are you're caught between powerful and conflicting interests, with no real advocate or guardian angel.

Taxation offers a bird's-eye view of the situation. Do you really believe that the ultrarich pay Uncle Sam what they're supposed to every April 15th? Of course not. In one recent issue of *Worth* magazine, a consultant to the nation's wealthiest philanthropists spoke bluntly about why most wealthy people donate to nonprofit organizations. "The motivation is 100 percent taxes," she said. "That's what these people brag about to me—how much they're saving in taxes. There is this ethos among the rich: We don't pay taxes, taxes are for schnooks. Let the schnooks pay to run the government. . . ." The comment I hear is that people would rather give their money to charity than to the government.

Granted, these are cynical comments. But they don't strike me as entirely unfair. Years of professional experience has taught me that the top 1 percent of this country's wealthy have insulated themselves quite successfully from the long reach of the U.S. tax collector. Typically, these people hide their money through a combined strategy of deposits in foreign banks and domestic investments along with big charitable contributions.

At the other end of the spectrum are the working poor, and believe me, they've been the only real beneficiaries of President Clinton's tax reform measures. Back in 1992, then candidate Clinton traveled around America saying tax reform should start with a tax cut for the middle class. But almost immediately after assuming office, that promise underwent radical transformation. Instead of a tax cut, the middle class got "expanded income tax credit."

But look at the specifics: To collect a $1,000 credit, a family of four must earn no more than $23,746 in gross income. When that family's total income reaches just over $28,000, the credit shrinks to a mere $100. And at $28,495, it disappears entirely. Clinton calls this middle-class tax relief? It's low-income tax relief and does zip to help middle- and upper-income Americans. Although the president talks of simplifying the tax code, he staunchly defends a system in which the wealthy pay higher tax rates—rates that he increased in 1993 by raising the top bracket from 31 percent to 39.6 percent.

Make no mistake, by almost any standard of measurement, the quality of life for successful U.S. professionals and entrepreneurs continues to decline rather than improve. Baby Boomers have seen social security and sales tax rates more than double in their lifetime. Over the past twenty-five years, the average "wealthy" family income went up 24 percent, from $70,000 to almost $90,000. But it hasn't mattered much because the rate of personal debt has reached an all-time high. Most upper-income Americans find that their income gain has been swallowed up entirely by the escalating cost of car loans, home mortgages, insurance premiums, and credit card debt.

THE U.S. GOVERNMENT BOUND AND GAGGED

We've already established that the government can do little to change this national crisis. Indeed, that's the most pitiful part of the whole story. When all is said and done, there's only a small portion of the federal budget that any president or congressional session can control. That's because before the government can spend a dollar on even the wisest program or investment, it must fork over money to cover federal deposit insurance, interest payments on its huge debt, and all "entitlement" programs.

Just to put this in perspective, consider the fact that by the end of the Reagan years the portion of the federal budget that could be controlled (that is, reduced) by the president or the Congress was a meager 33 percent. Everything else was untouchable. By the end of Bush's presidency, interest and entitlement spending had grown, leaving only 27 percent of the budget for controlled spending. Let's look at this from another angle. The Congressional Budget Office (CBO) reports that the government's discretionary spending for 1993 was $547 billion. By 1998, CBO projections estimate that this figure will rise to about $584 billion—or virtually no increase in real terms. Entitlement spending, however, will soar from $770 billion in 1993 to $1.1 trillion in 1998. That's a 43 percent increase! And there's no place for America to go for that money!

All this means is that any progress toward fiscal equilibrium is made with baby steps. In theory, everyone agrees that federal spending should be reduced and our total debt repaid. Just how we can accomplish this feat remains unclear. To believe that government can do it is like still believing in Santa Claus. The truth is, our government is fairly powerless. Both bound and gagged, the president and Congress are helpless to improve the situation in any significant way. The nation is bleeding to death from years of fiscal abuse. But like a surgeon without operating instruments, Uncle Sam can do nothing but prolong his patient's misery. This country needs to be recast at the most fundamental level. No president can do that. No congressional session can do it, either. The American economy is out of control and careening toward destruction. The whole situation is almost laughable, sadly.

Doomsday is approaching, and the average U.S. citizen can feel it coming. America's median family income is no higher today than it was in 1969. Even though the Clinton campaign slogan "Are you better off today than you were four years ago?" can be answered "yes," it's only because you have more credit, not more wealth. And consider these facts. In 1995, a U.S. family earning the median income (approximately $39,000) paid a social security tax of nearly 8 percent and an average sales tax of 7 percent—or a total of slightly less than 15 percent. After these taxes, the family's income was $32,774. Back in 1965, these tax rates added up to less than 8 percent, which left $33,818 in income. So the average American family is making $1,044 less after thirty years. Rather than being better off than you were four years ago, you're worse off than you were thirty years ago! Excluding the income tax rate (which has remained essentially unchanged), after-tax income in 1995 was lower than that in 1969. In other words, twenty-six years of plodding improvement in family incomes was wiped out by the silent demise of the American economy.

The bottom line is sobering to say the least. The net worth of more than 25 percent of all American families is less than $5,000. Another 6.5 percent have less than $10,000 in real assets. And still another 12.5 percent have less than $25,000. Summed up, nearly half of all families in this country have less than $25,000 to their name, counting everything they own minus debts.

Look around you. If you're like the majority of upper-income citizens, you're watching your financial safety net get smaller and smaller. For many Americans, it may have already disappeared altogether. Perhaps you're making in the neighborhood of $100,000 a year, but after you get done paying your taxes to the absolutely ravenous federal and state governments, financing your kids' education, and servicing your credit card debts, you wonder where "the rest" is—the money you had hoped to put into investment savings. You've been told to fund your IRA, but you can't find anything to put in it. In no way has your standard of living improved. You can't save enough to pay your mortgage, put your kids through school, or anything.

Although the officials in Washington would never admit it, this nation is in Chapter 11. The U.S. government is broke. Bankrupt. The government owes more than it has. What's more, we will suffer the consequences. You and I and millions of other Americans. No wonder a widely respected University of Michigan survey of consumer sentiment shows that the average citizen is turning darkly pessimistic about this country's economic future.

THE "WIMPY" STYLE OF GOVERNMENT

Most analysts agree with me that entitlement spending—medicare, family assistance, farm subsidies—is killing this country. Like so many problems, this one developed slowly. But today it's reached the critical point. Social security is a perfect example of how we've allowed ourselves to slip into this mess. When social security was initiated by Franklin Roosevelt in 1935, it was designed to work a lot like private insurance. In a sense, it was government forcing people to save for their old age. Uncle Sam was a fair banker back then, too. In the effort to entice workers into liking the process, he offered them a respectable rate of interest on their accumulating nest egg. Retirees would get back all that they put into the fund, he assured America, plus interest and accrued investment credit.

It was a fascinating economic experiment with tremendous potential. That is, until 1939, when Congress got itchy about all that money just sitting around with nobody to spend it. So, while they continued to call it social security, they really turned it into a "pay as you go" plan. Tax payments from the current workforce would finance the benefits of those already retired—which at that time was a ratio of about fifty workers to one retiree. With this change, the government's pension account lost its protection from congressional raids. Like

Wimpy from the Popeye cartoons, Uncle Sam gladly promised to pay Tuesday for a hamburger today.

As if this weren't bad enough, it was also in 1939 that Congress added to its social security obligation a benefit commitment to the dependents of retired workers as well as insurance for their survivors. Roosevelt's original idea had been to provide a supplemental retirement income for workers in commerce and industry only. But lawmakers just couldn't leave well enough alone. Over time, they added more and more beneficiaries and increased the benefits to those already receiving social security.

In 1956 they added disability benefits for covered workers. Then in 1965, medicare and medicaid were tacked onto the list of social security responsibilities. In 1972, benefits were "indexed" to keep inflation from chipping away at their purchasing power. That meant that cost-of-living adjustments were added to the basic benefit checks on an ongoing basis. By 1983, the government was borrowing from the social security fund you contribute to in order to send a monthly check to retired military personnel (who already had their own generous pension system), farmworkers, domestic workers, government workers (who, like the military, were already covered under a separate pension plan), as well as widows, widowers, orphans, the disabled, and their dependents!

Of course, in borrowing from the public pension system Uncle Sam is risking your money. It is collected for a specific reason: to be deposited in a trust and held on account to pay future retirement benefits to the people whose salary dollars helped create the capital pool. The government simply ignores that fact.

For today's young and even middle-aged workers this means that, upon retirement, there isn't going to be any money left in the pot to pay for their benefits. In fact, economists claim that between the years 2015 and 2020, even with moderate economic growth, social security costs will exceed its income. So by the time today's forty-

It appears that increasing numbers of U.S. investors don't want to tie up money within American industry, either. That's because investors in general are reluctant to invest in a country that relentlessly addresses its problems with big government solutions. Meanwhile, other countries, especially in Asia and Latin America, are curtailing the scope of government, and their economies are growing rapidly as a result.

year-olds reach retirement eligibility age, the fund will be completely broke. Average Americans know it, too. In one recent national survey, this nation's young adults claimed to have more faith in the existence of unidentified flying objects (UFOs) than in their chance of collecting social security!

And it gets worse. What the budget masters in Washington have done to social security, they also do to other federal trust funds: military, postal workers, railroad, and civil service retirement; medicare surplus; and highway and airport trust funds. They borrow from these trusts to cover daily operational costs for welfare, food stamps, and farm price supports, and then replace the money with IOUs. Well, let's face it: An IOU from Uncle Sam is a lot like a trunk full of Confederate dollars. It may sound good, but it's positively worthless.

Don't get me wrong: I have no argument against the good intentions underlying these federal allocations. But, by the same token, I don't hear anybody describing ways to secure the future financial commitments our government has made to its citizens. Eventually the chickens will come home to roost, and when they do there will be an uproar in this nation the likes of which the world has never seen. When millions and millions of Americans discover that there is no money left, real or pretend, to pay them what they had been counting on, I pity the poor guy sitting in the Oval Office.

There have been efforts to prevent that day of reckoning. As far back as 1982, with social security already heading straight for the red, Ronald Reagan appointed a commission that met and recommended—surprise—higher payroll taxes to bring in more revenue to support retired recipients. Today, with the problem more out of control than ever, Bill Clinton is doing the same thing. Despite the fact that the government already takes in 400 percent more in taxes than it did just one decade ago—thanks largely to the tax increases that occurred under Reagan and Bush—Clinton asked for and got the biggest tax increase in U.S. history.

WE'RE WASTING AWAY

With so little of the overall budget actually available to them, you would think the government would take scrupulous care of what they can control. Wrong! Not only do they throw money around like sailors on a weekend furlough, they don't even bother to take the spending advice that they themselves pay to hear.

For example, in the early 1980s Ronald Reagan commissioned the President's Private Sector Survey on Cost Control to investigate ways of eliminating waste in federal spending. The recommendations were presented in 1984: nearly 2,500 separate instances of budget waste and mismanagement that could have been eliminated by simple presidential order.

Guess what our politicians did about that waste? You're right: almost nothing! Instead of realizing the nearly $2 trillion in potential annual savings that was suggested, the government only tipped its hat at cost cutting. To date, less than $250 billion in needless spending has been eliminated.

It's not as though waste in government was difficult to uncover. The Cost Control report found that one-third of all U.S. tax dollars was consumed by inefficiency and waste in the federal government alone. Here's a short list of other examples:

- **The Nose Study** A study funded by the federal government to determine the average nose size of airline stewardesses.
- **The U.S. Forest Service** The world's largest road builder, the service spends roughly $500 million of its annual budget each year to build and maintain roads on federal lands so that private timber companies can harvest what they want to buy. Still, the agency makes so little from these timber sales that in 1991, for example, it lost $1.8 billion.
- **Federal Office Furniture** Each year, the government spends $4 billion to buy hardwood desks, reclining chairs, mahogany tables, sofas, and oriental rugs—all for the offices of bureaucrats. A huge warehouse in Washington is packed with slightly used furnishings rejected by choosy new tenants when they take office.

All of these expenditures seem ridiculous. It's downright laughable until you stop to realize that the government is tossing your money around on trivial, meaningless projects while America stands on the brink of complete financial ruin. As a nation, we have become the laughingstock of the economic world. Foreign investors don't want to put their money into ventures owned and operated by a people who appear to be so easily duped and abused by their own government. And who can blame them for feeling that way? Would you want your money wrapped up in projects run by people that dumb? Or acquiescent?

It appears that increasing numbers of U.S. investors don't want to tie up money within American industry, either. That's because investors in general are reluctant to invest in a country that relentlessly addresses its problems with big government solutions. Meanwhile, other countries, especially in Asia and Latin America, are curtailing the scope of government, and their economies are growing rapidly as a result. Every investor, domestic and foreign, prefers markets in which government is downsizing, because the prospects for economic growth (and profit) improve.

Every research study on the subject shows the same trend: Our national debt coupled with excessive government spending has caused investment from every sector to decline every year. In 1980, for example, investment in U.S. plants and equipment accounted for nearly 15 percent of our gross domestic product (GDP). By 1992, investment was down to 9 percent—and falling.

THE COMING APOCALYPSE

No matter how you figure it, things don't look good. The U.S. economy is collapsing, and taking a lot of good people down with it. At the blink of an eye, as soon as interest rates head up, the economy will burst like a huge bubble.

But you don't have to be one of the victims. Get mad. Get furious, in fact. You have every right to resent the way in which your government has forfeited your financial security and future just to make the federal budget appear acceptable from one year to the next. After you've exhausted your anger, do something about it. You need to accept that the domestic scene is hopeless, and you need to create a financial escape route for yourself and those who depend on you. Stop beating your head against a brick wall. America is crumbling, and you need to get out.

And you can. By exploring the full range of money-making opportunities that exist within various foreign markets, you can come to see that there is a very real alternative to the dead-end investments available within the United States. As a global player, you'll be able to watch the crisis in this country with enviable indifference. While other Americans with less foresight watch their savings evaporate on Wall Street, you'll watch your money grow in highly liquid investments all around the world.

You may decide on a European offshore fund in February. By May, you might choose to transfer funds into a very short-term money market account in Luxembourg, where you'll earn a handsome interest rate. Then in the fall, you may even opt to funnel your profits into the short-term financing of a fast-food business in Sao Paulo. All the while, you'll accumulate profits, expand your network of international financial contacts, and—as an added bonus—enjoy international travel, from the capitals of Europe to the sun-drenched beaches of South America.

Chapter 2

The Beacon Offshore

Ahead, and only a short distance away, lay Shangri-La . . . a new world stirring in the ruins, stirring in hopefulness, seeking its lost and legendary treasures.

— **James Hilton, *Lost Horizon***

I am sometimes accused of using scare tactics to make my point. I suppose it's a fair criticism. I do spend a lot of my time on the lecture circuit warning people that the U.S. economy is in deep trouble. The economy simply does not provide opportunities for profitable investment. Even if our economy turned around today, it would take years to have a positive impact on your personal finances. That means you should only expect meager investment success (at best) if you opt for the kind of portfolio diversity that is regularly presented as the best strategy in today's financial magazines.

Today's investment marketplace is a veritable wasteland: traditional savings accounts offer a pitiful interest rate of 3 percent; even the most appealing interest-bearing accounts offer just 4.3 percent profit on your deposit; the Dow Jones averages fluctuate meaninglessly from one month to the next; the government continually spends your tax dollars to invent new ways of monitoring you and scrutinizing your financial activities. It is a place where the poor get poorer even though the rich can't seem to get richer. It turns you into a kind of Sisyphus, pushing uphill forever. For almost nothing in the end.

In stark contrast to this bleak domestic picture there exists a wide array of exciting, profitable, and creative international markets. They allow you to make money anytime of the day or night. They let you completely sidestep the suffocating red tape that has totally stifled this country's market. They bring you into contact with businesspeople and investors from virtually every part of the world. Best of all, these markets make it possible for you to earn a lot of money in a short amount of time without excessive taxation or undue government interference.

This offshore world is not a fantasy. Foreign financial centers really do exist and many of them have been created expressly for people like you. But beyond their physical reality, these offshore markets also exist as a state of mind. By that I mean that "offshore" is really a way of looking at the investment world. It's an all-encompassing financial perspective, liberated from territorial boundaries and legislative decrees. It transforms the globe into one enormous economic system made up of different but interdependent financial markets. In this world your assets are entry tickets into one (or all) of these markets.

LOOK AT ALL THOSE WEALTHY PEOPLE OFFSHORE!

In talking with prospective clients all around the country, I find that a great many people consider offshore banking and investment to be reserved for the ultrarich, the billionaire jet set. Actually, offshore havens are attracting more and more of what I call the working affluent, possibly several million people in this country alone!

Of course, the offshore market has always appealed to major U.S. corporations—huge conglomerates big enough to survey the global environment, identify good investment opportunities, and "set up shop." These large corporate interests were the first to invest offshore because they were big enough to risk a loss. If the offshore concept failed, they could lick their wounds and move on to other profit and tax protection approaches. But, as it turned out, the offshore business approach proved to be a gold mine for the conglomerates. That's why virtually every Fortune 500 company today is actively investing offshore—McDonald's, Nike, Wal-Mart, Du Pont, to name just a few. And every one of them is making money.

Particularly in the early years, offshore money havens went out of their way to attract the megawealthy. By and large, these folks were looking to move their assets out of high-tax jurisdictions or unstable political environments. I've met a lot of "old money" people offshore. They frequently use foreign financial centers to carry out even the most routine transactions. I think they're attracted by the privacy and discretion of an offshore involvement. Accustomed to exceptional service, they also appreciate the speed and special handling that come with most offshore services.

Excessive tax burden has propelled many wealthy artists offshore. For example, I remember reading about an internationally respected musician, a guy so famous that his albums are sold throughout the world. He could do his work anywhere. Yet, as he explained, "in today's music world, geography is not decided by place but by local taxation." Because of high taxes, recording is moving away from New York, Los Angeles, and London. "The equipment is the same anywhere. It's the taxes that matter." Several of today's biggest pop stars have built recording studios in beautiful Caribbean island retreats.

With greater frequency, however, I meet people from still another offshore consumer group. They are the

"Offshore" is really a way of looking at the investment world. It's an all-encompassing financial perspective, liberated from territorial boundaries and legislative decrees. It transforms the globe into one enormous economic system made up of different but interdependent financial markets.

up-and-comers: young U.S. entrepreneurs who want to explore efficient alternatives to the investment approach that dominates in this country. Uninterested in a lifelong commitment to any one trade or profession, they typically want to build their business fast, sell it for as big a profit as they possibly can, and move on to an entirely new project. As a group, they like to invest on two levels, for their business and for themselves personally. So they tend to use offshore centers for their commercial as well as private benefits.

Aidan is a perfect example. He's a successful graphics designer based in Los Angeles. When I first met him, he had just opened a spacious suite of offices in Beverly Hills. Servicing primarily motion picture studios, Aidan was the modern picture of success. He was on his way up in a fun and growing field. Yet, at our first meeting, he told me that he wanted a better return on his personal investment income. So we took funds from his various conventional, low-yield sources and started an offshore company. He chose a Caribbean haven in which to establish the company because he thought it would put him within convenient distance of Latin American investors looking for creative partnerships.

He was right. Within one year, Aidan had become involved in several small real estate ventures in Chile and had formed a partnership to create graphic design computer software to be marketed throughout Brazil. He had bought himself an absolutely beautiful vintage Porsche and was looking to establish a second offshore company. This time he chose a location on the Pacific Rim, where he hoped to explore creative Asian investment and partnerships.

Aidan is part of this new, innovative market—people in their thirties and forties who have just enough resources to invest in the offshore arena. I call these men and women the "inventurers." Like trailblazing adventurers of the past, they are bold and self-confident. They prove you can do the "untried but true" and come out ahead, time after time.

OFFSHORE: FINANCE A $7 TRILLION PHENOMENON

In case you are under the impression that this whole offshore industry is a small-scale phenomenon, let me set the record straight. It's enormous. It involves governments, multinational corporations, billionaires, and multibillionaires from around the world, and an awful lot of people just like you—hardworking, upper-income Americans looking for a better investment opportunity than they can find in the domestic scene. The number of people who use international private banking services has risen from eight million in 1984 to twenty million in 1997. Together, these folks represent a trillion-dollar industry!

Many financial forecasters agree that most of the money to be made by individual Americans over the next several decades will be made abroad. According to President Clinton's undersecretary of commerce, Jeffrey E. Garten, nearly 75 percent of the overall growth in world trade during the next two decades will take place in developing countries. "These emerging markets are likely to double their share of the world GDP in that time," he reports. "By the year 2010, their share of world imports is likely to exceed that of Japan and the European Union combined."

These Big Emerging Markets (BEMs) offer the best investment opportunities for American business, Garten maintains. These ten markets, listed in order of promise, are: China, Indonesia, India, South Korea, Mexico, Argentina, Brazil, South Africa, Poland, and Turkey. The U.S. government, of course, views the BEMs as fertile soil for well-established U.S. industry. In fact, officials speculate that business with China alone could create half a million U.S. jobs over the next six years!

For assertive independent investors, the BEMs shine like beacon lights on the economic horizon. With the right combination of intelligence, investing power, and creativity, a single entrepreneur or small business consortium could make an enormous amount of money. Goods and services that we have come to take utterly for granted here in the United States will be, for years to come, revolutionary advancements in these rapidly developing nations. For those able and willing to introduce them into these select foreign markets, the prospects for profit are incredible! For example, half of the world's population has never made a phone call. . . .

Of course, there are countries other than the BEMs that offer almost as much profit potential. Vietnam, for example, is one. Now that America's long-standing trade embargo against Vietnam has been lifted, the possibilities for lucrative investment are almost limitless. As one writer recently put it, "in the world of emerging markets, Vietnam is the flavor of the week."

The former Soviet Union also offers high-risk, high return market opportunities. Since Russia's dramatic political revolution in 1989, enormous fortunes have been amassed by people like Mikhail Khodorkovsky, chairman of the now famous Menatep Bank. When the communists lost power, Khodorkovsky and others like him went on well-conceived buying sprees—picking up everything from midsize companies to raw materials and even central bank money. They got all these investments at old market values. Then, within only months, they turned around and sold them at new, much higher market rates. It's been a fast and easy way for investors to make a killing in profits! But they are taking a big risk. Because law and order is practically nonexistent in Russia, it is also easy for an investor to wind up being the victim of a killing.

AND THERE'S A LOT IN IT FOR THE MONEY HAVEN

The offshore industry is booming. Why? Because it lets everybody come out a winner. Investors get rich. And the tiny foreign financial centers in which they do business are transformed from impoverished island states into thriving international business and vacation havens. For a case in point, let's consider Malta, a country composed of three small islands in the Mediterranean Sea, just south of Sicily.

Like most other offshore havens, Malta is quite small (122 square miles) and has a modest population of a few hundred thousand residents. Among its citizens are many U.S. and European expatriates. That's because Malta has a generous tax system. Independent for more than twenty-five years, this former British colony also attracts a good number of tax exiles from the United Kingdom.

Malta's economy, like any other, requires capital. Following independence, its government needed to generate money in order to fund economic development. Unfortunately, the fledgling state went through a period of political upheaval during which its financial stability went from bad to worse. Malta learned its lesson, however. By the mid-1980s, it had established a sound government that sought to secure an influx of capital by offering an impressive tax break to individuals purchasing island property.

In the late 1980s, the Maltese government announced new regulations designed to compete with other money havens. The first of those regulations cut the jurisdictional income tax rate in half, from 30 to 15 percent for foreign investors residing on any of the three islands. Another of the regulations modified local inheritance tax rules to ensure that estate duty is payable on only a small percentage of a deceased resident's assets. Again, the government's aim is obvious: To attract wealthy people from around the world who want to save taxes and leave the largest possible estate to their heirs.

Not every offshore haven contours its local laws and enforcement practices to this particular market. Still, such financial and legal accommodations are reflective of the economic benefits available through foreign financial centers. Typically, each haven—whether it's located in the Pacific, the Caribbean, the Mediterranean, or inland (such as Luxembourg)—specializes in a particular financial area and serves a specific market.

The bottom line is this: Offshore havens want the spending power that foreign investors and residents can bring. Without your wealth and the wealth of others like you, they would be forced to depend entirely on tourism

With the right combination of intelligence, investing power, and creativity, a single entrepreneur or small business consortium could make an enormous amount of money. Goods and services that we have come to take utterly for granted here in the United States will be, for years to come, revolutionary advancements in these rapidly developing nations.

for a capital base. And tourism could never begin to compare with the profits available through genuine foreign investment services. The result is that many places, Malta being just one example, deliberately and carefully develop into financial centers offering tax efficiency and state-of-the-art financial opportunity.

JUST SLIP YOUR FEET INTO THESE SHOES . . .

For many investors the biggest obstacle to venturing offshore is fear of economic isolation. A lot of them come to hear me speak. They read my books as well as others on related topics. They talk with other independent financial consultants. They ponder the possibilities of involvement in an international market. But in the end, they weasel out of their own best plans because they're afraid the offshore arena will be too big and too empty for them. "Who'll be out there with me?" one client asked not so long ago. "Sure, I want to make money, but I don't want to stalk around the globe alone looking for the next big killing."

You won't be alone. In fact, the offshore community of successful foreign investors and businesspeople gets bigger all the time. This community includes people from all over, people starting out with nothing, people with every conceivable strike against them—they see an opportunity that offers comparable potential, and they seize the initiative. Sometimes with the equivalent of just a few thousand dollars, they successfully start companies that produce desirable goods or provide necessary services to hungry foreign markets. And voilà: These rags-to-riches visionaries find themselves on the leading edge of the world's profit-making curve.

Thaksin Shinawatra is a case in point. In 1983, he was working as a lieutenant colonel in the Royal Thai

Police Department. But he had a crazy idea. He thought he could make a lot of money leasing computers. So he borrowed every cent he could from relatives and friends, and bought some IBM systems. He convinced the police department that computerizing their database would ultimately save time and money. By 1988, Shinawatra's computer leasing company was making $300,000 a year. So he decided to expand. He became a distributor for AT&T, as well as for IBM equipment, throughout Thailand. Most importantly, he landed a twenty-year license to operate the country's first cellular phone system. Think about it: In twenty years, he'll be richer than Midas! He's already worth $1.6 billion.

Some potential offshore investors worry that they lack the "sixth sense" that may be required to get rich abroad. Well, they should relax. The foreign market is full of engineers, doctors, and even scientists who got rich not because they had any particular investment savvy, but simply because they just had the courage to jump in. Consider the story of Valery Neverov, a forty-five-year-old physics teacher in Moscow. In 1989, as the Soviet Union collapsed, this underpaid public employee saw an opportunity. He gathered a dozen of his closest friends and, using his own money as well as theirs, started a company called Hermes.

Neverov's vision was a simple one, really. He wanted to finance oil trades. At that time, many directors of state-owned oil companies were eager to sell small shipments of oil on the side rather than deliver their entire production to the government at ridiculously low fixed prices. Many buyers, meanwhile, were willing to pay the higher market price just to avoid getting bogged down in the state procurement bureaucracy. So Neverov made a place for himself as a middleman. He bought oil slightly above the fixed price (making oil companies happy) and resold it on the open market (where there was a steady stream of eager customers).

In 1991, the official state price for oil was 9 rubles, but the market value was sixteen times that figure! Do the math and you begin to get a picture of Neverov's profit margin. "We commonly made several million dollars a day in clear profits," he boasts.

As the political environment changed, Neverov used his impressive financial resources to make even more money. Today, Hermes continues to do about $100 million a year in oil trading. The company also owns seven banks; a small oil field in western Siberia; and four Siberian forestry companies; plus small stakes in twenty-two oil production companies, refineries, and petrochemical enterprises. Neverov is one of the richest men in Russia—not because he was intuitive about making money. He simply seized an opportunity.

Then there's the story of Kenshin Oshima. When he was twelve years old, he read a book about the Rothschilds and decided to become a billionaire. Now at the age of forty-eight, his assets are valued at $1.2 billion. He made that money through his fast-growing finance company, which specializes in short-term business loans. Here in the United States, that doesn't sound like a billion-dollar idea. But in Japan, large banks don't generally like lending to small businesses. So what's a poor middle-sized business supposed to do? Next to the small loan sharks who charge outrageous fees and interest rates, Oshima's professionally run operation is extremely attractive. "You have to understand," he chuckles, "this business has rather a dirty image in Japan. So it doesn't attract a lot of smart people. I've learned it's easier to compete with stupid people."

Oshima's sarcasm aside, there's a valuable offshore lesson to be learned from his success story: In the foreign marketplace, enormous profit can be earned by providing a service or offering a product that other businessmen in the area consider to be beneath them. Oshima is also making plans for a garbage collection business and a string of funeral parlors that will operate throughout Japan.

Vijay Mallya, an internationally renowned East Indian investor, learned a somewhat similar lesson from his father. In the mid-1970s, the Indian prime minister tried to ban the sale of liquor. "My father was convinced that prohibition wouldn't work," Mallya says, as he sips a glass of chilled chardonnay in the study of his multi-million-dollar home just outside London. "Records showed that tax on alcohol was the biggest revenue earner for each state government. So sure enough, the stocks of breweries went down, and in 1977, my dad bought up everything he could." The strategy paid off. Today his company—now run by his son—controls 39 percent of India's beer market and 42 percent of the country's market in spirits.

Here again is a perfect example of the essence of investment success: You must be willing to capitalize on an opportunity as soon it becomes available. Had Mallya's father waited, another more aggressive investor would have probably beat him to the stock purchase counter. Or government policy would have changed and the chance of a lifetime would have slipped right through his fingers.

Remember, within the domestic stock market, activity is relatively slow. Daily ups and downs don't mean much. That's why it's impossible to get rich by relying on the Dow Jones. But within the international market, it's a whole different story. Markets all over the world are constantly shifting based on government regulation and political events. They create instant opportunities, but you must be prepared to quickly take advantage of them.

Sometimes, though, a fortune can be waiting right at your kitchen counter. That was certainly true for Roberto Gonzalez Barrera. He became a billionaire by producing and marketing Mexico's first dry tortilla flour, a convenient alternative to patting clumps of wet cornmeal or rolling dough by hand. Gonzalez also pioneered the idea

The offshore community of successful foreign investors and businesspeople gets bigger all the time. This community includes people from all over, people starting out with nothing, people with every conceivable strike against them—they see an opportunity that offers comparable potential, and they seize the initiative.

of ready-made and prepackaged tortillas, the kind we Americans can buy at virtually any neighborhood supermarket. Through his Los Angeles–based subsidiary, Mission Foods, he now operates nearly a dozen tortillerias here in the United States and distributes to grocers all the way from California to Florida.

These are just a very few success stories. I've included them here to make my point: From within developing nations around the world, individual fortunes are springing up in truly amazing numbers. In 1987, *Forbes* magazine did its first survey of world billionaires. Only six were Latin American, and two of them were cocaine lords, now dead. By 1994, the list had grown to include forty-two Latins and, by all appearances, every one of them was legitimate. In 1987, *Forbes* listed only fourteen Asian billionaires. In 1994, it listed forty-six.

You might as well face it: The possibilities for truly profitable investment are dwindling for most investors within the U.S. market. All but 1 percent of Americans have been shut out for good. Experts agree: The fortunes still to be made within our market will be made by people already sitting in the brocade upholstered board seats of major multinational corporations. There are not many Horatio Alger stories cropping up in this country anymore.

On the other hand, wealth and security abound offshore. By doing what these successful foreign investors have done—identifying a need and meeting it within an emerging market—you can reap all the same rewards they have. You can get extremely rich, in privacy and without unreasonable taxation.

THE BAMBOO BOOM

An even better example of offshore market ingenuity comes from the ethnic Chinese expatriates and the children of expatriates who were forced out of mainland China during Chairman Mao's communist revolution. This unique population of dislocated investors is enjoying remarkable success all across Asia and throughout the Pacific Rim.

An estimated sixty million Chinese live outside China. Most of them reside in Taiwan, Hong Kong, or Macao, where collectively they earn more than $500 billion annually—an amount equal to the gross national product of China. The remaining three or four million, scattered throughout the world, seem to find ways to make money wherever they call home. In Indonesia, for example, they make up less than 5 percent of the population, yet they own nearly 70 percent of the private domestic capital and run 160 of the 200 largest businesses. In Thailand, they constitute about 10 percent of the population, yet they control the country's four largest banks.

Remember that Chinese immigrants did not start out with any advantages. In fact, it's hard to imagine how really disadvantaged they were. They arrived in foreign countries just happy to have escaped China with their lives. Desperately poor, typically uneducated, and totally out-of-step with the cultures in which they found themselves, they often sought work as unskilled laborers. Success for them was a move out of indentured servitude and into a small food stall or curiosity wagon that they could operate on their own or with their family.

From that starting point, thousands of these immigrant Chinese have become rich because they brought with them a number of habits, values, and attitudes that gave them an operating edge over local competitors, such as self-reliance, a reverence for education, thrift, discipline, and family cohesion. They built family enterprises with low debt levels. They relied on mutual assistance associations for loans, trade information, the recruitment of workers, business introductions, and, most importantly, enforcement of the handshake deals on which so much of their business was based.

Even today, a Chinese businessman who violates an agreement is rarely sued. Instead, he's blacklisted. "If you don't honor your commitment," remarks David Li, chief executive of Hong Kong's Bank of East Asia, "the whole Chinese network will know and you're finished."

In the overseas Chinese world, family enterprise has always been the basic economic unit. The family is the company. The company is the family. So, traditionally, company founders prefer hiring even incompetent relatives to outside professionals. That's because "Chinese culture is vertical," says Linda Lim, director of the Southeast Asia Business Program at the University of Michigan's business school. "You are responsible to ancestors as well as to future generations," she argues. "It never ends. You must maximize achievement to glorify your ancestors and accumulate wealth for your descendants. It's an inescapable obligation to your lineage."

You may disagree with that culturally based explanation for Chinese economic practices, but you can't dispute the facts. Since Deng Xiaoping launched his economic open-door policy in the late 1980s, ethnic Chinese living outside China have invested more than $50 billion in their mother country. That accounts for about

> **Ethnic Chinese living outside China have invested more than $50 billion in their mother country. That accounts for about 80 percent of all foreign investment in China. They have formed more than 100,000 joint ventures in China, built export industries, and brought valuable management skills, technology, and international connections back to a country economically ravaged by communism. From Hong Kong to Jakarta, Taipei to Singapore, Bangkok to Kuala Lumpur, the Chinese overseas are the driving force behind China's economic development.**

80 percent of all foreign investment in China. They have formed more than 100,000 joint ventures in China, built export industries, and brought valuable management skills, technology, and international connections back to a country economically ravaged by communism. From Hong Kong to Jakarta, Taipei to Singapore, Bangkok to Kuala Lumpur, the Chinese overseas are the driving force behind China's economic development. Through their informal business networks and indestructible family allegiances, their economy without borders is one of the most dynamic forces for economic change in the world today.

In addition to the obvious benefits that they reap for themselves and their families, these creative Chinese investors have done a lot for the countries they now call home. For the most part, these small nations had very underdeveloped economies—that is, until they got an infusion of money and financial activity from all those ethnic Chinese investments. I do not exaggerate when I say that Chinese immigrants have been the catalyst for the economic success of many Asian nation-states. Without the energy, drive, capital, and fresh perspectives of Chinese immigrants, these societies would never have attained the prosperity they enjoy today.

Confronted with these facts, you have to ask yourself the obvious: If immigrant Chinese have proved themselves to be so gifted at industrial and commercial investment, then why did economic prosperity completely pass China by? Why did their native country remain weak and barely able to feed its own population until only recently? How can a people be capable of such impressive success in every part of the world other than the place from which they come?

The answer is as obvious as the questions: bad government policy. Government cannot create prosperity. It can, however, create conditions in which a society's economic energy and talents can flower. Mainland China did not create those conditions—not during the revolution, and not for many decades before it began. As a result, creative Chinese investors, both big and small, were forced to look elsewhere for opportunity. As we stand at the brink of the twenty-first century, the tremendous success of these investors is a powerful example of all that offshore foreign investment can be and all that it can produce.

YOUR ONE BEST OPTION

Consider the facts: economic security at home is drying up right before your very eyes, and the prospects for fundamental change are bleak. With offshore markets bursting with profit potential, you have only one viable option. You have to put your uncertainties in your hip pocket, lift your shirttails, and move out into the world of global finance, into the profitable offshore world.

In order to be successful in that international arena, you will need to combine raw intelligence with a little bit of basic instinct and a whole lot of know-how. Raw intelligence is a quality you're either born with or not. My sense is that if you've figured out that you need to read this book, then you were born with it. Basic instinct exists in all of us. We just have to learn to trust it, and that comes with experience. So the sooner you get started, the faster your investment sixth sense will develop.

But what about know-how? Well, that you have to acquire. You have to be in the right place at the right time, talking with the right people in order to learn what you need to know in the offshore market. Acquiring know-how is what this book is all about. So let's keep going. . . .

CHAPTER 3

THE OPEN DOOR: DOING BUSINESS OFFSHORE

By all measures, we are launched on a new era in which the entire world is to become the investor's oyster.

— THE GLOBAL MONEY GAME

As you prepare to globalize your own assets and holdings, bear in mind that many investors and entrepreneurs have paved the way for you. There are many role models out there and lots of success stories to help guide your offshore strategy. Remember, too, that there have also been abysmal failures for some offshore investors, so approach every potential offshore adventure with a combination of enthusiasm and caution.

Whenever I meet with a potential client, I present a panoramic view of the rugged but beautiful financial terrain that can be found offshore. My advice is always the same. First, believe that there are limitless financial opportunities outside our borders, because there are. Second, know that to benefit from them you must adopt an entirely new business style, a style that mixes entrepreneurial savvy with a well-conceived business plan.

Given the current global economic picture and reliable forecasts for the near future, the offshore strategy is an absolute prerequisite for financial success. As recently as twenty years ago, that was not the case. But as we approach the end of the twentieth century, a healthy step outside U.S. borders will be essential to your financial profitability and, of course, your security.

Let me share some interesting facts that form the basis of a persuasive argument for offshore investment. In less than twenty-five years, the world's stock market inventory grew 700 percent, from roughly $1 trillion in the late 1960s to more than $7 trillion by the early 1990s. How much of that market do you suppose is contained within the United States? In 1970, U.S. equities comprised fully two-thirds of the world's stock market. In 1997, less than one-third are American. In only a few short years the equation had shifted. Nearly 70 percent of the world's stocks (and more than 55 percent of its fixed income) are invested in overseas markets. Therefore, it makes little sense to limit your investing sphere to just the continental United States.

Presently, the offshore option can give you considerably more of a return than Swiss bank accounts. It really does offer something for everyone. Your options are unlimited, from owning your own offshore bank to operating your own international money fund or serving as an international broker for industrial spare parts. It's entirely up to you. The only obstacle is the boundary of your imagination. As long as you understand that real growth and profit are now outside U.S. borders, you will do well.

THE WINDOW OF OPPORTUNITY

Until quite recently, the U.S. government did not encourage businesspeople to operate offshore. It didn't necessarily discourage them either. For a variety of reasons Uncle Sam wasn't terribly interested in international diversification. Now that has all changed.

Part of this change came about because more individual American investors began to see the light. As James Thorneburg, a businessman from Statesville, North Carolina, put it, "I looked at the marketplace and convinced myself that you're either going to be global or you're going to be nobody."

Not too long ago, while leafing through *Business Week,* I came across a very expensive special advertising section. It was a multipage, full-color section that had been purchased by the U.S. government to sell the offshore concept, to encourage American businesspeople to go offshore. The idea was endorsed in a letter by a former U.S. secretary of commerce. I smiled at the spread. In fact, it made my day. Here was a member of the president's cabinet giving exactly the same advice that I've been giving for the last twenty-five years!

The secretary went on to say:

> The dollar has declined substantially against the currencies of our major trading partners, and government efforts to open world markets to U.S. goods are paying off. . . . Recognizing that today's economic climate is ideal for improving our position in the world markets, the President has launched . . . a major new campaign to take advantage of a window of opportunity that has opened. . . .

Of course, the real story had to be read between the lines. Americans have not successfully managed to keep the dollar strong. The domestic economy has been going haywire for some time. So it's important to get out there and do something now, before it's too late. The secretary's comments reinforced my own thinking about offshore investment. The "window of opportunity" that he referred to is opening wider every day. More and more individuals, companies, and investment groups are benefiting from the offshore option.

It seems that everyone is trying to get in on the act. I've been an international financial adviser and consultant for nearly twenty-five years and I've never seen so many people waving the offshore banner. I believe the international marketplace has never been so open for profit making. In part, recent data on the size and purchasing power of the international market has encouraged this surge in activity. Experts tell us that the rest of the world produces four times the U.S. GNP. Fully 95 percent of the planet's population lives outside the U.S., and it's growing 70 percent faster than we are.

Sam Ferguson, president of Ferguson Industries, is an example of the new breed. His company helps finance and build fertilizer plants in various foreign countries. With close-cropped hair, dark horn-rimmed glasses, and a classic white Stetson, Ferguson looks more like a small-town businessman than an economic trailblazer. But aside from his Texas manner, he's an offshore activist. "If I weren't in international sales today, one of three things would have happened: I'd have closed my doors when the domestic market dwindled away; I'd have developed an entirely different line of products; or I'd have a very small company with a very small staff and take what we could sell."

Ferguson's business style is straightforward. "We simply recognize no geographical boundaries," he

Given the current global economic picture and reliable forecasts for the near future, the offshore strategy is an absolute prerequisite for financial success. As recently as twenty years ago, that was not the case. But as we approach the end of the twentieth century, a healthy step outside U.S. borders will be essential to your financial profitability and, of course, your security.

explains. "Any country is a sales prospect. . . . In our first year of exporting, foreign business was about 2 to 3 percent of sales. Today, about 65 percent of our business is export, and overall we make a better profit on our international business than we do on domestic sales."

Kathleen Bond, an experienced hand in offshore business and the manager of the international division of EIL Instruments, Inc., believes people like Sam Ferguson are still in the minority. She says that far too many Americans continue to have a "border mentality." They don't understand, she argues, that "you can do business as easily in Saudi Arabia as you can in Chicago."

I don't know if that's totally true. Doing business abroad does require special skills. Nevertheless, they are skills that can be easily acquired and honed. Too many people wear border blinders about doing international business. I am constantly amazed by how many intelligent, hard-driving business people simply will not acknowledge that financial opportunity exists outside our continental borders. I suspect their myopic vision may really be a defense. Maybe they prefer to deny the offshore market than to admit they're afraid of it.

Every day I encounter more evidence that the offshore option is the way to go. For example, recognizing that more and more people are conducting worldwide business from their U.S. telephones, AT&T has established an "International 800 Service." As its promotional material explains, "It's a fact that today's economy is not local, regional, or even national. It is global."

AT&T's International 800 Service acknowledges the pivotal role of offshore centers in today's international economy. Of the nearly thirty countries that can utilize the service, almost half are bona fide offshore jurisdictions, with all the relaxed legal and tax laws that are associated with such foreign financial centers. These include the Bahamas, the British Virgin Islands, the Cayman Islands, Hong Kong, the Netherlands, Panama, and Trinidad and Tobago.

AT&T has no genuine need to help you reach out and touch someone—they wouldn't be pumping money into trying to sell this service if they hadn't researched their potential market. They've glimpsed the future, and they know that it will be supported by a booming offshore economy.

OFFSHORE FINANCIAL GIANTS

Aside from international corporate activity, I've seen a tremendous increase in the number of individual financiers who roam the world in pursuit of profitable business deals. Among them are Ted Turner, George Soros, John Templeton, and Rupert Murdoch. Murdoch, the Australian communications magnate, emerges with one of the most visible profiles. His empire is spread over four continents: Europe, Australia, North America, and Asia. Although Murdoch is not a run-of-the-mill offshore investor, I believe we can learn a lot by observing his game.

Murdoch's global portfolio, currently valued at more than $12 billion, took nearly forty years to build. He began with two struggling newspapers that had belonged to his father. Today he owns—among other things—more than 100 newspapers and magazines, a satellite cable outlet, book publishers, his own airline, a U.S. television network, and a national cable channel. Not too long ago he purchased Triangle Publications, publisher of *TV Guide,* for $3 billion. He is, in a word, BIG.

What interests me most about Murdoch's style is the way he can manipulate and enhance his financial standing by simply exercising the international option, and by using national tax and legal differences to his advantage. With money strategically located around the world, he can take advantage of opportunities that are possible only with interglobal linkages.

For example, when he purchased Metromedia he financed the deal by having his company, the Australia-based News Corporation, issue shares on another of his holdings, the California-based 20th Century Fox. At a price of $2 billion, the project was an expensive gamble. But by financing on a global basis, Murdoch made it work. As *Business World* put it:

> Murdoch's luck held. When interest rates dipped, his company was able to raise $800 million by floating several bond issues in Europe and stretching its bank credit lines. . . .

Several differences between American and Australian accounting principles have made it easier for Murdoch to borrow. In the United States, for example, preferred shares of Fox were treated as debt and the dividend payout was deducted as though it were an interest expense; but Down Under, these shares were lumped with shareholder equity. On paper, this reduced News Corp.'s debt load and enabled it to exercise more leverage. Asset revaluation is another Australian accounting technique that has facilitated borrowing for Murdoch. Periodically, News Corp.'s mastheads and television licenses are reappraised. If they have grown in value, the increases are added to shareholder equity, thus strengthening the balance sheet.

That's the beauty of international investing. By moving offshore, you can expand your pool of available capital and, in the process, strengthen your own investment power. Of course, few of us have the savvy or resources of a Rupert Murdoch. He truly is one of a kind, able to structure packages that most of us could never design nor afford. Nevertheless, his sense of scale and ambition are an inspiration to any aspiring offshore investor.

Another fascinating international investor is George Soros. Among the world's most celebrated financial wizards, Soros is best known for the nearly $1 billion that he made in the space of just a few days of currency speculation in 1992. By betting correctly on the collapse of the British pound, Soros made one of the biggest profits ever registered in the global market. That distinction alone makes him a man worth watching. A Hungarian Jewish refugee who is said to currently manage more than $11 billion in assets, Soros has also established himself as a somewhat eccentric philanthropist. Drawn to the rebuilding of the nations of the former Eastern bloc, he has already given away $500 million and plans to give away $500 million more. He lives by a simple credo: "I was born poor, but I won't die poor."

For anyone who has begun to consider the international option, Soros stands as a role model for a number of reasons. He's fearless. He's quick to act. He knows the value of starting small and working up to high-stakes investment games. Perhaps most intriguing of all, Soros has developed a complete theory on how to get rich in the international market. Although his general concept of "reflexivity" is very abstract, it teaches investors to be ever on the lookout for "boom/bust sequences." In everyday language that means that Soros thinks you can make money when you correctly pinpoint a social imbalance that will precipitate radical change within a financial market.

In one *Wall Street Journal* article, he tried to outline his theory by observing that: "When people lose confidence in a currency, its decline tends to reinforce domestic inflation, thereby validating the decline. When investors have confidence in a company's management, the rise in share price makes it easier for management to fulfill investors expectations. . . . I call such initially self-reinforcing but eventually self-defeating connections 'reflexive.'" Elsewhere, Soros has reasoned that: "The greater the uncertainty, the more people are influenced by the market trends; and the greater the influence of trend-following speculation, the more uncertain the situation becomes." In times of such uncertainty, this financial genius has learned to act without hesitation. He tests the market's direction—which allows him to strengthen his conviction that he's correctly identified a trend—and then does exactly what everyone else isn't doing.

Byron Wien, U.S. equity investment strategist for Morgan Stanley in New York, is a close friend and adviser to Soros. He explains the theory of reflexivity in much simpler language: "His idea is that things do very well and then they do badly," argues Wien. "You should know that while they're doing well, they're about to do badly and . . . the important thing is to recognize the inevitability of trend change. The key point is the identification of the inflection point."

In my view, the international player has an immediate advantage with Soros's style of trend watching and investment response. If you have financial reserves strategically balanced across a number of markets, then you have an obvious interest in keeping up with the social and political shifts that affect those markets. If you choose to be like Soros, vigilant and thoughtful, then you can interpret world happenings through financial eyes. Instead of seeing a politician's victory (or defeat) from a social perspective, you begin to see it as the catalyst for very specific financial trends and developments. You begin to move your money around, exchange it and invest it—all based on this entrepreneurial worldview.

Philip Evans Kamins is another tale of rags to riches. Born in Chicago in the 1930s, Kamins's parents divorced when he was twelve and he had to go to work to help support the family. At sixteen he got a job with a local plastics scrap dealer and, you might say, the rest is history. Kamins is among this country's ultra-affluent, but he didn't do it through elite social connections or impressive academic credentials. In fact, he took night classes in finance at Northwestern, but never graduated. This is a guy who got rich by using his keen intuition for upcoming business trends. He got in on the ground floor

That's the beauty of international investing. By moving offshore, you can expand your pool of available capital and, in the process, strengthen your own investment power.

of the plastics explosion, and he's played all his cards right. Now worth close to $500 million, he is on the Forbes 400 list of the richest people in America. On top of all that, he is an offshore enthusiast.

He's also been a client of mine. Kamins first contacted me in the late 1970s to discuss the feasibility of an international bank involved with his plastics company. I endorsed the idea wholeheartedly, and within a few months the entire project had been completed. Kamins doesn't have time to build personal relationships with even a fraction of his business contacts. Still, I do take a special interest in him, simply because of his celebrity. I've made it a point to keep track of his success. Has the bank worked? I am not in a position to say. However, I can say that someone like Kamins does not enter into this type of financial arrangement without it paying off for him in some tangible way. If nothing else, it allows him some measure of confidentiality in his bank-controlled business dealings.

Individual investors such as Murdoch, Soros, and Kamins aren't the only ones getting in on the international financial boom. *Euromoney* reports that "offshore investments by U.S. tax-exempt pension funds are estimated to have grown from $4 billion in 1980 to over $60 billion by 1990—a compound rate of about 50 percent per year. More importantly, many institutional investors are just beginning to make investments in the world's smaller capital markets."

By and large, these institutional investors are known for their conservative style. So, why are they going offshore? Primarily because their risks are lower overseas, especially in the smaller capital markets that aren't tied to the returns generated within the giant markets. Dollar returns, even after currency exchange, are rather high. You can also obtain company shares at a lower price on the local market, whether or not the company competes internationally.

Murdoch, Soros, and the pension fund managers are only a few of the seasoned investors who scan the globe for financial opportunity. They are joined by tens of thousands of men and women throughout the world who are part of a rapidly expanding new breed of investors and entrepreneurs. They have erased the concept of national borders from their operating manuals. For them, the global economy is simply one vast, interlocking financial playing field.

ANYONE CAN PLAY

Certainly, it's important to be aware of the global investment giants and to realize that their fortunes depend on the offshore option. But I want to make it clear that anyone can become part of this offshore bonanza. For most of my clients and readers it's easier to identify with the many middle-market investors and businesspeople who have grown rich from international ventures—people whose assets range between $500,000 and $20 million.

One particular success story involves a man named Charles McKay, a fifty-six-year-old entrepreneur who lives in Florida. Based in south Dade County, McKay has worked hard to be successful. A twenty-five-year veteran of offshore investment and business operation, he's a product of the shifting fortunes of the investment battlefield. But when he talks about international moneymaking, a gleam comes to his eyes and his face beams. "There's nothing quite like it," he says proudly. For him, the initial allure was travel and big money. Always enjoying foreign places, he was determined to find a way of turning that enjoyment into money.

McKay started out in 1963 with a small-sized company that manufactured building materials for Florida-based contractors. There was nothing particularly remarkable about the company, nor about McKay. But he had two things going for him: He spoke a little Spanish and he had a good idea. He wanted to take his product line and market it throughout Latin America. In the beginning, he hit the pavement himself—actually walking the streets of various South American nations, meeting potential clients and drumming up business.

His efforts succeeded. Today he trades commodities—everything from used factories and lumber to exquisite marble and frozen American orange juice. Like other global players, he doesn't need to speak Spanish anymore. And he doesn't have to leave the United States unless he wants to. Instead, he conducts business and monitors his offshore investments—which span the Western Hemisphere and the Middle East—from his home office through sophisticated communications technologies and various methods of instantaneous money transfer.

That's the simple yet elegant essence of the offshore option: being able to manage your business and personal affairs from the onshore location of your choice while continuing to enjoy the legal and tax benefits of offshore locales. McKay's current offshore operation is a company called International Equipment Services, which he describes as a "turnkey operation." It's a multifaceted venture based in Miami with activities that shift from country to country depending on need. For example, he might operate for awhile in Ecuador, then move to Venezuela or Guatemala. He may make a deal to purchase a plant in one country, ship it to another for dismantling and refurbishing, and then to somewhere else for reassembling.

Like many offshore strategists, McKay prefers to move fast. And many people find it difficult to keep pace with him. "He's a crazy man," one observer says. "He's running off in all directions at once and you think this guy is nuts, until you see him bringing home all the bacon." That inclination toward fast investment turnaround and the willingness to act immediately on a good idea are qualities he shares with most offshore enthusiasts.

Perhaps best described as an "international trader," McKay lives by one simple motto: "Innovate or evaporate." By having a stake in the offshore market, he has managed to do more than survive erratic shifts within the U.S. economy. He's capitalized on them. In effect, he is poised for future strategic investment, wherever it looks the brightest.

The offshore option provides Charles McKay and every other offshore player with another attractive benefit: flexibility in all aspects of their business and personal financial affairs. It doesn't matter whether you're seeking a safe harbor for your overtaxed assets, or a relaxed legal environment where you can increase your profit margin by as much as tenfold. An offshore involvement guarantees you a flexible business tool.

For example, what if you wanted to sell your U.S.-based business? How could you benefit from selling it to an offshore interest? At one level, an offshore involvement would put you in close and continuous contact with an international network of businesspeople—all of whom are looking for appealing investments, and one of whom may find your business to be exactly what he or she is after. More specifically, by having an offshore holding company or bank, you can structure the sale of your own company to an international buyer while maintaining confidentiality, avoiding unnecessary tax burdens, and earning a generous profit.

In the late 1980s international buyers acquired an estimated 3,750 American businesses for prices ranging from $1 million to $50 million. All reliable indicators suggest that the future will bring more of these transnational purchases. According to R. M. Rodnick, chairman of an international merger and acquisition company based in California, "The volume of mergers and acquisitions of smaller to midsize, privately held American companies by international investors represents a growing trend."

STAYING AHEAD OF THE "POWER CURVE"

One-time financial guru William Simon is famous for saying that "a good market man stays ahead of the power curve." By that he means that if you want to play with the big guys and win, you need the ability to predict the future. Some investors, such as George Soros, claim to do that with theoretical formulas. I've known a few who maintain that there's a natural knack for investment success and either you have it or you don't. Most global players, however, credit their fortunes to diligent, hard work that keeps them abreast of economic change around the world. With careful thought and measured action they've learned to read these indicators like a road map to forthcoming ups and downs in the world economy.

Just as there are many different investment styles, there are many different offshore locations—each offering its own individual set of benefits. They all have their fair share of admirers—some faithful fans and others just fad enthusiasts. Over the years I've seen a lot of foreign locales come into vogue and then pass out of favor. Usually they become popular because their government actively pursues outside investment. Offshore center policy and practice is specifically tailored to attract money from around the world. Then, after a time, another foreign government designs an even more appealing investment environment. And the whole dynamic repeats

That's the simple yet elegant essence of the offshore option: being able to manage your business and personal affairs from the onshore location of your choice while continuing to enjoy the legal and tax benefits of offshore locales.

itself. For many years, I have been a strong believer in Pacific Rim growth. Yet, there are also other regions that allow assertive offshore investors to enjoy a high rate of return on any number of investments or activities.

It's easy, for example, to use an offshore base to invest in Japan, Great Britain, France, Mexico, the Netherlands, Hong Kong, Spain, or Singapore. Or, you can decide to base your offshore operations in a British Commonwealth location, where you are positioned to take part in some very interesting developments. One of these recent opportunities is the Canadian market.

Internationalizing doesn't always transport you overseas to one of the world's exotic financial markets. Sometimes it can take you to neighboring nations, such as Canada. Recent economic growth and new legislation have made it much easier and more appealing for U.S. investors to become a part of the Canadian financial boom. Keep in mind that the Canadian stock market performs better than the U.S. market and that the Canadian securities market is the sixth largest in the world.

Arthur Johnson, author of *Breaking the Banks,* has found that the largest North American market for venture capital is the Vancouver Stock Exchange. Johnson also notes that "More than 30 percent of the shares traded in Canada are those of resource companies. Metals, oil, and forest products are the mainstay of the economy. Traditionally, the profits of these companies rise at the end of a booming economic cycle and on expectations of rising inflation; hence the market's takeoff after the bull has been on a global tear." In today's fast-paced market, that's vital information.

Two other high-potential areas are Australia and New Zealand. Large sums of money are starting to flow throughout this region, primarily because both nations can offer higher interest rates than those tendered in the United States. New Zealand recently passed new tax legislation that will help give it a competitive edge over Australia. In October 1988, the corporate tax rate was cut from 48 to 28 percent for resident companies and will be reduced to just 33 percent for foreign corporations. A series of cuts in import tariffs will reduce rates from a whopping 50 percent to just 16.5 percent! And double taxation on company profits paid as dividends will also be eliminated.

As you may have already guessed, these British Commonwealth locales are not the only game in town. For instance, any international investor would be wise to remember that in 1993 western Europe removed all trade barriers between neighboring countries to create one gigantic market. The formation of the European Union (formerly known as European Community) created a market of more than 320 million consumers. This has, in turn, created further opportunities for investment. Securities, bonds, stock options, and other vehicles are increasing in volume and in value as companies restructure through creative mergers and acquisitions.

As these businesses expand to meet new challenges, competition for funds will accelerate. That suggests the probable need for international investors who can lend money, fund bond issues, and finance expansion. There will also be opportunities for U.S.-controlled projects that offer specialized financial services such as international banking and insurance. As the new European market expands, so too will its profit potential.

Looking south to Latin America, there is growing investor interest in the conversion of international bank loans into equity investments. This occurs when a bank trades the loans it holds in a particular country for an equity position in a company based in that nation. As reported in *Euromoney,* "The obvious reason for making such investments is that the realized value of an equity investment may eventually exceed the expected value of the loan converted. Such is the beauty of an equity investment: the upside is unlimited."

A few years ago, Bear Stearns, a leading U.S. investment and trading firm that serves international corporations, governments, and institutional and individual investors, saw the loan conversion market in Latin America as a potentially big moneymaker. So it set up a Latin American Finance Group intended solely to arrange complex debt swaps among multiple counterparties in Latin America. The result has been impressive, and Bear Stearns's clients are elated. The point is, this firm used its expertise to anticipate an opportunity and to capitalize on it earlier than the competition. That's the real secret to success in the international market: Keep your eyes and ears open, and move with certainty as quickly as you can.

THE FOUR STEPS TO OFFSHORE SUCCESS

It's dangerous to oversimplify offshore investing. The process of internationalization is not without its challenges and risks. Nevertheless, I think there are four basic steps to making a prudent and profitable move offshore.

- **The First Step** is to shed your border mentality. If you continue to see the world in terms of artificial boundaries, you will fail to take advantage of the new international economic climate. I like the way Sam Ferguson phrased it: "We simply recognize no geographical boundaries."

- **The Second Step** is to watch what the smart money is doing. Investors and businesses with deep pockets can afford to stake out new territories and take greater risks. However, by tracking their moves you can shape your own strategy. Whether it's George Soros's passion for his theoretical "boom/bust sequence," Rupert Murdoch's creative use of varying accounting methods, or Bear Stearns's decision to trade Third World debt for private sector equity, the masters of the game usually offer fascinating insight into what works and what doesn't.
- **The Third Step** is to explore the landscape in all directions. Currently, there's a rush to capitalize on emerging market activity in exotic locales. However, there are plenty of opportunities in less exotic places: Canada is just waiting to be mined with the proper strategy, and, since 1993, unique profit opportunities have abounded in the European Union. Keep in mind that the United States makes up less than one-sixth of the world land mass but that more than 80 percent of the world's financial and investment opportunities

The First Step is to shed your border mentality. If you continue to see the world in terms of artificial boundaries, you will fail to take advantage of the new international economic climate. I like the way Sam Ferguson phrased it: "We simply recognize no geographical boundaries."

are offshore. Investors definitely limit their financial horizon by confining themselves to the United States.

- **The Fourth Step** is to change your perception about the real value of the dollar. In fact, the value of the dollar is constantly declining and the only way to stay ahead of it is to maintain your assets' buying power—that is, to spread your risks on an international basis.

THE TIME HAS COME

If you're still unsure about whether or not to conduct business offshore, consider the following points. During meetings with potential clients, I find these points to be the most persuasive arguments for establishing an offshore involvement.

1. Remember that tens of thousands of small and mid-size businesses and investment groups are involved in the global economy. The recent devaluation of the dollar, higher yields in overseas markets, relaxed legal regulations, and a greater international flow of money have created more investment and business opportunities for Americans.
2. Going offshore should not depend on the domestic economy. As one successful offshore investor put it, "International diversification should be part of any investor's portfolio. Waiting on domestic opportunity could mean lost opportunity." In my view, the state of our current domestic economy suggests that waiting for good times at home could mean waiting a very long time.
3. Information on offshore investment is available from several sources. More new information on off-

shore business is being generated. Whether it comes from the government, international organizations, the media, specialized advisers, international newsletters, or computer databases, the amount of information and resources available is rapidly increasing.

4. Language is no longer a barrier. Twenty-five years ago, when Charles McKay took the offshore initiative, his ability to speak Spanish was a decisive advantage. Today, English is the language of international commerce. Most offshore investors work through English-speaking agents or brokers that they hire abroad. Keep in mind that foreign businesspeople often speak some English, or they have access to people who do.
5. International licenses, tariffs, and certificates are manageable. Offshore advisers, international brokers, agents, and distributors (both here and abroad) know how to deal with locally based bureaucracies. At the outset of any offshore involvement, it is wise to work with an experienced firm or individual in order to ensure that all the proper paperwork is in hand and in appropriate form.

Going offshore, whether it's to conduct your own business or to invest in international markets, may seem overwhelming at first. So, talk with a consultant. Weigh the benefits and the risks. But don't hesitate too long. Make the move before it's too late.

CHAPTER 4

THE PROFIT INCENTIVE

Uncertainty is a fact of life . . . but you can prepare for the unknown.

— HARRY BROWNE, *INVESTMENT ADVISER*

The number one concern among virtually all my clients is profit. People always want to know how much money they can make offshore, and how fast they can make it. They want to see the bottom line, and they want it to point toward substantial economic benefits.

One man who comes to mind as a prime example of the profit motive is Federico Solis. In 1980 he walked into my office wearing an exquisite Brioni suit. He cut an impressive figure. Beneath the stylish international exterior was a man intent on making a financial killing.

Freddy had a great idea. He wanted to serve as an intermediary for big money on a global basis. To accomplish his aim he established a private international bank based in Vanuatu. Before owning his own bank he couldn't get the right people (he called them the "big boys") to return his calls. Now doors were opening for him as never before.

The gist of the story is that Freddy made it work. He used his bank to obtain letters outlining a company's credit needs. These were written by the chief financial officers of major corporations in the United States. Freddy guaranteed them better rates than they were getting.

With these valuable letters in hand he flew off to Europe where he presented them to the directors of leading banks throughout the continent. In particular, he found banks in France, Germany, Switzerland, and England to be quite receptive. His one rule was to meet only with the top man at every institution. If Freddy couldn't meet him, there would be no deal.

The results were astounding. Nearly every banker committed to loans and credit lines at the rates Freddy had promised the borrowers. For him, the payoff came in large commissions on each single financial package that he put together. After one year of concerted effort, Freddy's plan paid off. He made $4.5 million and the profits have continued to go up since then.

Today, at just barely 45, Freddy Solis is a little gray at the temples but his worth has doubled. He estimates his net worth at $60 million. We recently spoke on the phone. He's now using his bank as a broker for loans between governments and banks. He told me that within the week he would be meeting with the finance ministers of two nations to help them negotiate loans for development projects in their countries. Then, with a chuckle, he told me that the commissions are bound to be astronomical.

Freddy originally came into my office with a simple idea: to make money on an international scale. He chose the offshore route as the means to test his idea. It succeeded because he worked at the idea every day for nearly a year. He once told me, "Success is a combination of the desire to succeed and the use of the right tool at the right time." For Freddy, that tool is an offshore vision. He was transformed from someone with a great dream to someone who could put his dream into action and realize a great profit.

Over the past twenty years, the argument for offshore investment has become almost irrefutable. First of all, it hardly makes sense to limit your investment game to domestic options. I tell my clients that the entire offshore industry was built on a single principle: Let your money work wherever it can work best. A quick look around the international financial scene should show you all you need to know about how this nation compares to the rest of the world. Here's my prediction: If you become a part of the global marketplace, like Freddy Solis, within one year your pocketbook will show the difference!

THREE WAYS TO MAKE IT OFFSHORE

If you plan to be among the winners in tomorrow's international economy, you must do three things. First, explore all the options available to you offshore.

Some people like to approach the global market one step at a time. That's fine. It can be reassuring to see profits inch up, little by little. Other investors want to plunge ahead, pumping a larger share of their assets into higher-risk, higher-yield projects. That's fine too. They are typically well rewarded for their daring.

Most of the people I work with want something in between these two extremes. Only by learning about the various opportunities that exist can you design the offshore investment plan that's right for you.

Secondly, diversify your portfolio. A first major step in this direction is, in fact, to move assets offshore. When you're used to a domestic investment plan, it is an essential transition to send those first funds outside the United States.

Over the past twenty years, the argument for offshore investment has become almost irrefutable. First of all, it hardly makes sense to limit your investment game to domestic options. I tell my clients that the entire offshore industry was built on a single principle: Let your money work wherever it can work best.

But after you've made the mental shift and expatriated a portion of your money, you must take the next step. Big offshore profits always come from global diversification. Don't keep all your eggs in one basket, they say. I've found that to be a good motto in the international marketplace. If you spread your money across a multitude of markets and keep it busy in a number of nations, you position yourself to earn money on the big bonanza—wherever it occurs.

Thirdly, offshore profit demands that you take action. It's not enough to read all the right books, subscribe to all the right magazines, and talk with the best consultants. After you have gathered together all the information you feel you need, take the leap forward. Don't waste time hesitating. I firmly believe that the most modest offshore approach is better than none at all. So don't convince yourself that you aren't prepared to play. If you've found your way to this book, you're ready.

When these three essential elements come together—when you explore, diversify, and act—then you have the makings for a genuine offshore success story. And somewhere along the line, an amazing thing will happen. In a subtle but unmistakable way, you will become a different person. Ultimately, that's what I like best about my work: watching people take on a unique sense of confidence that comes only from seeing their ideas and effort turn into bottom line profits.

Bill Hollings, a client of mine, is a perfect example of this transformation. From our first meeting, after a two-day seminar that I conducted in Dallas, Bill struck me as a classic American entrepreneur. Everything about him—his beige gabardine suit, his neat dark-brown mustache, his modest manner and cool Texas drawl—conveyed an image of honesty and exactness. He instantly came across as the kind of guy you'd trust with your money.

Over a drink that evening, Bill outlined a fairly simple international business plan. He intended to purchase an offshore bank and use it for two things. First, he wanted to increase his personal assets. Second, he sought to increase his company's visibility. At that time, Bill was operating a first-class limousine service in the Dallas–Fort Worth area. By establishing an offshore presence, he figured he could hobnob with the rich and famous. In the process, he hoped to expand his client base.

Within a few weeks Bill had received the official license and charter for his bank in Vanuatu. Within months he had built it into a thriving, full-service financial center. To begin with, he developed three zero-risk investment programs for people who wanted to benefit from an offshore involvement but who were too cautious to purchase their own company or bank. These investment programs were structured to let every client find his own level of comfortable risk.

Like most good businessmen, Bill had a sixth sense about promotion. It wasn't long before he had produced some really persuasive yet understated outreach materials. These brochures and postcard mailings added a level of professionalism and credibility to the well-conceived nature of his three offerings. For many investors, the promotional pieces were the initial contact with Bill's bank. What they saw was a serious, sensible service institution that addressed their needs.

After only a year of successful operation, Bill decided to concentrate more of his energy on the offshore marketplace. It had already been very good to him, and he was convinced that it could offer him more than a better limousine service. His bank could be a phenomenally successful business in and of itself. So he started delegating a lot of his Texas business operation to associates in order to devote the bulk of his time to offshore ventures.

He also began to get creative. His tendency to do things in the most traditional manner gave way to a more innovative business style. For instance, he started using his Vanuatu-based institution to structure and broker large transnational loans. It didn't take long before he was bringing together borrowers and lenders from all over the world in a wide array of interesting partnerships, mergers, acquisitions, and start-up ventures.

Soon Bill grasped that he was armed with an amazing financial instrument. He had a weapon that could get him through any door. Soon after, Bill read in the Dallas newspapers that the famous Hunt family was running into some major financial problems and was ultimately facing bankruptcy. He instantly saw an opportunity. Never one to waste time, he picked up the phone and called them directly. Not only did he get through, but he designed a loan package that made him a bundle of money.

Three years after Bill's entry into the global arena, he called to tell me that since buying the bank he'd earned over $25 million. Not bad for thirty-six months' work and an initial investment of $30,000. But what I like best about his story is the way it shows that offshore business can make millionaires out of fairly ordinary people. More importantly, it reveals the way that global moneymaking affects people. Bill did not enter the international marketplace as a dynamic man. He was an intense, methodical entrepreneur who had very modest goals for an offshore banking business. Nevertheless, the power and vitality of the offshore environment itself had an effect on him. It freed him from the excessive restrictions that characterize business operations within the United States, giving him the tools to make more money than he himself had ever imagined.

These days, Bill is regularly invited to all the high society balls in Dallas. He is no longer surprised but still elated to receive gold-engraved invitations to many of the premier events of the year. The word has spread that William T. Hollings is a man to be reckoned with and respected. Through the brilliant use of his offshore bank, Bill has moved up into an entirely new social stratum, commanding a Texas-size dollop of influence and prestige.

Step One: Open an Offshore Bank Account

Especially for beginners, it may be reassuring to learn that offshore finance does not need to involve high-stake ventures. In fact, it can be as simple as opening a bank account in a foreign country. You don't have to take the bulk of your assets and move them halfway around the world. By doing nothing more than establishing a personal checking or savings account with a bank outside the United States, you can earn a significant profit. Even more important, you can get a taste of the amazing financial opportunities that exist outside the domestic marketplace.

If you're thinking about the possibility of an offshore account, be aware that every foreign financial institution (regardless of its size or jurisdiction) must provide certain services in order to maintain its legal status as a bank. Your business is extremely important and desirable to any offshore bank. They need your money and your confidence in order to stay in operation. So they'll go far out of their way to keep you satisfied.

It's a very different story here in the United States. All major domestic banks stay in business because of their investment portfolios. In other words, your individual checking or savings account is not a matter of great consequence to them. They're glad to have your business, of course, because it means more money in their coffers with which to invest in real profit-earning ventures. Nevertheless, if you walk out the door today, taking all your money with you, nobody is likely to lose sleep tonight over your departure. This discrepancy between on- and offshore banks results in real benefits to anyone who maintains an account in another country.

To begin with, offshore banks are safer. The myth that U.S. banks offer safety because the government provides insurance for all deposits up to $100,000 means that banks here have the option of being bailed out by the government if they don't follow good management practices. At one time, this insurance was a real protection. But today, with the whole banking industry experiencing failure after failure and the federal government short of funds, we are facing the prospect of little or no protection. A U.S. bank that fails today may return, at most, fifty cents on every dollar to its depositors.

A depositor also has to factor in the additional cost of operating a bank in the United States. Ten to twenty percent of a U.S. bank's earnings are now allocated to regulatory compliance. American banks are spending upwards of $100 billion a year to comply with a labyrinth of federal, state, and local regulations. By patronizing these banks, you support the outlay for regulatory compliance and get back less in return.

Like all aspects of offshore business, private ownership abroad comes in various shapes and sizes. One of your options is to set up or purchase an offshore corporation.

Conversely, offshore banks do not have such regulatory burdens. As independent entities, they must operate efficiently and economically, or they will fail and fold. They don't have the option of falling back on government. In addition, unlike the domestic banks, offshore institutions must maintain a higher ratio of liquidity—the ratio of liquid assets to debts. Their reserve requirements are much higher than onshore banks. In other words, offshore banks are financially stronger, safer, and better managed as a whole than most domestic banks.

Basically, when it comes to the protection of your property, assets, and capital, you're the one who has to set the standards. In terms of banks, the higher standards most of us require in today's economic environment are being provided by offshore banks.

There are other benefits. Offshore banks offer a very attractive interest rate—several percentage points above what you can find at the best U.S. institution. Normally, the longer you keep your money on deposit, the more interest you earn. Overall, there is a higher liquidity ratio at offshore banks. They are in a better position to provide liquidity to their customers.

"Float time" is another benefit. Have you ever wondered how all those traveler's checks turn into big profits for American Express? It's simple, really. Everyday, people around the world exchange their cash for insured American Express Traveler's Checks. Literally millions of dollars are cycled through this process week after week, and, believe me, that money doesn't sit idly for months after happy vacationers cash one $50 check at a time. Instead, it is intelligently invested into high-interest T-bills and money-market accounts. In other words, during the time between purchase of insured checks and actual onshore bank clearing, American Express is earning interest on your money.

As an individual offshore customer, you can make money from float time in a similar way. For example, if you establish an interest-bearing checking account in a foreign jurisdiction, you can use it to pay your domestic bills. After being deposited by your creditors, your checks begin a long trip back to your offshore bank for clearing. Ordinarily, you can expect that process to take between thirty and forty days. During that time you will continue earning interest on the money already paid out in those checks—that float time benefits you.

It's fairly easy to open a foreign bank account. You can do it yourself—by sending a money order or cashier's check made out to the bank along with instructions on what kind of account you want to establish. (For more detailed information, please refer to Chapter 11, page 219.) There are a lot of international investment magazines and journals available now, and all of them contain ads for offshore centers that would like nothing better than to get your unexpected check in the mail one day.

The problem with mail transactions, of course, is your nervousness while you wait for a letter of confirmation from the bank. So I suggest that you let technology do the work faster and with more reliability. Work with a consultant who can implement the initial transaction for you via fax machine. This also gives you someone nearby you can turn to with questions and concerns during the early days and weeks of managing your foreign account.

You may also be interested in opening "twin accounts" with your offshore bank. This is a specialized service that combines a "current" (checking-type) account with a high-interest deposit account. Most of your money is held in the high-interest deposit, but a small balance is kept on hand for everyday withdrawal. In addition, if you are ever overdrawn, the bank automatically transfers money from your deposit account to cover the difference.

For the savvy investor, there are also fiduciary accounts to consider. They let you make investments in the bank's name and earn interest profit at the same time. For instance, let's say you maintain a savings account in a private Austrian bank. You can direct your banker to invest all (or part) of your holdings in U.S. dollars and West German marks. The dollars will be purchased in New York and held in a U.S. bank under the facility's name. The deutsche marks will be held in a German bank in Frankfurt.

For the record, it appears as though your offshore bank is acting on its own behalf. Nevertheless, all profits earned on the currency exchange and any interest earned on the deposit are paid to you.

Step Two: Develop an International Investment Game Plan

When you're ready for the next step in profit-earning potential, I suggest you think about investing in a number of offshore funds. All these funds are straightforward mutual funds based in tax-haven jurisdictions or in low-tax nations. Since they operate outside the investor "protection" and tax regulations of this and other major countries, these funds are able to invest in a broader range of instruments than onshore domestic investment companies. This flexibility makes them extremely attractive to investors worldwide.

To get the most from global diversification, I agree with other financial consultants who recommend that you put at least 15 percent of your portfolio into non-U.S. securities. You can choose either cash or fixed interest securities (such as bonds). You can transform your U.S. dollars into any of the world's major currencies or into equities.

Frankly, though, too much choice can be difficult to handle, especially if you're a beginner and are operating in unfamiliar territory. For example, do you trust yourself to know the right moment to switch from Japanese to European funds? And picking the big winners from among some 50,000 stocks and bonds traded on more than 100 exchanges in three dozen countries can be overwhelming, even for the most experienced offshore investor.

My advice is to rely on professionals. If your offshore financial consultant knows this field, let him or her handle it for you. If not, your consultant should know someone who does because the size of the market is astounding! There are now at least seventy U.S.-based international equity funds, and more than five hundred offshore funds. In addition, there are numerous global funds investing foreign bonds, currencies, and other types of securities.

In general, I recommend these international mutual funds because they offer you a kind of one-shot investment strategy. They make it possible for you to put your money on the table and then sit back while experts invest it in precisely those markets where it's most likely to make a fast and handsome profit.

Be aware that there are differences among international funds. Some are what we call "closed-end." That means they can trade only on a stock exchange and have no redemption capability. Its ability to appreciate may be more dependent on market forces and demand for the funds rather than performance. Nevertheless, some of them have done very well. In fact, one closed-end fund, the Taiwan Fund, outperformed all international funds through the late 1980s and early 1990s, returning a phenomenal 230 percent!

In my view, the Pacific Rim nations—where double-digit hikes in corporate profits and GNP gains of 6 percent have become commonplace—are also good bets for the late 1990s. To help keep tabs on this region, I recommend that you subscribe to the *Far Eastern Economic Review,* a monthly publication covering business and investment activities in the nations of the Pacific Rim. The articles and advertisements featured in each issue

Offshore banks do not have such regulatory burdens. As independent entities, they must operate efficiently and economically, or they will fail and fold. They don't have the option of falling back on government. In addition, unlike the domestic banks, offshore institutions must maintain a higher ratio of liquidity—the ratio of liquid assets to debts. Their reserve requirements are much higher than onshore banks. In other words, offshore banks are financially stronger, safer, and better managed as a whole than most domestic banks.

can be of enormous help to any investor with interests overseas. Also, the magazine regularly gathers corporate annual reports from many of the world's leading companies, and offers them to readers at no cost. By sending away for reports on Asian-based firms, you can get a very good sense of just how well their stock is likely to do over the coming months.

The point is, nearly all the international funds have surpassed U.S.-based global funds, largely because they face less regulation and fewer investment restrictions. So jump in, because the water is warm. And the profits are hot!

Step Three: Make a Tactical Decision to Own an Offshore Corporation

If you follow steps one and two that I've outlined above, I guarantee that you'll rapidly feel ready for something more substantial. Once aware of what the offshore marketplace can offer, investors become extremely eager to broaden their horizons. In other words, you'll want to begin running your own offshore operation instead of participating in someone else's.

Like all aspects of offshore business, private ownership abroad comes in various shapes and sizes. One of your options is to set up or purchase an offshore corporation. What would you do with it? That's entirely up to you. Frankly, you don't have to do anything with it if you don't want to. You can just let it operate as your broker in the international marketplace.

Once you assume ownership of an offshore corporation, you'll be legally entitled to use your firm for a wide variety of activities. For example, it can invest in stocks, commodities, CDs, real estate, or foreign currencies. It can also import and export all around the world and serve as a holding company to protect patents and trademarks.

Many companies based in offshore jurisdictions are used for manufacturing. Starting a company in order to manufacture products can also serve to bring you many benefits such as providing a vehicle for raising capital. However, you usually have a legal obligation to manufacture the product in question: computer parts, clothing, toys, etc. Unless this is your intent, I suggest you stay away from offshore corporations purchased on the basis of proposed manufacturing of goods.

Some individuals have also started offshore safety deposit companies. These are designed to serve individuals who want to keep their valuables safely stored offshore. These companies operate in a similar fashion to safety deposit companies in this country. Owners are able to charge fees for their service.

If this whole process seems a bit overwhelming, don't worry. You can enjoy all the benefits (and disadvantages, unfortunately) of an offshore corporation without having to personally run the company. Reputable and well-connected offshore consultants can make professional management services available. Typically, they'll refer you to a firm based outside the United States. Montreal and Hong Kong are home to a number of these financial management groups offering a full line of investment and administrative services as well as insurance for the tax-free status of the corporation.

Working with one of these firms offers another important benefit. It makes your firm "legitimate" in the eyes of Uncle Sam. You see, without an offshore management firm, it might appear that you are running your offshore company from within the United States. That could prompt the IRS to claim your business is nothing more than a "paper corporation" designed to avoid taxes. However, with overseas management there's no doubt that your firm is truly a foreign entity—a mandatory prerequisite to convincing the federal government that it has economic substance along with technical form.

Another offshore business that you may want to investigate is a Reinsurance firm—or "captive" insurance company, as they're more often called. These firms have been in business for years all over the world. To benefit from them, you must have a company here in the United States that purchases liability insurance.

By establishing an offshore insurance firm, you can instantly insure yourself against a number of high-risk contingencies such as malpractice, striking employees, fire, and flood. Instead of paying premiums to a U.S. insurance company, you simply pay them to yourself, in the name of your offshore company. Your domestic corporation will save a lot of money because it won't be contributing to the profit and administrative overhead of an underwriter. And, perhaps best of all, since insurance premiums are tax deductible, you will begin writing tax deductible premium checks to yourself! The more insurance you buy, the more money you make.

Talk with your consultant about the captive concept. Obviously, it won't be useful to most individual investors. Even small consortiums are probably out of this picture.

You should also be aware that if you establish one of these entities, you will need to function as a bona fide reinsurance firm. That's thanks to tax authorities here in the United States who got so upset by the captive concept that they pushed through legislation to force all U.S. corporations to accept third-party reinsurance risks into their foreign insurance pool. In this way, they prove themselves to be true reinsurers and not just ingenious tax evaders.

Step Four: Establish Your Own Offshore Bank

Establishing your own private offshore bank, in my view, offers the ultimate in offshore moneymaking potential.

For starters, virtually every offshore bank exists to service its owner's personal financial needs. As a bank owner you will enjoy all the customer benefits associated with offshore banking without paying a thing, because you'll be servicing yourself. In addition, you will gain an appealing new level of financial privacy because much of what you transact will be processed in the bank's name rather than in yours. In a sense, you will become an invisible economic entity protected from the radarlike vision of Uncle Sam and his investigators.

There are, however, more sophisticated profit perks that come with bank ownership. For example, all banks—foreign and domestic—borrow money from their depositors. When you open a checking account at any commercial bank, you are really loaning that institution your money in exchange for a checkbook. Currently, U.S. banks are paying about 5 percent interest on checking accounts. That means that banks must earn at least that

Establishing your own private offshore bank, in my view, offers the ultimate in offshore moneymaking potential.

much in investment return on your initial deposit if they are to break even. But banks are not in business to just break even. Typically, it loans your money out to third parties at the prime lending rate (in 1997, that's between 9.5 and 14.5 percent depending on the borrower and the situation) and keeps the difference as its profit.

Your private international bank can work in exactly the same way. Deposits can be accepted; loans can be made. The beauty of the concept, from your perspective, is that your bank makes money from both transactions. You earn a little bit from your depositor's money and you get a little more from everyone who borrows from you. In my view, this is the basic concept behind a two-way street to wealth and prosperity.

Once you get enough depositors (who learn about you primarily from aggressive advertising in international financial publications and from third-party associates), your bank can begin to extend credit. It can issue letters of credit and financial guarantees. In other words, it can allow borrowers to deposit a fixed sum of money for a specified period of time (usually ten years). The interest on that deposit is paid into a "sinking fund" that enables the bank to issue money amounting to the deposit plus interest to the borrower.

You profit in three ways. First, your bank charges a nominal fee to issue the letter of commitment. Second, it charges several percentage points to actually issue the loan guarantee. Third, it gains the use of the client's secured deposit during the period of time the guarantee is pending. If the borrower doesn't have enough capital to make the initial deposit, your bank can lend him the money at a higher rate of interest than it pays to establish the sinking fund. Or if the loan is obtained from a third party, your bank can charge an additional handling fee. So you stand to make money in still a fourth way.

Your offshore bank charter also allows you to provide back-to-back loans. In this particular transaction, funds deposited by one corporate subsidiary are used as collateral for a loan to another subsidiary of the same parent company. It's a fairly common banking process that lets diversified corporations transfer their profits from one business arm to another—usually from a high-tax base of operation to a low-tax jurisdiction. When the parent company is the owner of the offshore bank, the profit incentive is even more compelling because all handling costs and percentage points charges are within a kind of revolving money door.

Finally, your offshore bank can offer secured lending. Nearly all offshore banks take advantage of their right to lend money. The most frequently issued loans are for venture capital, high-risk projects involving high interest rates. Within the United States, strict laws restrict lending activity at extremely high interest rates. Private offshore banks are not limited by these legal parameters. Instead, they can lend at whatever the free market will allow, sometimes 10 percentage points higher than loans made by conventional lenders.

THE MAGNIFICENT SEVEN

Aside from the profits that you earn taking deposits and making loans, your offshore bank provides seven distinct moneymaking benefits. I call them the "magnificent seven" because, like the famous movie, they are an unbeatable combination. Each one of them calls for its own skills and financial connections. As an offshore bank owner, you will want to work with a professional consultant who can help you network with the right foreign representatives in your chosen jurisdiction. Then your only responsibilities will be to serve as the bank's North American adviser and to dream up new and creative ways to spend the money you make.

Profit Benefit Number One: Investment

When all is said and done, offshore banks make money because they invest their deposit reserves in high-yield ventures. Intelligent investment inevitably earns the bank more money than it is required to pay its depositors, no matter what rate of interest it offers. This earning power is possible because foreign banks are not bound by the investment restrictions that limit onshore banks. Instead, they can invest in any number of opportunities, from real estate to high-ticket consumer goods and securities. In my opinion, this single benefit is reason enough to purchase your own offshore bank.

Profit Benefit Number Two: Currency Exchange

Many offshore banks offer a currency exchange service to customers living in countries such as South Africa, where currency conversion is prohibited by law. The bank earns a profit because it charges a handsome commission (sometimes as high as 20 percent of the deposit) on the transaction.

Profit Benefit Number Three: Commodities Brokerage

If you like fast-paced business, you might enjoy the wheeling and dealing that comes with this service. I have one client in Tampa, Florida, who makes it a cornerstone of his offshore profit strategy. He uses his expertise as a fresh produce distributor to broker commodities to a wide array of North and South American businesses. Through his offshore bank in Vanuatu, he issues letters of credit to coffee merchants and produce distributors throughout Colombia, Guatemala, and Venezuela. When one of them has a significant surplus, he simply issues his own credit to the dealer. The terms specify that delivery will be made to one of the bank's clients, to be named at a later date. He then shops his network of Latin American and U.S. businesses until he finds an interested buyer, and has his bank negotiate a profitable sale. He tells me he earns between $40,000 and $50,000 on more than a dozen such transactions each year.

Profit Benefit Number Four: Secret Numbered Accounts

Frankly, I think that from a customer's perspective these anonymous accounts are an overrated dinosaur from the offshore Stone Age. Nevertheless, a lot of people around the world put considerable value in them. Usually they are residents of politically turbulent nations who feel a real need to keep a sizable portion of their assets in a secret account that cannot be linked to them or their families.

Not all foreign jurisdictions allow for the Swiss-style numbered bank account. So if you want to provide this customer service, be sure to pick a locale that does. It will definitely help you attract an entire community of international clients and the profits that go along with their business.

Profit Benefit Number Five: Trusts

Most offshore banks find it profitable to offer trust company services. Acting as a trustee under deeds of settlement or will, receiving assets on behalf of clients, and managing them in accordance with their instructions can be a lucrative business. I know that some offshore banks charge up to $10,000 to administer a trust.

Aside from the profits that you earn taking deposits and making loans, your offshore bank provides seven distinct moneymaking benefits. I call them the "magnificent seven" because, like the famous movie, they are an unbeatable combination.

Profit Benefit Number Six: Cash Management

The goal of any bank is to ensure that capital is legally invested and utilized in high-yielding opportunities such as commodities and real estate. Unfortunately for U.S. institutions, onshore bank laws prohibit financial facilities from making such investments with their long-term deposit reserves. Offshore banks are far less constrained. They can legally invest all their capital, long- and short-term, in any opportunity they choose.

Profit Benefit Number Seven: Arbitrage

"Arbitrage" means the simultaneous buying and selling of the same (or equivalent) securities in different markets. A smart offshore banker can monitor various currency values in a number of markets and take lucrative advantage of the arbitrage process. To put it simply, the investor can buy low and sell high—all in the same moment—and keep the difference as a profit.

For example, an offshore bank might buy deutsche marks for its account in Frankfurt and immediately sell them for Italian lire. Then, if it can find a broker (perhaps in Zurich) who needs lire, the bank can trade again. And this time, it will get more value than it started with.

THE BOTTOM LINE

By this point, you may be wondering how to become part of the offshore market. For some of you, this is as easy as sitting down and writing a check for the purchase of your own bank. For many others without money to invest, it takes a level of creativity to go out and actually obtain your very own offshore bank.

One of the most encouraging examples of such individual creativity and determination I've ever encountered took place at one of my seminars. One of the attendees was a young entrepreneur named Eric Foxman. Although he was very excited about the prospect of offshore banking, Eric did not have the money to purchase a bank. However, to his credit, he came up with a way that allowed him to become a bank owner.

He convinced a number of investors at the seminar to place a certain amount of money down on the bank. When Eric had enough funds, he purchased the bank in his name with the investors as his partners. The point is that you don't necessarily need the money to start a bank. There are always ways to obtain what you need if you are creative and determined.

A few months ago I received a letter from Eric. He wrote that "everything has gone better than he dreamed." His partners are happy, he's earned enough by managing the bank to purchase a substantial percentage of the bank, and customers are flocking to its services.

Now you're wondering, how much money can all this put in your pocket? It depends on which offshore financial options you combine in your international investment plan. If you choose to work with just a single foreign bank account, you can probably count on several percentage points more interest than you're earning here in the United States. If your deposit reserves are high, that could mean thousands of dollars a year.

If you add to that foreign account a number of intelligently selected global mutual funds, you've upped your profit potential by tens of thousands of dollars. This two-pronged effort is probably a good plan for the extremely cautious offshore investor.

However, I hope for your sake that you decide to be aggressive, because by purchasing your own private international bank, you can surpass those modest profit projections by leaps and bounds. Remember, Bill Hollings made $25 million in just three years! Freddy Solis quickly doubled his worth. For each of them, all it took was a modest investment up front, some creative thinking, and one offshore bank.

Chapter 5

In Pursuit of True Financial Privacy

The greatest degree of privacy in this society is achieved by the very rich, the very poor, and the very crooked.

— **Bill Petrocelli, *Low Profile***

After profit, the second major concern that brings prospective clients into my office is financial privacy. Over the years I've heard a staggering number of horror stories from people whose lives have been indelibly marked by corporate and governmental intrusion. Based on what they've told me and on what I've read about U.S. law and economic policy, I am convinced that there is a complex, seemingly invisible information system in this country that has been set up to unearth, store, and disseminate even the most personal facts about your life.

If you're like many Americans, you probably assume that the Constitution ensures your inalienable right to privacy. Unfortunately, you're wrong. The Fourth Amendment—most often cited as the national guarantee of confidentiality—specifies only that "the right of the people to be secure in their persons, houses, papers, and effects against unreasonable searches and seizures shall not be violated and no warrants shall issue, but upon probable cause. . . ."

The men of 1787 who drafted this legal tenet clearly meant to protect privacy as it pertained to property. They wanted a right to unthreatened ownership of land and personal possession. But as an article in *Time* magazine recently pointed out, our founding fathers lived in a world where people shared common norms of morality. They didn't need to sort through the questions that plague a global information service economy. They didn't need to worry about how one man might decide to use (or share) private financial information about another. They didn't foresee an era in which sophisticated communication systems could instantaneously interact, calling up, comparing, and exchanging information about you or me within a matter of minutes.

In other words, they didn't foresee the 1990s. Today, the greatest threat to your individual privacy may have nothing to do with property theft. It has to do with access to information about you and your activities. Where you live and work, the names of your children, your medical and psychiatric history, your arrest record, the phone numbers you dial, the amount of money you earn, the way you earn it, and how you report it to Uncle Sam after it's yours—these are the information tidbits that will undoubtedly remain stored in lots of different places as long as you keep your money within U.S. borders.

An offshore financial involvement offers you the one and only escape from this government-endorsed conspiracy. Just as you can legitimately make more money overseas than you could ever hope to earn in this country, you can also look forward to enjoying your foreign profits in an atmosphere of complete confidentiality. In money havens scattered from Hong Kong to Vanuatu to the Netherlands Antilles, you can benefit from ironclad secrecy laws that strictly forbid any bureaucratic review of your personal financial records. That means you can legally guard your assets from the overzealous inspection that has become part and parcel of U.S. banking and investment portfolio management.

HOW DEEP CAN THEY DIG FOR DIRT?

If you're like most upper- and middle-income Americans, the federal government alone maintains nearly twenty separate files on you. According to one recent analysis, Uncle Sam currently has computer tabs on three billion files, a virtual treasure trove through which an army of eager bureaucrats can search and snoop. The state in which you reside probably holds another dozen or so active computer files on you. And the Census Bureau routinely updates its records. Any minute of any day, its computer system can spit out your basic data: sex, race, ethnic origin, marital status, employment situation, and place in the household pecking order. Most important, it can legally pass any or all of that information along to other interested branches of government.

Then, of course, there's the Internal Revenue Service. The IRS knows how much money you make, and where it comes from. The Social Security Administration probably knows more than you do about your employment earnings history. If you served in the armed forces, you're permanently listed in the archives of the Veterans Administration as well as your service branch.

Are you a borrower? If so, then at least one credit bureau (and probably several) keeps a file on you. Lenders nationwide can request from any one of these independent business operations a slew of information about your income, debts, employment history, marital status, tax liens, judgments, arrests, and convictions. The largest of these data collection firms, TRW, maintains files on some 120 million Americans at any given time.

Still another category of consumer investigation companies collects information about the health habits and lifestyles of likely employment and insurance applicants. How do these agencies get their information? Mainly from the friends, neighbors, employers, landlords, and other casual professional associates of those they are investigating. The big daddy of this business is Equifax Services based in Atlanta. Equifax sells reports to prospective employers and insurers on well over twenty million people each and every year.

This booming information industry has gone the way of all big business—toward specialization. For example, the Chicago-based Docket-Search Network sells a service called "Physician's Alert." It consists solely of information on patients who have filed civil suits. Its clients, naturally enough, tend to be doctors in high-risk specialties like obstetrics and orthopedics.

Then there's Moscom, the world's leading supplier of call accounting computer systems. Through Moscom's software system, employers can connect their workers' telephones to a personal computer system and track all on-the-job phone calls. The service gives executives a bird's-eye view of their company's telephone bill. But in the process they are spying on their employees—who they call and how long they talk. Is it such a stretch to envision a future decision to eavesdrop on what they're talking about?

Sometimes the information that's conveyed through these systems is painfully accurate. For example, I was once hired by a professional caterer named Jackie who had spent years living with the negative financial consequences of a past mistake. She was still fairly young when I first met her—maybe in her mid-thirties. She came to see me because her five-year-old business, a good catering service hired primarily by the Los Angeles entertainment industry, had finally taken off and she was becoming quite successful. Along with her partner, she had nurtured a select clientele and they were grossing about $1 million a year. They wanted to take a percentage of their profits and invest them offshore. Their goal was a healthy return with a fast turnaround.

During our second meeting Jackie happened to mention that she had actually started the business out of her small West Hollywood apartment. Now she leased a separate facility, but still lived in the apartment. It seemed odd to me that someone making her kind of money—and obviously aware of strategic financial planning—wouldn't own a home. So I asked her about it. It turned out that while she was still in cooking school she had bought a brand-new Porsche sports car. "It was great while it lasted," she told me. "But on an assistant chef's salary, I couldn't keep up the payments for long." Before she could get out from under a mountain of unpaid bills, the car was repossessed.

In hindsight, of course, it's obvious that Jackie shouldn't have bought a car she couldn't afford. But by the same token, it doesn't seem fair that six-and-a-half years later her credit rating was still suffering a death blow from that earlier mistake. She had tried to buy a house, she told me, but the repossession of the Porsche stood out like a glaring red light to every potential lender. None of them were willing to take the risk.

An offshore financial involvement offers you the one and only escape from this government-endorsed conspiracy. Just as you can legitimately make more money overseas than you could ever hope to earn in this country, you can also look forward to enjoying your foreign profits in an atmosphere of complete confidentiality.

I think it's even more shocking to learn about the victims of inaccurate information transfer. For example, one California woman was unable to buy health insurance because an emergency-room physician treating her after a diabetic attack wrongly diagnosed her as being an alcoholic.

Not long ago, I also read a story about a fellow in New York who had received a notice of his dishonorable discharge from the Army—a very odd occurrence since he'd never been in the service. Finally, he found the source of the problem: a former college roommate had been using his name. "I realized that my social security number was stored in I don't know how many databases across the country," he said. His ex-roommate had everything from bad credit to jail records all under his name. Unable to persuade credit agencies to change his records, he was forced to apply for a new social security number and driver's license. How's that for adding insult to injury?

TECHNOLOGY: BOON OR BANE?

The extent to which misinformation exists is, unfortunately, a matter of sheer speculation. According to some estimates, as much as 50 percent of all FBI records are inaccurate or incomplete. State criminal records are said to be anywhere between 12 and 49 percent accurate. And only 13 percent of all federal agencies bother to audit their own systems for accuracy.

That is particularly alarming when you stop to consider the following: It's Uncle Sam himself who weaves the most complex web of information on U.S. citizens. There are about eighty-five federal databases on 114 million people. And it's not just the volume of information that's frightening. Advances in computer technology are making it easy to do what was impossible just a decade ago: cross-match information at the touch of a keyboard.

A network of fifteen federal regulatory and enforcement agencies routinely mixes and matches data—ostensibly in an effort to detect fraud and waste in welfare and social service programs. Divorced fathers who fail to pay child support can be identified. The Department of Education can compare data that comes from various record systems to locate wage earners who have defaulted on their student loans. By comparing its lists with state driver's license records, the Selective Service can ferret out the names of young men who have failed to register for the draft. And the IRS can flag taxpayers who underreport by matching tax returns with information from employers, stockbrokers, mutual funds, and insurers of stocks and bonds.

In fact, the government's most aggressive investigating agency is the IRS. Its debtor master file, created in 1986, is routinely used to withhold tax refunds owed to borrowers who default on federal loans. So far it lists about 750,000 people who owe money to the Department of Education, the Department of Housing and Urban Development, the Veterans Administration, and the Small Business Administration.

Business Week reported that Uncle Sam even experimented briefly with buying lists from direct mail companies, just to find out if the spending habits of targeted individuals were in sync with their reported income.

While that program was dropped almost immediately, the basic concept behind it—computer profiling—is now common practice within government. The idea is to spot combinations of data that characterize the types of individuals likely to engage in specific behaviors or activities. The Drug Enforcement Administration, for example, has worked up profiles of the types of people who are most apt to violate drug laws. The IRS knows the characteristics and behavior patterns of people most likely to underreport income. All this collecting, computerizing, searching, matching, merging, sifting, and reporting is meant to spot criminals, cut costs, and increase efficiency. Fine, but what about risk of error and intentional abuse?

Uncle Sam would like to convince us that the benefits outweigh those risks. And, in fact, national computer monitoring has produced some impressive results. IRS officials report, for example, that the new technology helped them recover $2.5 billion in 1985 taxes alone—money that would have gone uncollected without the computer cross-matching. From the perspective of a typical U.S. taxpayer, however, the system means that the federal tax collector has added one more trick to his already long list of investigation tactics. By flipping through an array of different computer information files, he can now pinpoint even more Americans who owe another few thousand dollars. Or more.

THE LETTER OF THE LAW

What does the law have to say about this blatant invasion of privacy? What are your rights when it comes to keeping your financial life confidential?

The truth is, you don't have many. And the ones you do have are steadily eroding. The bottom line is that while the U.S. Supreme Court has recognized your constitutional right to privacy in some cases, it has repeatedly failed to extend that right to "informational privacy." In other words, you have very limited ability to curtail the collection, exchange, or use of information about you or your personal financial situation.

There are, in fact, laws that authorize the invasion of your privacy. One of them is the Bank Secrecy Act of 1970 (Public Law 91-508). Its name is a deceptive misnomer

There are, in fact, laws that authorize the invasion of your privacy. One of them is the Bank Secrecy Act of 1970 (Public Law 91-508). Its name is a deceptive misnomer because instead of protecting confidentiality, it gives our government outrageous authority to review and investigate personal and business bank accounts.

because instead of protecting confidentiality, it gives our government outrageous authority to review and investigate personal and business bank accounts. The law requires all U.S. banks to maintain records of deposit slips and the front and back of all checks drawn over $100. Since it would cost so much to keep these records on hand, banks are allowed to routinely microfilm all your checks—regardless of value. So they do. All of them!

The law also demands that banks maintain records of any credit extension (other than a real estate mortgage) that exceeds $3,000. Banks must report all cash transactions, deposits, or withdrawals in excess of $3,000. They are required to ask you for your social security number or taxpayer identification number before any new checking or savings account can be opened. If you do not supply this number within forty-five days of the request, your name, address, and account numbers are put on a list for inspection by the Treasury Department.

The law takes routine government inspection a few steps further by requiring that you supply federal officials with your own share of sensitive information. For instance, you must report any transfer of money across U.S. borders if it exceeds $10,000. You must also acknowledge the existence of any foreign bank accounts when completing your annual tax return.

Advocates of the Bank Secrecy Act like to say that it aims at fighting organized and white-collar crime. Maybe that's true, but I seriously question who suffers most from the letter of this law. Criminals and thugs, who are often masterminds at circumventing legal mandates, or innocent Americans who have never heard of the laws that conspire against their rights to privacy? I have to agree with the late Supreme Court Justice William O. Douglas who said, "I am not yet ready to agree that America is so possessed with evil that we must level all constitutional barriers to give our civil authorities the tools to catch criminals."

Several individuals and groups have challenged the constitutionality of the Bank Secrecy Act, but in each case the Supreme Court has ruled in favor of the federal government. In one of the most significant rulings, the highest court in this nation said categorically that we are not entitled to any "expectation of privacy" in bank accounts or records. Furthermore, one of the justices wrote that in each and every one of our banking transactions, we take the risk that the information will be conveyed by the banker to the government.

On the bright side, some action has been taken to reduce what privacy expert Mark Skousen calls the "wholesale government inspection of bank records." In his book *Mark Skousen's Complete Guide to Financial Privacy,* he reviews some of them. The most important of those he discusses, I think, is the Financial Privacy Act, passed by Congress in 1978. It requires that government investigators notify an individual and give him the opportunity to challenge the search of any bank, savings and loan association, or credit card record before that record is turned over to the government. If Uncle Sam wants to review records without notifying the customer, he must seek a court order barring the bank from notifying its customer of the investigation.

In actuality, a lengthy time delay is the only benefit of the law. Some of the people who have challenged the government's request to see bank records have waited up to nine months before their case was heard in court. And once heard, virtually every judge has ruled in favor of Uncle Sam.

You should also know about the Anti-Crime Act of 1986. In my view, it has given ominous new powers to U.S. Customs, allowing agents the right to search through baggage and mail without a warrant or permission. This new authority applies to departing as well as returning travelers. So, at their discretion, airport Customs officials can now rummage through the things you take out of this country as well as the things you bring back into it.

The Money Laundering and Drug Control Act of 1986 is another frontal attack on personal privacy. This one makes it illegal for bank employees, stockbrokers, real estate agents, automobile dealers, jewelers, and other businesses to accept deposits from anyone engaged in an illegal business. Granted, it sounds fair so far. But the law also states that deposits are outlawed even before legal conviction. In effect, businessmen and bankers are being told to discriminate against anyone who appears to be guilty! That, it seems to me, is diametrically opposed to the principles upon which this nation was founded. Yet it's now the law of the land, passed by Congress and upheld by the courts.

The conspiracy continues. In August of 1994, under unrelenting pressure from the Clinton White House, Congress passed another anticrime bill that contains provisions that will again wipe away our precious constitutional right of privacy, provisions that will, in effect, take us back to the worst consequences of the Bank Secrecy Act. It lets the Treasury Department and other federal agencies forward to the Justice Department records of any "suspicious financial transactions" without notifying the bank customer.

Don't be mistaken about why all this concerns me. I don't condone illegality. I don't think people should evade

To maintain financial and personal privacy in your correspondence, consider renting a post office box. This, together with a registered trade name, can do a lot to ensure at least a significant amount of confidentiality.

the taxes they owe to this country; I certainly don't think that white-collar executives should be allowed to use public or private corporation funds to make outrageous and underhanded profits for themselves. On the other hand, I wonder why our government has decided that the only way of identifying bad guys is to snoop around freely through the personal business matters of law-abiding citizens.

Even more to the point, I wonder why any American with the economic option of moving offshore and into an atmosphere of utter financial privacy would choose to stick around and take the abuse. You deserve something better, and there are plenty of foreign financial centers willing to make you an offer that's hard to refuse.

AN OUNCE OF PREVENTION . . .

To ensure your own financial privacy, you must do two things. First, you must minimize the amount of information that gets created about you. Second, you need to verify and limit access to the information that already exists.

That may sound like elementary advice, but remember, the experts say that we ourselves provide government and private industry with most of the data they maintain on us. In fact, one study concludes that more than 72 percent of the time, investigators obtain their information from the very people they are monitoring.

Because you will probably want to keep some portion of your assets within the United States, I urge you to take a minute and consider ways that you can protect yourself from unnecessary invasion of privacy. Just to get you thinking along the right track, here are some practical suggestions . . .

First, be aware that not all domestic banks are alike. They all fall under U.S. banking regulations, but some are more privacy oriented than others. For example, a number of financial institutions have recently started photographing and fingerprinting customers before completing even the most routine transactions. Don't do business with that kind of place! Instead, look for a bank that's willing to ensure the highest possible level of financial confidentiality.

A good way to identify the right institution is to ask for a written contract that sets down the ground rules for your professional relationship. Make sure your contract includes at least these two provisions: (1) the bank must notify you whenever anyone asks to see your records; and (2) you reserve the right to periodically see and correct any records the bank may keep on you.

Secondly, when banking, try to keep a low profile. Think about it. By reviewing nothing more than your monthly checking account statement, an investigating agent could learn a lot about you—where you shop, the restaurants you frequent, the names of friends and relatives, your religious and political affiliations, even the private clubs at which you have a membership. On careful study, the account provides a panoramic view of your everyday lifestyle.

You should aim to reduce the clarity of that view. For instance, use your checking account for only ordinary, everyday expenses—mortgage or rent payments, utility bills, car loans. For more sensitive purchases, open and maintain a second account, preferably offshore. Better yet, handle these through a registered trade name. Simply set up a company and conduct your discreet transactions through its checking account. It's easy to implement this strategy. Your business must be registered, of course, either at the county or state level (or both). It's perfectly legal as long as you register it and use it without intent to defraud, and it will give you a flexible, low-key way to legitimately preserve your privacy.

To keep a low profile, you should probably avoid the wide array of privacy-insurance gimmicks that are around these days. Ultimately, things like invisible ink (meant to protect your checks from the bank's photocopy machine) and red checks (again, intended to limit reproduction) are only going to work against you because they bring attention to you and your account. That's not your goal. You want to preserve privacy, so, you must try to blend in, become invisible within a system that constantly searches for the slightest deviation from routine procedure.

When it comes to investments, be forewarned that some—like interest on bank accounts and dividends from a brokerage account—are automatically reported to the government. Others are known only to brokers, bankers, and fund managers. Still others are not reported to anyone. Within this last (and most appealing) category, there are a number of subdivisions. For example, information about your commodity futures, options, and nondividend-paying stocks must be made available for disclosure, but only if someone asks for it. Data relevant to a foreign bank account is reportable to the government, but you are the one who reports it. And investments such as municipal bonds, gold and silver, foreign currency, diamonds, art, and other collectibles are not reportable to anyone, not necessarily known to anyone, and not available for disclosure until the investment is sold.

To maintain the privacy of your investments consider the benefits of working through a registered trade name. Brokerage firms accept corporate accounts, and these accounts are used by individuals as well as by large corporations. A professional corporation can trade under its own name and, if titled properly, will ensure the anonymity of the real owner. You should know that your privacy is maintained only at the trading level. Outsiders can still gain access if the brokerage firm chooses to reveal the true owner.

To maintain financial and personal privacy in your correspondence, consider renting a post office box. This, together with a registered trade name, can do a lot to ensure at least a significant amount of confidentiality.

Finally, keep tabs on your credit records. There are about two thousand separate credit bureaus in this country, and they all carry data that could potentially be used against you. Under the Fair Credit Reporting Act, you can demand to know what is in your file. If you disagree with any of the information you find in it, you can insist that another investigation be done. If that second go-around doesn't resolve the matter, you can enter your own statement of explanation as a permanent part of the credit file.

IN SEARCH OF THE REAL THING

I opened this chapter with a quote from Bill Petrocelli's excellent book *Low Profile.* To repeat: "The greatest degree of privacy in this society is achieved by the very rich, the very poor, and the very crooked." His entire argument is wrapped up in that short excerpt.

Within the United States, it's possible to work diligently and ferociously safeguarding the limited privacy that our legal system still allows. Frankly, the incredibly rich don't need to bother. They're already protected by sophisticated investment plans—usually including offshore involvements. The very poor don't make much effort either. They're too busy making ends meet, while Uncle Sam isn't vigorous in pursuit of information about them. They don't have enough money to make it worth his while. Finally, of course, there are the very crooked. They don't spend time protecting a legal right to privacy because illegal activity keeps them pretty well occupied and camouflaged.

That still leaves a lot of Americans who need to fight for privacy. This group includes people like you: upper-income professionals and businesspeople whose level of success makes them aware of how the government systematically deprives them of personal financial privacy but who hesitate to take any drastic action.

It's for all those people that I've written this book. By moving a portion of your money offshore, you can give yourself an immediate escape route. You can stop chasing that elusive goal of onshore privacy and, in the process, you can walk away from the frustration and aggravation that are part of that quest. You can find out what life is like on the other side of excessive government regulation and bureaucratic red tape. You can, for the first time in your life, discover what true financial freedom feels like.

Again and again throughout this book I've said that if you want to design an international investment plan that's tailored to your specific needs, you must establish a one-on-one, professional relationship with an experienced offshore financial consultant. When it comes to structuring a foreign involvement that's sensitive to your genuine concerns about privacy, the same advice holds true.

Let's review the four basic privacy benefits that apply to almost every offshore venture and can be implemented in virtually any foreign financial center.

Privacy Benefit Number One: Insurance Against a Banking or Economic Crisis in the United States

Domestic banks are in bad shape—worse shape, in fact, than most foreign banks. Of course, your money is insured up to $100,000 by the Federal Deposit Insurance Corporation (FDIC), but what would happen in the event of a universal banking crisis? Federal agencies could never handle the massive run on banks that would ensue. Having some money tucked away in a safe and secure foreign account may be just the protection you need.

Remember, too, that in times of trouble, governments tend to persecute the financially independent by means of price controls, rationing, foreign exchange controls, prohibition of foreign accounts, confiscation of property, and high taxes. War, and sometimes just the threat of war, can bring with it the sting of government restrictions.

History has also taught that discrimination can rise up and target even the powerful within a society. At various times, in various places, Jews, Blacks, Asians, Protestants, Catholics and many other groups have been singled out for attack. Unfortunately, governments are not immune to their own prejudices. Under federal authority, people around the world have had their property taken away. Sometimes they have also been imprisoned and even killed.

That's why smart investors living in politically and socially explosive countries often keep the bulk of their money offshore. Overriding (and rational) fears of government expropriation push them into a no-choice position. As Americans, we can be far less fearful. Nevertheless,

One of the most important privacy benefits you get from an offshore involvement is protection against overly aggressive competitors. Countless fights have taken place in U.S. courtrooms, many of them involving large sums of money and vengeful antagonists. The inclination to sue at the least provocation is approaching an epidemic. And the likeliest targets are the people with the most money.

there is growing concern about creeping federal authority over individual economic liberty. As a result, quiet transfers of money and assets have become common.

If the essence of financial privacy means limiting the information that is available about you, then it seems wise to act before the fact. Don't wait until a period of unrest brings you and your assets under federal scrutiny. By then, it will be too late. You won't be able to protect what you've got because Uncle Sam will probably decide to "protect" it for you.

Privacy Benefit Number Two: Protection of Your Bank Records

Government officials can gather the following information and material on you or just about anyone: checks (both front and back copies), bank statements, signature cards, loan applications, deposit and withdrawal slips, and all bank communications. Even more to the point, they can get it without their suspect ever knowing about the probe.

Domestic banks typically release records in the event of civil litigation, criminal proceedings, SEC investigation, and any IRS audit. A private foreign bank, on the other hand, can protect you from any such invasion. By owning your own offshore bank, for instance, you ensure that all your financial decisions (and the papers that authorize them) are beyond the reach of domestic rules and regulations. Provided your dealings are structured as bank transactions rather than as individual or corporate ones, Uncle Sam has virtually no authority over the size or frequency of your money maneuvers. You can also avoid reporting requirements by using offshore banks to transact your financial dealings in their name. Although the U.S. Treasury is informed of these dealings, it does not know the individuals involved—only the banks' names. The actual bank owners remain anonymous.

Privacy Benefit Number Three: Limits on Excessive and Unfair Marketplace Competition

One of the most important privacy benefits you get from an offshore involvement is protection against overly aggressive competitors. Countless fights have taken place in U.S. courtrooms, many of them involving large sums of money and vengeful antagonists. The inclination to sue at the least provocation is approaching an epidemic. And the likeliest targets are the people with the most money.

Let's say you become involved in a business situation that ultimately leads to a lawsuit. If you bank within the United States, a court may award your competitor legal access to any or all of your financial records. In the process, your privacy may be seriously jeopardized. If, however, your records are kept offshore, they are impervious to court orders.

Privacy Benefit Number Four: Separation of Your Present from Your Past

Have you ever been the target of ugly gossip or intentional misinformation? It's sometimes based on nothing—just lies and innuendo. Other times, the story has a kernel (or more) of truth. And that's even more difficult to handle.

Most of us have a few skeletons in our closet. When it comes to financial privacy, however, those bones take on particularly ghoulish contours. Past mistakes—from a car repossession to a personal bankruptcy, draft evasion, or a minor criminal record—can haunt you for a very long time. Credit bureaus maintain all their information for at least seven years, often even longer.

The truth is, we do not live in a perfect world. People do not separate the past from the present. They are not willing to judge associates only on the grounds of firsthand experience. If, for whatever reason, you are interested in separating your past from your present, financial privacy is a must. You will never have it within the domestic financial environment. Offshore centers, however, can guarantee that today is what matters. Yesterday is essentially irrelevant.

There is a more subtle concern that some people have about separating their personal identities. Even if they have no past mistake to hide, they want or need to make a clear distinction between various current financial involvements. For example, doctors have a very particular professional image in this society. To protect their medical practice they must appear above and beyond many of the investment projects that the rest of us can implement.

What would you think of a doctor who decided to invest in a bar? Probably not much. Yet he has every right to experiment with profitable ventures. By handling his affairs offshore, he can keep a desirable distance between his Manhattan medical practice and his Miami Beach bar and grill.

As Much or As Little As You Like

Privacy is a relative concern. It can mean virtually nothing to one person while it means everything to the next. Only hermits know complete confidentiality, and they pay a high price for it. They're isolated from everything. Nobody knows anything about them but, then, they don't know about anybody or anything.

Most of us don't want privacy when it costs that much. At the same time, very few of us want to just hand over the details of our financial lives to the IRS and other federal officials. Instead, we want some middle ground, some halfway point between hypersensitive secrecy and flagrant economic exposure.

Offshore involvements, everything from a checking account in some Caribbean tax haven to a private international bank or corporation, allow you to have as much privacy as you need. If you want to declare everything to Uncle Sam, there's no law forbidding you from doing so. If, on the other hand, you want a strict guarantee of confidentiality in all your personal financial dealings, you can have it.

The point is, by moving assets offshore you regain control. Within the United States, you must play according to federal rules—rules that get a little less citizen-oriented every year. Offshore, there are entire jurisdictions organized to play by your rules. You design the game, and you get to be the winner.

CHAPTER 6

OFFSHORE TAX PROTECTION

When plunder becomes a way of life for a group of men living in society, they create for themselves, in the course of time, a legal system that authorizes and a moral code that glorifies it.

— FREDERICK BASTIST

Someone once said that there are only two absolutes in this world: death and taxes. That's certainly true for U.S. citizens. In my opinion, concern over excessive taxation is the third major motivation for offshore banking. More than half my clients initially move into the offshore world—at least in part—to legally reduce their tax load.

Rob and Bonnie Marsh are a perfect example. Several years ago, they walked into my office and related an all too typical tax nightmare. For nearly four years, they had owned and operated their own business, leasing office equipment (such as fax machines, modems, copiers, computers, and cellular telephones) to small companies and private individuals. When we first met, they had two locations in Los Angeles and were planning to open a third.

Everything had been going well, they said, until a recent meeting with their accountant. Due to changes in

All indicators suggest that tax rates will continue to rise, with a significant jump expected every year through the rest of the decade.

the tax law, they owed an enormous corporate tax. I didn't ask them for an exact figure but Rob kept mentioning the "unfairness of a $75,000 tax bill."

That was only the first level of their problem. Rob and Bonnie also faced a huge individual income tax. They asked me about the consequences of not paying the debt promptly. I told them what I tell all clients in that situation: The worst creditor in the world is the IRS. Beg for the money. Borrow it. Even sing for your supper if you must. But pay the IRS what you owe them because they can make your life miserable until you do.

I sat there, watching and listening as they explained their situation, and I was reminded that success brings a lot of complex responsibilities. Rob and Bonnie were both very smart, and obviously industrious enough to transform a good business idea into a thriving company. Yet they had forgotten an essential part of good business operation. They had forgotten tax planning. They had done a great job at making money, but they had completely overlooked the task of safeguarding their profit. They had become successful, but they hadn't managed their success very well. And for that error they were going to share a lot of the money they had earned with a crass relative: Uncle Sam.

After a couple of meetings and some in-depth conversation about the international market, Rob and Bonnie decided to purchase an offshore bank. On the one hand, they reasoned, a privately owned facility would be a boon to their business. For example, they could use the bank to finance the leasing of their equipment offshore.

Since most of it was made in Japan or Korea anyway, they could save themselves the markup that comes with buying imports.

On the other hand, their own offshore bank could offer a convenient, legitimate way to structure both personal and business tax savings. Specifically, they arranged to make their bank the sole owner of their onshore business. In the process, they divorced themselves personally from the company's profits but still ensured themselves total control over its financial management. How did they fare? At our last meeting Rob and Bonnie said they had cut their overall current tax burden by more than 60 percent!

SURVEYING THE TERRAIN: TAX REFORM

Speaking from a tax perspective, things have come a long way since 1776. And you might say they've moved in the wrong direction! It's ironic, really, to think that this country was born out of history's most successful tax revolt. Until 1913, there was absolutely no income tax levied against any U.S. citizen.

Today the United States is home to the most complicated and burdensome tax laws in the world. A New York City Tax Committee Report from the late 1960s found that this nation's tax code was beyond the understanding of most tax specialists. And that was more than twenty years ago! The situation has only worsened since then. Indeed, the tax problem is now considered so severe that every federal administration, each new session of Congress, and virtually all political candidates make the promise to work toward relief for individuals as well as businesses, and to simplify the tax code. Whether it was Ronald Reagan when he ran for president in 1980; or George Bush in 1988 and his "No New Taxes" pledge; or

Bill Clinton with his two-term smoke-and-mirrors approach to federal deficit busting, which is really packed with myriad tax increases.

I especially recall Reagan's big tax scam: the 1986 Tax Reform. Now most experts agree that his 1986 Tax Reform Act has not managed to deliver what he promised to ensure: lower taxes for most Americans. Granted, the law does represent the most massive overhaul of our tax system in decades. But for a piece of legislation that was described as both simple and fair, it's turning out to be amazingly complex and arguably only for tax lawyers.

According to a recent study by the Congressional Budget Office, the Tax Reform Act has not had a positive impact on most taxpayers. The study reveals that, on the whole, Americans have paid about 25 to 30 percent of their income to taxes—at least the same portion if not more than they paid in 1977. That means no real tax relief in nearly two decades!

The *National Review* has put the situation into even clearer focus. "Recent research has worked through the net impact of the total tax package," the journal reports. And the evidence is overwhelming: "All income brackets above $50,000 pay more in taxes under the new tax laws. Considerably more." Let me translate that into concrete figures. Taxpayers who earned $200,000 and above in 1988 saw their tax liability rise as high as 12.9 percent over what they would have paid under the old law.

Unfortunately, the outlook for the next few years is not uplifting. All indicators suggest that tax rates will continue to rise, with a significant jump expected every year through the rest of the decade. Many of you have already learned that the promised tax rate of 28 percent for 1988 was actually a phantom pledge because the Congress sneaked in a surtax of 5 percent on income over $43,150 for individuals and $71,900 for couples filing jointly.

In addition to higher income tax rates, a number of other tax hikes have been proposed and are already on the table for discussion. Although I won't predict the specific outcome of that discussion, I suspect that increases will most likely come in the form of higher excise taxes, increased energy taxes, and the probable value-added tax also known as a VAT.

Regardless of the specific tax hikes, one thing seems certain: There *will* be further tax increases levied against U.S. citizens. After sixteen years of borrowing money and running up annual deficits of between $100 billion to more than $200 billion, the federal government literally has no choice but to tax its citizens as harshly as the law and legal system will allow. For those who keep assets within the domestic economy, that means more income passed on to Uncle Sam and less available for lifestyle, children, business, and savings.

But perhaps the most frightening thing about so-called tax reform is its impact on the U.S. capital gains tax. For a country that is supposed to believe in capitalism, America has become nothing less than a hostage to a pathetic capital gains tax structure—thanks to the 1986 reform.

To fully understand the significance of the transformation, let me remind you that there are two distinctly different ways to earn money in this country. The first way is return on labor: salary, wages, and fees for professional services. This is your income, the money you live on and a portion of which you pay the IRS as your personal income tax. The rate at which you are taxed on personal income depends on how much you earn. I suspect that most of my readers are likely in the 28 percent tax bracket, meaning that once all legitimate deductions are subtracted from your income, you pay Uncle Sam a little less than one-third of your total earnings.

There is a second way to earn money. It's called return on capital, or "passive" income. It's the money you make each year on your investments. Those investments can be interest on savings deposits, loans, or bonds; rental income; patents; stock dividends; or royalties. Put simply, the 1986 Tax Reform Act has played havoc with the tax rate imposed on this second kind of income. It has resulted in the largest increase in the capital gains tax rate ever imposed by the federal government.

Before the tax reform measure became law, the top rate of capital gains tax in America was 20 percent. That's outrageous enough, if you ask me. Many countries, in order to encourage capital investment, do not even tax capital gains. But in 1988—just two years after passage of the new law—the maximum rate shot up to a staggering maximum effective rate of 38.5 percent for short-term investment profits. As of January 1988, capital gains were taxed just like ordinary income and, so, were permanently linked to each taxpayer's personal income tax bracket. For affluent Americans, that means millions and millions of new dollars tucked into Uncle Sam's pocket each and every year.

In my opinion, the federal government has gone way over the edge on this matter. In the 1990s, Americans pay one of the highest tax rates in the world on income generated by capital. I don't think our economy can function for long under the weight of this new capital gains tax structure. Something will have to give, and soon.

A study done by Arthur Andersen, a topflight accountancy firm, reveals that of the eleven industrialized nations, only Australia and Great Britain have higher long-term capital gains taxes than the United States. West Germany and Japan, for example, don't impose any capital gains tax. In a desperate attempt to reduce its insurmountable debts, the United States is trying to implement a tax law that would be laughed out of virtually every other capitalist nation on earth.

When Bush was president, and even in 1997 under the strange bedfellow political axis of the Clinton White House and the Gingrich-Lott Congress, there has been a push to cut the tax rate on capital gains to 15 percent on assets held for at least one year. Although this still seems high to me—when offshore options offer so much more appealing a tax structure—it's definitely a move in the right direction. At a time when most of the capitalist world is moving toward cutting capital gains taxes in an effort to promote equity investment, we need to get in touch with economic reality.

EXPLORING THE OPTIONS

So what are intelligent Americans supposed to do with their money? Fling open their wallets, pockets, and checkbooks to pour it into the lap of the IRS? Some experts argue that you might as well because it's becoming harder and harder to protect your onshore assets from the government's invading eye. So hard, in fact, that even smart guys have started to make stupid mistakes. For example, the *Wall Street Journal* reported a few years ago that one well-respected investment banker kept $700,000 in cash in a closet, and that he used it to pay his baby-sitter.

Aren't there better ways to deal with that kind of cash? Not nearly as many as you might think. To show you what I mean, let's run through some of the choices that would confront you if you woke up tomorrow morning with just that amount of cold cash sitting on your dresser.

The obvious place to put $700,000 cash, you might be thinking, is in a bank account. But remember, we've already established that there's a law requiring banks to tattle on anyone who deposits or withdraws more than $10,000 in currency. So why not hire runners to open accounts at seventy-five different banks and deposit just under $10,000 in each? Because there's also a law that makes such a practice illegal. And each deposit increases your chances of being caught because banks are also required to report transactions under $10,000 from anyone who "looks suspicious."

Once upon a time, bearer municipal bonds offered a way to invest a big "stash." No more. The 1982 tax law bans new issues of bearer tax-exempts. A shrinking pool of pre-1982 bearer municipals can be bought secondhand, and banks are not required to report depositors who cash in the coupons. But the game is up when the bond matures. Redeeming the bond at either a bank or a stockbroker causes a 1099-B report to go directly to the IRS.

Buying stocks won't work, either. Just like banks, brokers are required to report deposits over $10,000. Charles Schwab, a leading stock brokerage firm, won't even take cash at its teller cages. Merrill Lynch won't take more than $100.

What about using that $700,000 the old-fashioned way? You could spend it. The truth is, you could try. Theater tickets and restaurant meals are safe. But that's a lot of Broadway musicals and caviar. So what about bigger purchases, you say. Well, don't try to buy a Mercedes with it because car dealers (and all businesses) must file a form 8300 with the IRS on all cash purchases over $10,000. Large winnings and purchases of gambling chips at casinos are also reportable.

On a final note, let me pass along one more news item. The IRS has hired 2,500 additional auditors every year for the last few years. That means Uncle Sam has increased his "police force" by a hefty 26 percent!

As you may have already suspected, I do have another solution to propose. You could take your $700,000 and move it offshore. By purchasing your own international bank, and making it the owner and manager of your assets, you would sidestep the whole IRS mess and keep a lot more of the money you'd make in a more profitable environment than the U.S. market.

THE OFFSHORE TAX ADVANTAGE

Is offshore tax protection really feasible, given the government's increasing mania for stricter enforcement? Of course it's feasible! And do you know why? Because in today's economy, it's absolutely necessary. Americans, on the average, are better educated and more self-directed than ever before. In growing numbers, they see the possibility of a genuine transnational economy. Like never before, they're learning to shop around for the best investments and the best places in which to make them. Typically, that takes them outside U.S. borders.

With billions of dollars at stake, foreign jurisdictions are extremely eager to create low-tax enclaves for disgruntled Americans and other high-tax nation residents. It's the simple law of supply and demand. A lucrative foreign market, which has nurtured tax havens that have existed for many years, has also led to the creation of a number of new tax sanctuaries.

There's another important reason why offshore tax protection exists. It's the reflection of a basic human

Regardless of the specific tax hikes, one thing seems certain: There *will* be further tax increases levied against U.S. citizens. After sixteen years of borrowing money and running up annual deficits of between $100 billion to more than $200 billion, the federal government literally has no choice but to tax its citizens as harshly as the law and legal system will allow. For those who keep assets within the domestic economy, that means more income passed on to Uncle Sam and less available for lifestyle, children, business, and savings.

instinct: positive self-interest. Intelligent men and women who work hard to achieve something usually want more success and more protection for the success they've already achieved. Perhaps it's true that a fool and his money are soon parted. But smart people want to hold on to theirs.

Isn't that what you'd want to do with that $700,000 sitting on your dresser? You'd want to protect it as best you could from taxation and creditors, and, if possible, you'd want to make it earn you even more money. To show you how offshore economics can help achieve both goals, let's examine one scenario for managing just half of that imaginary fortune. I'm cutting the figure down because I want you to see that it takes only a reasonable investment to produce amazing offshore results!

First, you should take about $40,000 and purchase an offshore bank charter and license in, let's say, the tax haven of Vanuatu. I suggest that you commission an experienced native resident to work as your part-time bank agent. I also urge you to set up a well-equipped home office—complete with photocopy machine, a fax, two telephones, and a top-notch computer system.

Once your office and the offshore facility are operational, you can really get to work. You would be wise to have your agent work in tandem with one of the better international investment management firms to identify lucrative foreign investment and partnership opportunities. Canada is home to a number of these firms, so ask around. And check out the possibilities with your offshore banking specialist. After careful review of your options, you might aim to spend in the neighborhood of $200,000 on intelligent selections within six months.

All of your investments would technically belong to the offshore bank, of course. So any profit made on them falls under Vanuatu rather than U.S. tax law. In other words, the IRS could not impose any U.S. capital gains tax on your profit. And because Vanuatu does not tax on capital gains, your bank could legally keep each and every one of its hard-earned dollars.

One way to access this profit is to borrow money from your bank. The bank, of course, will charge you the highest possible interest rate. You pay the interest, which is wholly deductible, and deposit the money back in the bank. Immediately, the bank can extend another loan to you. Now you'll begin paying the bank interest on the second loan as well as the first, and it, too, is wholly deductible. The interest payments received by the bank are tax-free so, as they accumulate offshore, you can reinvest them over and over again with no tax penalty. (The United States imposes a 30 percent withholding on the interest paid to a foreign corporation or financial entity, but this withholding can be eliminated with proper tax planning.)

You need not be content with a bank that has only you for a customer, though. Through professional advertising in a number of international investment journals, you can also begin attracting depositors to your offshore bank. Using the same six-month time frame, I would say $100,000 in deposits is a very conservative estimate of what might come your way. That money, in turn, could be used to make loans to individuals and small businesses. And, of course, loans imply additional interest income for your bank.

So, at the end of one year—for an initial investment of around $300,000—you could have established an international presence, entered into a number of lucrative foreign business ventures, avoided tens of thousands in taxes, and actually earned some cold cash in the form of deposits and interest income.

What about the money that's left over? If you're smart, some of it will have gone to a top-notch international financial consultant. Plan, too, on all the extravagant meals you want at your favorite restaurants. And by all means, figure in money for at least one quick trip to your Caribbean tax haven. I can tell you from experience, vacation spots don't come much better!

HOW TO STRUCTURE OFFSHORE TAX BREAKS

From a tax expert's point of view, a single and important distinction rests at the heart of offshore banking's appeal. Tax avoidance and tax evasion are two very different things. When you avoid tax, you decide to use all legal means available to reduce your tax burden. When you evade tax, you opt to use illegal means to achieve the same end.

Any reputable accountant will encourage you to avoid taxation. In fact, if your accountant isn't working with you to plan intelligent tax avoidance strategies, I'd suggest you look for a new accountant. His job, after all, is to help you design legal and appropriate ways in which to reduce your taxable income and increase your nontaxable investments.

If, on the other hand, your accountant were to sit back while you intentionally failed to report a part of your income so as to reduce taxes, he would be tacitly going along with a criminal action. It is against the law to hide any percentage of your money—no matter how small—from Uncle Sam. It is not, however, illegal or immoral to move your money outside the government's sphere of tax authority. And that's where the beauty of offshore banking comes into clear focus.

A privately owned bank in a foreign jurisdiction lets you have the ultimate in business confidentiality. It separates you from your money in a way that protects you from the reach of IRS. At the same time, it allows you absolute control over the movements and activity of your money.

An offshore corporation or bank is as much a legal entity as you are. Therefore, to the IRS and other governmental agencies, its assets, liabilities, and income are its own. In practical terms, that means you can sell your investments—subject to certain rules—to a foreign bank (which, of course, you own) and immediately make the bank responsible for any tax due on the profits from those investments. In addition, any future appreciation will be transferred to the bank. Since the bank incurs no tax at a corporate level—your investments operate tax free! The key is proper tax planning. To make this work, treat the bank as a business. It accumulates assets. It can be used to finance local operations and to fund export activities.

In order to make this offshore tax avoidance formula work for you, remember the three basic characteristics of true tax shelters:

- They are separate from their creator by guaranteeing that the income they receive from their investments cannot be considered part of his or her income.
- They are domiciled in countries where the tax situation is much better than in their creator's home country.
- They can be indirectly controlled by their creator, and their assets managed by him as he sees fit, without tax liability in his home country.

I should point out that the economic perfection of this tax avoidance strategy will not last forever. The U.S. federal government is not blind to the realities of offshore banking, and it's not thrilled that foreign financial centers are offering U.S. citizens a legal way to circumvent taxes. Nevertheless, for the time being, Uncle Sam can't do much about it.

Over the past several years, the United States has extended tax treaties to a number of well-known tax haven nations. In each case, the aim has been to establish an open dialogue between our government and theirs on

An offshore corporation or bank is as much a legal entity as you are. Therefore, to the IRS and other governmental agencies, its assets, liabilities, and income are its own. In practical terms, that means you can sell your investments—subject to certain rules—to a foreign bank (which, of course, you own) and immediately make the bank responsible for any tax due on the profits from those investments.

the subject of U.S. investor involvement in the offshore financial community. There's a major obstacle to the usefulness of these treaties, however. Tax haven jurisdictions have far more to gain by protecting bank owners—who pay handsome licensing fees and governmental service charges on certain transactions—than by finking on them to the IRS.

Historically, tax loopholes are short-lived. Chances are, the offshore banking loophole will eventually shrink to a mere shadow of what it is today. Still, for U.S. investors who act quickly, there's time for incredible tax savings. And, quite frankly, even if the U.S. government does manage to gradually suffocate offshore banking's tax appeal, it would take decades—perhaps an entire century—for the offshore tax situation to get half as bad as it has already become here in the United States!

The longer you wait to plan your tax avoidance program, the more money you lose. Every day that you delay costs you a percentage of your earnings. I always tell my clients to view taxes in concrete terms. Just like the money in your pocket, taxes represent your time, your energy, and your talent. What percentage of those personal commodities are you willing to give the IRS? Once you've made that determination, you must assertively act to protect the rest.

If you feel that you are working to build something that will last, something that will be there when you decide to retire, something that you can count on in an emergency, and something you can pass on to your heirs, then tax planning, with an offshore instrument as the centerpiece, must be a priority.

THE "BARRIERS" AND THE "EXEMPTIONS"

There's an interesting history behind the tax advantages of offshore banking. Back in the late 1950s and early 1960s, federal officials became alarmed by the alluring tax benefits available to U.S. investors abroad. Their fear was simple enough: If too many investors moved assets offshore, the IRS could lose millions in annual revenue. So, as a precautionary move, President Kennedy urged Congress in 1962 to prevent Americans from using tax havens. Within months, legislation was introduced that taxed every American citizen who owned a controlling interest in any foreign corporation.

It wasn't long before the U.S. banking industry got wind of the proposal and quickly moved to modify it. Virtually every major bank in this nation lobbied against the tax law. If their foreign subsidiaries were taxed at a shareholder level, they explained, then they would be unable to compete effectively against their foreign competitors.

Congress was convinced, and it basically built in a series of tax breaks for American-owned banks operating outside the United States. These special privileges continue to apply to any merchant bank that purchases and sells stocks as an underwriter; acts as an investment adviser, merger consultant, or business manager; or engages in a broad range of manufacturing and business activities outside U.S. borders.

Let's take a look at some of the taxes that you can effectively avoid by owning an offshore facility. I think the list is impressive.

- The Controlled Foreign Corporation (CFC) tax is a major barrier to tax avoidance. It applies to all foreign corporations closely held by either a U.S. corporation or individual. Normally, when no more than ten U.S. citizens own such a foreign company, they are all subject to the current federal tax on their proportionate share of that company's worldwide interests, dividends, and royalties. In other words, the CFC tax allows Uncle Sam to take a hefty share of "passive income" from each of these shareholders—all of whom are treated as if the corporation (as a separate legal entity) did not exist.
- The Foreign Personal Holding Company (FPHC) tax was adopted many years ago to attack incorporated pocketbooks that operate in tax havens and receive passive income. The tax is imposed only in the case of passive income generated by a foreign corporation that is owned by no more than five U.S. citizens. In such cases, each shareholder is taxed as if the corporation did not exist.

  Typically, this barrier to tax avoidance is insurmountable, but under its provisions foreign banks receive special exemption from the IRS if they can show that the bank was created for some express purpose other than pure tax avoidance.
- The Accumulated Earnings (AE) tax applies to both foreign- and U.S.-based corporations that are owned by U.S. citizens. Put simply, it taxes all accumulated earnings that are considered "unnecessary" for the business of the corporation. The AE tax burden can be as high as 38 percent on undistributed U.S.-source accumulated earnings in

excess of $150,000 per year. It also imposes a penalty tax on those earnings that cannot be justifiably retained.

An offshore bank can qualify for exemption from this tax because all banks—in the everyday course of business operation—accumulate earnings. That's the way they make the portfolio investments that keep them afloat.

- The Personal Holding Company (PHC) tax, imposed at the rate of 70 percent, applies to foreign- as well as U.S.-based corporations that are owned by less than ten Americans. It is incurred directly by the company and not by its shareholders. In the case of a tax-haven corporation, it applies to closely held haven businesses, and is imposed on all relevant U.S.-source passive income.

  Offshore banks may be able to avoid this tax if their income is not considered to be "passive."

- Foreign Investment Company (FIC) tax is imposed annually on U.S.-owned foreign corporations that exist primarily to invest in stocks or commodity futures. An offshore bank is exempt from this tax so long as it functions as more than an international brokerage house.

- Passive Foreign Investment Company (PFIC) tax was enacted in 1986 because the U.S. Congress was concerned that some taxpayers were able to avoid many of the IRS traps by careful tax planning. The PFIC rules add a surtax on all distributions to U.S. shareholders from a foreign company unless the company is actively engaged in business and most of its assets are used in that business. A foreign bank registered in the United States can avoid the PFIC rule. Also, the PFIC rules can be avoided or their impact minimized through careful tax planning.

- Effectively-Connected-with-U.S. tax is a nebulous-sounding federal practice. It basically imposes a tax on the U.S.-source income of any foreign-based but U.S.-owned corporation if that income is "effectively connected with a U.S. business." An offshore bank is exempt from this tax because its activities, to a large extent, are treated as if they were conducted offshore through a resident agent.

JUST A WORD OF WARNING . . .

Remember that even within the international market, laws apply. A vast majority of the people I meet in my work see offshore banking and business as a legitimate escape from our overzealous U.S. tax system. Occasionally, however, I hear about someone who views it as something else: a way to conduct profitable but illicit business activity.

Howard Fisher, a well-known tax attorney based in Los Angeles, likes to tell a particular story about one of these offshore rogues. I'm going to borrow the tale because it has important lessons to offer. First, it shows how tempting it can be to break the law when you enter the foreign market. It's like being set free inside your favorite candy shop: with so much to choose from, it can be hard to watch your weight. I also like the story because it shows how offshore financial trouble can come from the least likely source. And, finally, the story shows how you can operate legitimately on all the major levels, but ultimately be destroyed by the small but illegal details.

Gucci is, for most discriminating shoppers, a familiar name. Luggage, briefcases, purses, and innumerable accessories—all of them expensive—are the products made by the firm. Most shoppers don't know, however, that the company's founder, Dr. Aldo Gucci, made part of his fortune with help from an illegal offshore scheme.

When Gucci entered the offshore market, he was a successful middle-aged physician who wanted to use his hard-earned capital as a ticket into the lucrative world of foreign investment. So he hired a high-priced Manhattan tax attorney and told him to establish a company called "Gucci USA." It would design and market some of the most expensive leather accessories in the world, he said, and market them throughout the United States and the rest of the world.

Next, based on some pretty "creative" advice from his attorney, Dr. Gucci decided to establish a foreign-based subsidiary. The foreign company was to develop concepts for new products, research the marketability of those products, and attempt to sell the designs to interested manufacturers abroad. After considering the options, he selected Hong Kong as the offshore jurisdiction for the subsidiary because of its tax allure, and within a few months he had signed a licensing agreement with his own Hong Kong company, stipulating that it would receive 10 percent of Gucci USA's gross annual income to use as operational funds.

It's one thing to outsmart the IRS at its own game. It's another to break the law. How can you tell the difference? When you cannot comfortably trace your actions with clear explanations for why you did what you did, you've probably crossed the line from shrewd offshore venture strategy into criminal business operation. That's an extremely important distinction.

On one level, it was a brilliant scheme, but *only* on one level! Imagine being able to take 10 percent of an enormous gross annual income, move it out of this country without ever paying tax on it, use it to make millions offshore, and keep the money within a foreign financial center that imposes no tax on capital gains. It was illegal, of course, because the Gucci subsidiary never really functioned at all. It was a paper front that allowed Dr. Gucci to funnel unreported personal and corporate income into an offshore tax haven.

Nevertheless, the idea worked for fifteen years.

And ultimately, when Dr. Gucci was caught, it had absolutely nothing to do with a thorough IRS investigation. He was caught because his own children turned him in. They felt that they were not getting their fair share of his burgeoning financial empire. So they decided to make money another way. They went to the IRS and gave them the name of their father's front company. They also provided the name of its bank, Chase Hong Kong, and its bank account number. In exchange, they asked to collect the reward that's typically given for such information: up to 10 percent of the amount of unpaid tax due on accumulated profit.

As long as they were at it, the Gucci kids also decided to tell Uncle Sam who held the shares of the Hong Kong Company: two Panamanian-chartered companies. And if that wasn't good enough for the government, they even told officials where the actual shares were held.

Guess what the IRS did with all this information? Go directly after Dr. Gucci? No, because the government couldn't convince its star witnesses, Gucci's kids, to testify in open court. What's more, the IRS didn't have anything that could be used to indict Dr. Gucci. So Uncle Sam went after his bank. The IRS went to Chase Manhattan in New York, the parent bank company, and asked them to make Chase Hong Kong provide records on Dr. Gucci's transactions. When Chase New York refused to comply, the IRS decided to sue them.

Of course, the bank lost its case. So it took it all the way to the appellate court. And, again, it lost. In fact, I suspect that it knew all along that it would lose. But it also knew that if it rolled over too quickly on a big client like Gucci, its name would be mud with every major international investor.

Just to end the story, let me tell you how Dr. Gucci was ultimately nabbed. When all the dust settled, they got him on a technicality. He was shown to have had a "defective license agreement." In other words, they showed that there had not been enough activity within Gucci's Hong Kong subsidiary to prove it a legitimate business entity. In fact, during the fifteen years that the agreement was in place, only three drawings or plans for new products had been produced by the firm. They had all been sent to the United States for approval, but none of the three ever resulted in an actual product. And the killer was that all three drawings had been prepared by an employee in New Jersey!

As soon as Chase New York turned over its records on Gucci USA, Dr. Gucci pleaded guilty and he wound up spending eighteen months in a New York halfway house.

I've shared this story because it illustrates the fact that offshore crime really doesn't pay, at least not very often. And definitely not forever. Certainly there are international players who find illegitimate ways to make big money up front, but over the long haul, they pay a high price for the profit. They must constantly worry about exposure, and more often than not they end up paying Uncle Sam anyway—from a prison cell especially designed for white-collar crooks.

It's one thing to outsmart the IRS at its own game. It's another to break the law. How can you tell the difference? When you cannot comfortably trace your actions with clear explanations for why you did what you did, you've probably crossed the line from shrewd offshore venture strategy into criminal business operation. That's an extremely important distinction.

THE SPIRIT OF AMERICA

There are tens of thousands of people throughout this country who mind their own business, apply themselves, and make a real contribution to our economy. But with the passage of each new tax law, they must hold on tighter in the effort to keep an equitable fraction of the fruits of their labor.

Every year, the president, the Congress, and the Supreme Court give IRS officials more money, more laws, and more leeway to collect revenues from us all. They get better computers, more agents, and more auditors. It's a virtual army against each individual and each family.

Ironically, however, it's the very complexity of the U.S. tax system that offers wise Americans the one remaining way out from under excessive taxation. With the help of an experienced financial consultant, you can turn the ambiguities and inconsistencies of our tax code to your own advantage. You can break away from the uninformed majority and revolutionize your economic life. I believe that in making such a move, you reflect the finest spirit of this nation: individual ingenuity and the pursuit of personal betterment.

Right now, offshore banks and some foreign companies let you legally move assets outside the U.S. and beyond the reach of Uncle Sam. While the special tax breaks they provide may not last forever, for the moment there are fortunes to be made abroad.

CHAPTER 7

PROTECTING YOUR ASSETS

The simple answer to the question, "Do I need to protect my assets?" is yes, unless you don't care about the wealth you have accumulated.

— HOWARD FISHER, *INTERNATIONAL TAX ATTORNEY*

Most successful Americans want a very basic kind of financial freedom. They want to be able to spend the largest possible percentage of the wealth they have accumulated in whatever way they see fit, and they want to be able to leave what remains upon their death to their heirs.

There's nothing terribly complex or bewildering about such a liberty. In fact, it complements the economic ethics that built the United States of America: a guarantee of free enterprise and the promise that every generation might prosper beyond what it came from, to ensure a better life for those it leaves behind.

Unfortunately, it's only a small minority of affluent Americans who ever manage to enjoy this kind of economic freedom. The reality for everyone else is far more sobering and grim. Even upper-income professionals often find themselves working twice as hard as their parents just to accumulate half as many assets. Recent surveys find that only 20 percent of all U.S. citizens can afford to buy a home. Two-car families now require in the neighborhood of $1,000 to $1,500 a month just for midsize, mid-luxury transportation. Private education costs between $5,000 and $15,000 per year per child—and that's just for elementary school. We're not even talking about the stratospheric costs of sending your children to college. As one friend of mine with two sons in college recently informed me, "Tuition plus room and board means I have to deduct $50,000 a year from my income before I can even think about eating or keeping a roof over my head."

Put simply, true asset protection does not exist in this country or anywhere in North America for that matter. Just for starters, there's Uncle Sam to attack the kitty. After he takes his share, you've probably lost a full one-third of what you had to begin with. Then there's state tax to pay, social security tax, gasoline tax, consumer tax, and, of course, estate tax on anything you inherit. Figure in the additional cost of liability insurance and loss—both of which are everyday components of doing business for a lot of wealthy and affluent Americans—and you begin to see why even the most highly paid professionals don't live as well as their parents did in the 1950s and 1960s. In fact, they don't live as well as

True asset protection does not exist in this country or anywhere in North America for that matter. Just for starters, there's Uncle Sam to attack the kitty. After he takes his share, you've probably lost a full one-third of what you had to begin with. Then there's state tax to pay, social security tax, gasoline tax, consumer tax, and, of course, estate tax on anything you inherit.

they themselves did in the 1980s. Things just get worse and worse with no end in sight.

All these irrefutable realities create the strongest argument for developing an offshore financial strategy. Outside the United States, and beyond the reach of excessive U.S. government interference, there are little-known ways to safeguard what you have, and use it to make more.

WHEN IS SUCCESS A LIABILITY?

When I was a kid, my family lived next door to a man named Hal Leon. Mr. Leon was not a particularly exceptional guy, but he was one of the nicest people I've ever met. He seemed to love his family and like his neighbors. He was always the first to offer help when you needed it and the last to interfere otherwise. He was a lawyer, which in our neighborhood made him sort of a big shot, but he never held his credentials over anyone. As I recall, his only apparent source of pride was an enormous backyard garden that he tended himself.

I was in the fifth grade when I first overheard my parents talking about Mr. Leon's car accident. Later it came out that the incident had left a young girl blind in one eye. I remember that everyone talked about it a lot, but nobody ever seemed to approach him directly. So it was only through the neighborhood gossip that I learned, over the course of many months, that he was sued by the girl's parents, lost his case, and was hit with an overwhelming liability debt.

For a while, nothing seemed to change. But during my sixth grade year, I remember that Mrs. Leon went to work—an odd development in our suburban area, where wives were inevitably full-time homemakers. Eventually I heard that they had gone bankrupt. Bankruptcy was a word only uttered in hushed tones when I was a child, and at the time I wasn't really sure what it meant. I did know that it was the explanation for the Leons moving away and selling their big station wagon to someone else on the block.

When I was a child, lawsuits happened only to the very rich and the very delinquent. Millionaires were vulnerable because their pockets were so deep that they almost cried out to be pilfered. Ne'er-do-wells were vulnerable, too: drunks, quacks, and scam artists who either allowed bad habits to blur their better judgment or deliberately set out to deceive and steal.

Today, things are very different. Lawsuits happen to just about everybody. Experts predict, in fact, that one out of every four adults in this country will be sued during the coming year alone. Some of those suits will be for wrongful damages, like the one against Mr. Leon. But like all spheres of economic activity, lawsuits have "matured" over the past several years. For example, there will probably be 50,000 personal injury lawsuits involving damages of $1 million and more filed this year—twice as many as were filed even fifteen years ago.

In 1990, the average general practice doctor spent between $10,000 and $15,000 a year on malpractice insurance to cover up to $1 million in award damages. Today, that same doctor is paying at least $50,000 a year for coverage of up to $3 million! And that's just for GPs! Medical specialists such as heart surgeons and orthopedic surgeons pay far more. It's the newest craze. Litigation has replaced baseball as America's favorite pastime. People sue their doctors, their hospitals, their general contractors, their plumbers, electricians, gardeners, and television repairmen. They sue their landlords, and they sue their tenants. They sue their automobile dealers and their insurance companies. One group of failed investors recently sued their bank for lending them too much money—the cause, they argued, for their financial demise. One couple sued the Roman Catholic Church when their son committed suicide because, they maintained, he had received inadequate counseling from his local parish priest.

It's absurd but not very funny. Not at all. Lawsuits hang like a threatening storm cloud over most of us. Any successful businessperson should fear them because at any moment, without any warning, they might be slapped with a multimillion dollar lawsuit. It might not even be your own mistake that gets you in trouble. Negligence on the part of one of your employees—or even one of your customers—can do the job just as well.

Consider the following scenario. A midsize hardware store was sued for $1.4 million because a customer foolishly decided to test a power saw inside his crowded store and hit another shopper—seriously cutting both his arms, leaving him unable to work for nearly two years and permanently disabled. The store owner, as it so happens, wasn't even in the store at the time of the tragic accident. But as the owner of the store he was sued for negligence. Does it sound far-fetched? It shouldn't. Sad cases like this happen all the time, and they wipe out hard-earned fortunes in the instant it takes a judge or jury to rule in favor of the plaintiff.

By the way, lawsuits don't always result from a little guy suffering at the hands of a big guy. Sometimes, in fact, it's just the opposite. Strategic Lawsuits Against Public Participation (SLAPPs) are good examples of what I mean. Concerned citizens who campaign against local polluters or new developments are increasingly likely to be hit with one of these suits. They can be small, like the one filed against a West Virginia blueberry farmer. When he told local authorities that operators of a nearby coal mine had polluted a river and killed fish in it, the mining company sued him for $200,000.

SLAPPs can also be quite big, like the one filed against the League of Women Voters in Beverly Hills. In a recent election, the league supported a ballot initiative to stop a fully planned condominium project. League officers also wrote two letters to a local newspaper criticizing the measure. The developers took decisive action: They sued the league for $63 million.

Perhaps the worst aspect of the lawsuit mania that plagues us is that it can be completely indiscriminate about who it destroys. A woman named Violet Hanson once came to see me, desperately wanting to take advantage of the offshore option. In conversation it came out that her house and life savings were likely to be confiscated to pay off angry creditors. I should admit up front that I have a hard time accepting the legitimate right of a creditor to take such personal assets, regardless of the offense. But what was particularly frustrating about this case was the fact that Vi herself had not done anything wrong.

Years earlier, she had co-signed on a loan that her son-in-law took out to start his own graphic design and printing business. The company had been doing well, at least apparently, so Vi had just forgotten about the loan. Well, in actuality, things were not going so well. The business failed, and along with her son-in-law's bankruptcy came her own. Vi's only crimes were a soft heart and poor judgment. But for those offenses, she paid through the teeth.

I remember how frantic and agitated she was. Her husband had worked his whole life to provide for their retirement. He had died just a few years before, and she was almost inconsolable at the thought of losing all that he had left behind. Her idea was to quickly establish a legitimate offshore presence and then transfer nearly all her holdings into a welcoming foreign center.

The trouble was, her excellent idea had come too late. Offshore asset conservation can be legally offered only if there are no judgments or liabilities against your assets. Vi's assets were already under steady attack. Fortunately, with some careful planning, I was able to deal with her predicament, but she was definitely caught in a bad situation.

Perhaps one of the worst cases I've come across had to do with a client of mine named Oliver Webster. He had inherited some virgin land in rural Tennessee from an uncle. Soon after he inherited the property, he was sued for $75 million by the local townspeople. The land had a gas storage tank buried on it. The tank was polluting the water for the whole area. The case went to court and Mr. Webster lost everything.

It is also possible to have all your assets frozen by police, not only for your own crimes but for other people's as well. By the stipulations of the Anti-Drug Act of 1988, authorities have the right to temporarily take or restrict your access to your own property (i.e., your own house, car, and all your bank accounts) if they think you received all or part of them from a relative or other associate who sold drugs. When will the assets be returned? When the suspect is found innocent or when you can prove that you have no reasonable way of knowing about the illegal activity and that the property was purchased with "clean" money. Even under the best of circumstances, that could take several months to prove. In the meantime, your financial ship is sunk.

A Little Protection Is Better Than None

My advice is straightforward: Move as many of your assets offshore as you can. Why? Because the more you keep offshore, the better protected you are from attacks by nuisance lawsuits, the government, and the courts. Nevertheless, I realize that not everyone is initially willing to commit the bulk of their hard-earned assets to an offshore protection plan. Frankly, I suspect that's only because they're new to the game. The more involved you become in foreign investment and business opportunities, the more willing you will be to see your money leave the veritable sieve that characterizes the domestic marketplace in North America. The conventional means of protection—for example, IRAs and savings accounts—no longer offer any real protection. In time, I predict that friends and relatives will be hard-pressed to interest you in any domestic investing.

In the beginning you will probably want to maintain a sizable onshore presence. So for those just starting the offshore adventure, I would like to offer some advice on how to best protect the assets you keep in the United States. My advice is limited because there are so few possibilities for genuine asset protection without extensive and creative planning. There are, however, four rules you should follow in all your onshore financial activities. If you adhere to them, your accumulated wealth will be as safe as it can possibly be within the United States.

Rule Number One: Beware of Joint Relationships

Marriage is a 50/50 proposition, right? And a 10-percent interest in a new venture means a 10-percent accountability for future losses and claims, right?

Wrong on both counts.

Most Americans suffer under the misconception that what is fair in one aspect of a relationship, whatever the nature of the association, is fair in all aspects of the relationship. Sadly, that doesn't hold true when it comes to the distribution of financial responsibility and accountability.

For example, a wife may have nothing at all to do with her husband's professional activities—in fact, they may be separated—but if his business gets into trouble, creditors will see her share of their jointly owned assets as fair game in their quest for recompense.

Likewise, if you are a 10 percent partner in a business venture that fails, you can be held 100 percent accountable for its losses. That means your home, your IRA, your stocks, bonds, savings accounts, and valuable

Today, things are very different. Lawsuits happen to just about everybody. Experts predict, in fact, that one out of every four adults in this country will be sued during the coming year alone. Some of those suits will be for wrongful damages, like the one against Mr. Leon. But like all spheres of economic activity, lawsuits have "matured" over the past several years. For example, there will probably be 50,000 personal injury lawsuits involving damages of $1 million and more filed this year—twice as many as were filed even fifteen years ago.

investments are all up for grabs in the scramble to pay off bad debts.

So be cautious. "Joint tenancy," the fancy term for co-ownership, between spouses and relatives can sound great in the beginning but it can turn very sour very fast. Prenuptial agreements, as unromantic as they are, can provide a good deal of asset protection down the line. Once dismissed in most court proceedings, many judges are now quite willing to review them and rule in accordance with the provision they outline.

Be careful, too, about joint business ventures. Often they are held to be nothing more than simple general partnerships with open-ended liability for anyone involved. If that "anyone" is you, it could mean big losses down the line.

Rule Number Two: Use Corporations Wisely

One of the cornerstones to all asset protection is this: You have to separate yourself from your money in order to avoid paying it to people you don't like. By establishing a U.S.-based corporation through which you handle your business activities, you distance yourself somewhat from the liability that might result from those activities. There are other alternatives in Wyoming and Florida, where limited liability corporations and limited partnerships are available under special laws.

I remember years ago when I first became involved in offshore financial consulting, I met a man at an international business seminar who kept telling me to incorporate. "Don't let the bastards get you," he said. "Make one mistake and you'll lose a little blood." Then he said something I'll never forget. "And they're all like sharks. They smell that little bit of blood and they go crazy."

He gave me good advice. I'm happy to report that I have not encountered trouble with my business associates. But that doesn't mean I couldn't. So for me, and for millions of other consultants and businesspeople, it's wise to operate through a corporation. If the time ever comes that a client or business associate does sue me, all my personal assets are independent of the business. Ultimately, they're still vulnerable by virtue of the fact that the same person owns them both. But they're not as immediately vulnerable.

One of the cornerstones to all asset protection is this: You have to separate yourself from your money in order to avoid paying it to people you don't like. By establishing a U.S.-based corporation through which you handle your business activities, you distance yourself somewhat from the liability that might result from those activities. There are other alternatives in Wyoming and Florida, where limited liability corporations and limited partnerships are available under special laws.

By the way, it's possible to need more than one corporation. This would certainly be true if, let's say, your business has two facets, and one of them is far more likely to bring on lawsuits. For someone who manufactures construction equipment and operates an architectural firm, two corporations would be in order—one for the relatively low-risk architectural venture and another for the high-risk construction business. With this arrangement one business could remain, at least temporarily, unaffected while the other withstands the shock of a legal battle and possible liability.

Rule Number Three: Spread Your Wealth

There's one surefire way to avoid paying costly tax and liability bills: technically rid yourself of your most valuable assets. Give a lot of your money to your children, other relatives, or worthy social causes; put it in trust; transfer it to a limited partnership of which you officially own just a small part. But get your name off of it. In this way, if financial disaster hits, much of the wealth you have accumulated will be beyond the reach of your business or personal adversaries.

The problem with this arrangement is pretty obvious. How can you enjoy the pleasures of wealth you give away? Well, for starters, most people work hard—at least in part because they want to pass along economic security to their kids, extended family, and important nonprofit causes. In addition, it is quite possible that assets given to children (especially through an irrevocable trust) can be relied upon in times of future economic need.

For example, if you place 100 percent of your real estate assets in a trust for your kids, you could easily have more than a million dollars in equity stashed away for your heirs' financial future. If, however, you run into financial trouble yourself—even if you lose everything you own—the trust and all that's in it will belong legally and lawfully to your children. Creditors will have no claim to it.

Assuming you have a good relationship with the trust's beneficiaries, you can count on them to instruct their trustee to loan you some money to get started again. If, on the other hand, you don't get along, you've got little recourse because nothing in the trust belongs to you. You have little or no control. As always, the key is planning.

Rule Number Four: Intelligently Distribute Assets Between Spouses

Just as a couple can, to some extent, safeguard their assets by entrusting them to their heirs, they can also protect against potential loss by intelligently dividing their assets within the marriage. Let me use an example to illustrate my point.

Lauren and Jake were in their early forties when they decided to initiate some careful estate planning. In talking with a number of consultants, they decided that Jake's sports equipment rental business left him relatively open to devastating lawsuits. So they strategically set up two trusts. One was established in Lauren's name, and into it they placed the bulk of their assets. The other was set up in Jake's name, which held his office equipment and their two cars.

It proved to be a brilliant move. Six years later, Jake was sued for more than $4 million when two customers had a fatal accident in a dune buggy he had rented to them. Their widows won the case and had the legal right to everything owned by the business and by Jake. That means the cars, of course. But virtually everything else was held in trust under Lauren's name. As a result, it was safe, and provided a second economic chance for the couple.

Thousands of married people lose everything each year because of a lawsuit brought against just one spouse. Don't let that happen to you. Plan wisely. And, while we're on the topic, remember not to put 100 percent of your assets in just one spouse's name. A court of law would probably find that to be an attempt to defraud creditors. If so, you could still lose everything.

THE OFFSHORE ADVANTAGE: AN OFFSHORE ASSET PROTECTION TRUST

Admittedly, there are limitations to each of these domestic asset protection plans. And in effect, all the limitations result from two mutually supportive conspiracies against American businesspeople and investors.

First, in any attempt to safeguard your money within the continental United States, you are up against the power of the federal government. Put simply, Uncle Sam doesn't want your assets to be protected because he wants the ability to get at them at any time.

Second, there is an insidious relationship between the U.S. financial sector and the U.S. government that works against your efforts to keep assets free from excessive taxation and regulatory interference. At one time, American banks could operate independently of the federal bureaucracy. Today, they cannot. The reporting requirements and legal restraints placed upon banks and savings and loans makes it truly impossible for you to have a private relationship with your financial institution. In fact, whether your onshore banker likes it or not, he is the greatest obstacle to your asset protection plan.

In the effort to circumvent these intricately intertwined problems, many investors have established onshore trusts, into which they've placed the bulk of their assets. "Living trusts" are the newest rage, it seems.

(These revocable trust agreements usually specify that all trust income be distributed to you, as the trust creator, during your lifetime. Then, upon your death, the trust's principal assets are left to your heirs.) I've personally seen a number of how-to paperbacks marketed specifically to affluent Americans who might want to investigate the trust as an appealing alternative to simple bank accounts and stock or real-estate investment options.

Living trusts do offer one real benefit: They let your heirs avoid inconvenience, delay, and the cost of the probate experience. (Many people are unaware that probate can be extremely expensive, up to 11 percent of the gross value of the estate in some parts of the country.) Nevertheless, if you are considering a living trust, my advice is to beware. For starters, revocable living trusts will not escape estate tax because by their very nature they let you keep control over the property—by being able to revoke or amend them and by retaining the power to withdraw any portion of the trust property at any time.

If that's not enough to dissuade you, there are other serious drawbacks to domestic trusts. For example, the U.S. courts consider any trust that has been created by an individual for his own benefit—even if actual control of all assets has been surrendered—fair game in a creditor's quest for recompense. In other words, if you place your assets in trust, but continue to benefit in any way from them, then someone who wins a legal judgment against you can go after those assets. And, in most cases, get them.

Moreover, the U.S. courts have held that creditors can go after assets in a domestic trust if the trust creator retains any measure of control over them—even though he or she may not actually enjoy the benefits of the trust assets. For example, if you set up a trust agreement, the courts would be likely to hold that your creditors could go after whatever assets you have placed in the trust.

If your estate is worth $350,000 or more, I strongly suggest you consider one of the best asset protection strategies I know about: the Asset Protection Trust. If properly executed and intelligently maintained, this single offshore venture can provide you with an unparalleled level of tax protection and financial invisibility. It may not protect you from becoming the target of a lawsuit or other claim. But it may place your assets substantially beyond the reach of any U.S. court, and severely limit anyone's ability to enforce a money judgment against you. In the process, it will also discourage potential creditors from making bogus claims, and save you the emotional and financial cost of addressing such claims.

One of the keys to a successful foreign trust is the selection of a friendly host country. By that I mean you should establish your trust within an offshore jurisdiction that, first and foremost, maintains stringent laws against enforcing foreign judgments. The whole notion of the trust is based on common law, which applied in only some countries—those formerly or presently associated with Great Britain. Most other countries operate under a separate set of codes, and while they have arrangements similar to trusts, they have different names and varied structures.

Second, there is an insidious relationship between the U.S. financial sector and the U.S. government that works against your efforts to keep assets free from excessive taxation and regulatory interference. At one time, American banks could operate independently of the federal bureaucracy. Today, they cannot. The reporting requirements and legal restraints placed upon banks and savings and loans makes it truly impossible for you to have a private relationship with your financial institution.

For example, the British Virgin Islands (BVI) has a well-established body of trust laws that protect any BVI-based trust from the scrutiny of foreign courts and creditors. Yet, like the United States, the BVI recognizes a properly structured trust as a separate legal entity—independent of its creators—and will not allow creditors of any of the parties to the trust to obtain the trust's assets.

It's also critical that your preferred foreign site have nothing equivalent to the U.S. "statute of frauds." In other words, you want to be sure that if you were to physically transfer your assets to the offshore center and then place them in trust there, courts and creditors here in the United States would be unable to claim fraudulent intent. Why? Because the laws that govern the creation of trusts in your chosen foreign center do not recognize such fraud.

A basic foreign asset protection trust can be set up with anyone as the direct beneficiary (including you as the creator of the trust). However, for maximum protection, it's better to choose someone else for that role. (Otherwise you could be seen to have too much of a beneficial interest in the trust and its activities.) If, however, you do decide to make yourself the beneficiary, be absolutely sure that you are entitled only to the trust's income and have no claim on its principal. That way, a creditor can theoretically attack only your income stream from the trust, not the actual assets.

Just like domestic trusts, all foreign asset protection trusts have a trustee, someone to administer the trust and hold its assets for the benefit of the beneficiaries. I have worked with clients who insist on being the trustee to their own foreign trust, but in every one of those cases I advised against it. Serving as your own trustee can be extremely dangerous. A court is much more inclined to invalidate a trust if its creator is also a trustee or beneficiary.

So, select an independent foreign trustee, either an individual familiar with your personal life and business needs, or a financial institution with which you have an ongoing relationship. If neither of those options seems appealing or appropriate, you can turn to one of many professional international management firms that specialize in the supervision of foreign trusts and other offshore entities.

When you initially establish the trust and name a foreign trustee, you should also name a committee of one or more "trust protectors" to serve as advisers to that trustee. And you should serve on that committee. Why? Because the protectors have the right to remove or replace the trustee, so, by remaining a part of the protector committee, you keep indirect but effective control over the trust's assets. And if a creditor should later decide to pursue you, you can simply resign as a protector, leaving the foreign trustee in sole control of the assets. (That way, there can be little merit in the argument that your resignation was somehow an impermissible transfer of assets after the creditor's claims were made.)

Establishing a foreign asset protection trust is not a terribly complex or lengthy undertaking, but it does require expert legal advice from a trust attorney. There are a number of special features that should be included in the trust agreement: anti-duress provisions and a spendthrift clause are just two examples. Don't risk making a mistake. Bring in a qualified specialist to work with you on the project. It will necessitate a financial outlay up front, but it's likely to save untold headaches and expenses down the line.

Finally, because it is generally required that you transfer title or ownership to the property of the offshore jurisdiction before you actually establish a trust there, the foreign asset protection trust is usually best for holding liquid assets: cash, stocks, bonds, and certificates of deposit. In addition, assets transferred to a simple foreign asset protection trust should generally be those not needed for your daily living or business needs. In other words, they should be your "nest egg," which you have been setting aside for future security.

ADDITIONAL LAYERS OF PROTECTION

A foreign asset protection trust can be a vehicle for people seeking nothing more than the basic right to safeguard their money. As an irrevocable trust, it is an entirely independent entity, and recognized as such under the laws of all fifty states and the U.S. federal government. If you take care to distance yourself sufficiently from the trust—so that a court will not find that the arrangement is a sham for holding assets under your direct control—no judge or jury can legally give your creditors assets that you earlier contributed to the trust.

A number of recent court cases demonstrate exactly how the use of these irrevocable trusts can work. In one of those cases, a woman with two grown children established an irrevocable trust into which she transferred most of her assets. The trust provided for the distribution of the entire net income to the woman for life, with the remaining principal to go to her children upon her death. When the woman was later sued by a creditor, the court upheld the validity of the trust, saying that "A creditor has no more rights and can secure no greater benefit from a trust than the beneficiary of the trust can obtain for himself [or herself]." In other words, since the woman herself could not ignore the provisions of the trust or regain the principal for herself, then neither could her creditors have it set aside to obtain the assets it contained.

But for some people an offshore trust alone does not offer enough asset control. Despite a trust's protective advantages, some people want (and need) more direct authority over how assets are maintained and profitably put to work. In particular, if you run your own business, have a professional corporation, or own real property within the United States, you will probably want to combine a foreign asset protection trust with a domestic limited partnership. Using both, you can ensure that your assets remain completely safe from creditors, and that you keep constant and total control over them.

Here's how it works. You establish an asset protection trust within a welcoming offshore jurisdiction, and you contribute virtually all of your property to that trust. Then, you set up a domestic limited partnership, personally taking just a 1 percent interest in the partnership but designating yourself as general partner. The foreign trust takes a 99 percent interest and pays for that interest by contributing to the partnership the following: your operating business, your family home, title to your investment real estate, and any other nonliquid assets.

Once the trust and partnership are funded, your total assets will consist of just a 1 percent interest in the limited partnership and the few personal belongings you have not contributed to the trust. As a result, very little of your total net worth is available to any potential creditor. Technically, 99 percent of that worth belongs to the foreign trust and has been contributed to the limited partnership.

So, if a creditor were ever able to obtain a judgment against you, your only asset would be a small interest in the partnership.

Another big part of the system's appeal lies in the control it gives you over assets that cannot be attached. Specifically, because of your role as a general partner, you will still be able to do with the trust's assets whatever you please as long as it's in the furtherance of the partnership's purpose. And as an additional perk, there is no authority that could allow a creditor to remove you

I should mention that there are even more elaborate offshore asset protection plans. Of course, they involve more initial research and additional start-up revenue. Nevertheless, for investors with a lot of vulnerability and a high or professional profile, they can be very desirable.

as general partner of the partnership. So you would continue to control all of your assets all of the time.

You may even be able to get money out of the limited partnership held in your offshore trust if you have the ability, in arm's-length transactions, to draw funds from it as salary for services performed and as fringe benefits. (If you go this route, however, be aware that these wages and benefits are vulnerable to creditors in any judgment against you.)

Even if there is a judgment against you, the most a creditor can obtain would be a so-called charging order against your partnership interest. True, the creditor could go after all the benefits that flow to you from the partnership, but because you own so small an interest, very little does flow to you. This charging order would also mandate that you treat the creditor only as an "assignee." That means, he would have no vote in the management of the partnership and would not be able to force you to make distributions from the partnership.

This final provision allows you to create the "poison pill," something to discourage even the heartiest of creditors. You simply include a provision in the partnership agreement that allows the general partner to retain the earnings of the partnership and not make cash distributions. If a creditor gets a charging order against the partnership, you can stop making cash distributions.

This move will no doubt irritate the creditor. But, frankly, that irritation pales in comparison to what lies ahead for the creditor. Let me explain.

Under U.S. tax laws, a limited partnership is deemed to have distributed its income to the partners at the end of each fiscal year—even if no cash distributions were made. Thus, the creditor is faced with the prospect of having to pay taxes on the income generated by his assigned share of the partnership's income despite the fact that he has not received any money at all! Faced with such a prospect, most creditors will not even bother to attack your interests in the foreign trust or the domestic limited partnership.

Finally, because 99 percent of the partnership belongs to the foreign trust, the assets from the partnership all flow automatically offshore and back into a trust that is governed by extremely favorable foreign laws.

I should mention that there are even more elaborate offshore asset protection plans. Of course, they involve more initial research and additional start-up revenue. Nevertheless, for investors with a lot of vulnerability and a high or professional profile, they can be very desirable. Unlike the foreign trust alone, a trust, partnership, and offshore bank can work hand-in-hand, forming a powerful triad. These complex protection strategies are not fixed plans. Instead, they constantly evolve and change to inhibit potential challenges of lawsuits directed against you. In essence, by keeping your money on the move, and circulating it through creative combinations of various offshore financial ventures (trusts, consulting companies, holding companies, and banks), you can obliterate all traces of your financial activities.

For such total financial invisibility, you will have to relinquish virtually all personal affiliation with and claim to your assets. You *can* control them. In fact, you can make them grow beyond your wildest dreams. But you can't call them your own because they are all absorbed by the offshore plan, never to emerge for future creditors to see.

HAVE YOUR CAKE AND EAT IT TOO

There's a popular expression we've all heard at least once: Less is more. Well, when it comes to conservation and responsible ecology, that may be true. But when it comes to money—your money—only more is more.

So as you find yourself successfully accumulating more, don't forget that unless you do something to protect yourself, a hefty chunk of what you've worked to acquire will be sacrificed to the U.S. tax collector. And what's left could be lost overnight in an ugly, and perhaps even unfair, lawsuit.

But take heart. Asset protection is available. To a very limited extent it's even available onshore within the domestic marketplace. Unfortunately, however, as citizens of the world's great experiment in free enterprise, we Americans have to look offshore for true safeguards.

That's the bad news.

The good news is that there really are places where you can protect your precious assets—and with some careful preplanning, even control them too. All you need is the commitment to give offshore money havens a try, and the willingness to work closely with a well-qualified professional consultant.

CHAPTER 8

EIGHT STEPS TO OFFSHORE SUCCESS

Spontaneous innovations in the marketplace arise to avoid government regulation and taxation. . . .

— DAVID GLASNER,
FREE BANKING AND MONETARY REFORM

Offshore money havens are no longer a luxury reserved for the ultrarich. Within today's global economic system, they are the prime investment option for anyone whose assets total $250,000 or more. That includes tens of thousands of Americans—all of whom want tax protection, impressive profits, and financial privacy.

Why do you think so many investors—large, small, and in-between—are moving toward this global business approach? Why have they decided to compete (and win) at the offshore game?

In part, the offshore boom results from a wide array of technological advancements. Thanks to sophisticated telecommunications and computerized banking services worldwide, people can make, spend, win, lose, and transfer money faster than ever before. A conscientious investor may, for instance, assess the value of currency in any nation on a given morning, decide when it has reached a danger point, and complete a cash-out program on all liquid investments held in that country by the following afternoon! This fast-paced movement of funds has made offshore investment very appealing to growing numbers of domestic businesspeople and entrepreneurs.

But there is an even more profound reason for the trend toward offshore investment: the changing profile of today's financial players. Regardless of their individual differences, the economic winners of the 1990s and into the next century will share a common view of the global marketplace. They will see it as a wide-open environment from which to pick and choose the most lucrative investment options. They will have taken what I perceive to be the most important step in attaining genuine financial independence: learning to see the world without national borders. That gives them an almost limitless profit-making arena.

If you take only one message from this book, I hope it will be the enormity of your potential investment sphere. You no longer need to restrict your financial activity to the traditional Swiss bank account, or to a paltry selection of onshore tax shelters. Conventional investment vehicles (such as bonds, commodities, and securities) have become relics of another time. The entire world offers lucrative ventures, and you can become a part of any or all of them. You just need to broaden your own investment horizon.

Experience has shown me that, for many reasons, Americans tend to see the world as a neatly divided assortment of cultures, countries, and currencies. We think of east as east, and west as west, and only at the United Nations do the twain meet. I can't tell you how many times I've consulted with extremely successful professionals and entrepreneurs from around the country, all of whom want to add offshore investments to their financial portfolio. Nevertheless, their personal sense of economic nationalism limits their ability to reap the benefits of the offshore solution.

They pay a high price for this limited vision. They miss the benefits inherent in the international option. From those who have avoided offshore activity altogether, I most often hear about profit margins that are far less than satisfactory. From those who have severely restricted foreign investments, I learn of stymied venture activity and meager earnings. In each instance I find myself thinking of the more assertive investors (from the United States and around the world) who have entered the offshore arena, those who are constantly taking part in creative new ventures and who are sharpening their global edge.

THE BIG MYTH ABOUT OFFSHORE BUSINESS

Despite its proven benefits, the offshore option still lacks a level of public credibility. For too many people, the words "offshore banking investment" conjure up images of money laundering, drug trafficking, arms smuggling, insider-trading schemes, and tax evasion. The media are partly to blame for this false impression. Every television network, newspaper, and weekly news magazine in the country has run stories on illicit foreign

The offshore boom results from a wide array of technological advancements. Thanks to sophisticated telecommunications and computerized banking services worldwide, people can make, spend, win, lose, and transfer money faster than ever before.

financial ventures. After all, these complex intrigues make for attention-grabbing headlines.

Admittedly, there is some truth behind the hype. Illegal activity has occurred, and it continues to happen. Although this criminal element accounts for only a small fraction of the total offshore investment community, it has managed to tarnish the reputation of an entirely legitimate financial option. Why? Because the global market is so inviting and so well tailored to unregulated profit, it has easily fallen prey to those with less than honorable intentions.

The Iran-Contra scandal of the late 1980s uncovered a world in which the profits from illegal drug and arms deals ended up in secret Swiss bank accounts. From endless hours of televised hearings, we learned that Col. Oliver North (a member of President Reagan's National Security Council who worked out of the basement of the White House) was funding the Contra rebels of Nicaragua with money from international drug sales and arms deals to the Iranian government. This scandal marked the end of Ronald Reagan's amazing and unquestioned popularity.

Iran-Contra and the Bank of Credit and Commerce International (BCCI) scandals added fuel to the fire of "offshore" illegality. How ironic that the most famous of all international financial scandals should involve the U.S. government itself! Federal authorities have been nothing less than rabid in their search for individual investors who may have improperly circumvented the law. All the while, the biggest scheme was happening right under their noses.

Later, the complicated narcotics mess with now-deposed and federally convicted General Noriega of Panama also contributed to negative mythmaking about offshore activities. Here was a man—the military leader of his nation—who accepted millions of dollars in bribes to allow the safe transport of drugs through his country.

He also tolerated the laundering of drug profits through Panamanian banks. *Southern Banker* magazine reported that "$200 to $300 million a month" was laundered through 140 Panamanian banks for the notorious Colombian drug cartel. Noriega personally pocketed "$10 million a month in protection fees."

The image of offshore banking certainly wasn't helped by revelations that Ferdinand Marcos, the late president of the Philippines, may have taken money from his country's budget and used it in the international market for personal profit. It's now estimated that during his reign Marcos may have stashed upwards of $310 billion in secret accounts throughout the world.

And during the summer of 1988, news broke that the Securities and Exchange Commission was investigating an insider-trading scheme and the use of Swiss banks. Respected firms such as Morgan Stanley, Goldman Sachs, First Boston, Merrill Lynch, Shearson Lehman Hutton, and Charles Schwab were all subpoenaed in the case.

I've related these stories not to aggravate an already sensitive nerve among prospective offshore investors. I've covered them because I want to honestly confront the fact that international business does include an underworld of illegitimate activity. What financial environment is without its bandits? Wall Street certainly has its share of thieves. So do the venerable financial houses of Hong Kong.

The point is, when there is money to be made some people will try to take more than their fair share by opting to break the law. As a rule, our government does not engage in illegal arms trades. Most heads of state are honest and concerned with the betterment of their people. Most business conducted by top U.S. securities firms is legitimate, open, and aboveboard. It is unfair to allow isolated exceptions to these rules to reflect negatively on the entire offshore option.

In and of itself, offshore investment is neither legal nor illegal. It becomes legal or illegal only by the way in which it is conducted. The great majority of offshore activities involve businesspeople and investors on the up-and-up. Most offshore operators are simply seeking safe harbors for their money and/or legal ways to avoid taxes; they are usually trying to take advantage of profit-making opportunities that are unavailable onshore.

EIGHT STEPS TO OFFSHORE SUCCESS

If you are taking the time to read this book, you're probably serious about an offshore financial involvement. Many of you may have already experienced the international arena; others are undoubtedly considering a "first venture."

In either case, I would like to offer you some basic advice: eight steps to success in the offshore world marketplace. There is nothing particularly unusual about them. In fact, you may have heard similar advice from other consultants.

However, there is one big difference. I've been out there for twenty years now. I've been on the front lines of the offshore investment expansion. The following steps are based primarily on my firsthand experience with real people. Working on the front lines has prepared me to offer you advice tempered by reality, not far-fetched academic theories.

Over the years, I've watched a lot of investors enter the world of offshore finance. While many of them have become tremendously successful in the process, I've seen some failures too. In my view, each of those failures can be traced to an unwillingness or an inability to follow these basic steps.

The first step to successfully entering the offshore arena is careful self-assessment. Know your own level of interest and comfort. I advocate an informed and assertive approach.

Step One: Decide If an Offshore Financial Move Is Right for You

Not everyone is cut out for international finance. There are people who simply don't want to do business in a foreign country. Even among those who do like the global market, there are decisive differences. Some are satisfied when they are "invisibly" involved in an offshore investment. Others aren't happy until they get right in the middle of it: taking frequent trips abroad and juggling the challenges of offshore business relations for themselves. So, the first step to successfully entering the offshore arena is careful self-assessment. Know your own level of interest and comfort. I advocate an informed and assertive approach.

This may be the time to point out how strongly I disagree with those experts who urge American investors to learn cross-cultural business skills in order to go global. The fact is, most successful U.S. businesspeople already have extensive cross-cultural experience. Anyone who lives in Manhattan and handles transactions in Los Angeles, New Orleans, Houston, or even Chicago understands that. The United States really consists of many different cultures functioning together as a single country. So the challenge, as I see it, is one of expanding professional skills that already exist.

In short, going offshore is committing to an entirely new way of making money. It's expanding your investment perspective, and capitalizing on financial opportunities whenever and wherever they occur. Remember—before you get involved, be sure you're really attracted to this very contemporary approach to personal investment.

Step Two: Develop a Strategy

Once you've decided that offshore action is for you, you must begin to develop a feasible financial strategy. You can't hope to make money, save taxes, or protect your privacy by merely stumbling around in the offshore marketplace. You must know what you're doing.

So take the time to ask yourself: what do you want from, say, a silent partnership in Tokyo? From your private brass-plate bank in the Caribbean? From an import/export firm in the Pacific? Each of these offshore ventures can be extremely profitable and each one is a distinct business activity with very specific demands and benefits. Developing a strategy involves serious consideration of your needs, your goals, and your future.

Every successful businessperson or investor that I've ever met has known the value of strategic thinking. It begins when you realize that it is essential to diversify in order to protect your holdings. Once that idea is firmly ingrained, it is time to lay out a well-designed plan of action.

Let's consider the strategy of well-known international investor George Soros (see also Chapter 3, page 47). It's true that he knows the value of financial flexibility. Soros has mapped out a plan that's designed to direct his daily, weekly, and monthly decisions for the next few years. His overall goal is to profit from the changing social and political situations in various economies around the globe. That goal allows him a wide arena in which to conduct his activities, but it also builds parameters around his playing field. He must take certain factors into account and then base his investments upon those assessments. In my view, that makes for the most successful strategy.

Like Soros, you also need to devise specific tactics that will make it possible for you to carry out your strategy. In order to meet his particular objective, Soros plans to trade and invest in very targeted markets and areas at very specific times. If, for example, your overall aim in using an offshore base is to lessen your tax load, then you must think of appropriate ways in which to carry out that strategy. These will be your tactics.

My advice is that those tactics should embody the golden rule of financial investment: Diversification. Like even the best things in life, each individual offshore venture can satisfy only so many economic needs. I strongly discourage anyone from imagining that there is a single international investment, acquisition, or new business concept that can legally address all your financial needs. That's why the best international investors have assets strategically working around the world, functioning in different ways in different places.

Step Three: Select an Experienced Offshore Adviser

Realizing the need for a practical strategy, you must now consider the services of a first-class financial expert. While shopping for an adviser, remember that a number of professional qualities characterize a really good consultant.

Superior Financial Skills You need someone who can develop an optimal strategy tailored especially to your needs. Don't accept a "one-size-fits-all" approach to offshore investment. Look for an adviser who is willing and able to help you design the plan that's right for you. Any reputable consultant will be well versed in handling foreign exchange matters, preparing proper documentation, and setting offshore operating parameters. Your consultant must also be someone who can help with the implementation of your business strategy, not just with the concept behind it.

Excellent Knowledge of Offshore International Investment Alternatives A qualified adviser will offer various investment vehicles, and will encourage you to compare them before making a final choice. Every investment has its own complexity and each requires careful consideration. You should be able to count on your consultant for help in balancing out the various accounting, tax, and legal issues involved in all your options.

A Wide Network of International Contacts Avoid fly-by-night operations. By and large, international financial consultants are honest and reliable, but there are a few scam artists who make it their business to identify inexperienced investors. A good way to know if you've met a real professional is to ask about his international business network. You want to look for an adviser who is well connected to people and institutions

My advice is that those tactics should embody the golden rule of financial investment: Diversification. Like even the best things in life, each individual offshore venture can satisfy only so many economic needs. I strongly discourage anyone from imagining that there is a single international investment, acquisition, or new business concept that can legally address all your financial needs. That's why the best international investors have assets strategically working around the world, functioning in different ways in different places.

abroad. Those contacts are your insurance that an offshore venture will be implemented legally and on the best possible terms for you.

An In-Depth Understanding of the Offshore Market and the Staff to Efficiently Execute All Transactions. Establishing an offshore operation and conducting transactions in another country often involves close and regular interaction with government officials. You need to work with an adviser who understands the intricacies involved in your preferred offshore location. What's more, your adviser should offer you an experienced and efficient staff, capable of serving as backup for your project. Also, be sure the adviser you select has the communication technology to execute complicated transactions quickly and accurately.

Once you have selected an offshore adviser who meets these criteria, it's time to reassess your strategy—this time with his or her input. By working through the plan you've designed for yourself, you can benefit from your adviser's feedback and guidance. Although you probably have a good sense for what's right for you, don't be bullheaded about taking your professional consultant's advice. After all, his advice is what you're paying for. Let your adviser help you refine and hone your offshore game plan.

Step Four: Put All the Proper Systems in Place

After you've clarified your priorities, mapped out your strategy, and identified a good adviser, it's time to put your systems in place. Before you attempt to negotiate your first deal, be sure you're prepared to do business the way it's done offshore. That means setting up a sound organizational structure to manage your international investments and/or operations. You need good people and the right equipment. That may sound like an obvious step, but you'd be surprised at how many new investors forget to take it.

You should now select your key people: an accountant, an attorney, and a clerical assistant. Depending upon the nature and scope of your particular strategy, you may want to hire them on a per-hour (or freelance) basis, rather than as full-time employees. This is an area in which a professional consultant can offer some experienced advice.

You will need the right equipment in place and operational. With the proper assemblage of a personal computer, modem, fax machine, and photocopier, you will be able to create a virtual electronic control center. From this ultramodern financial headquarters, you can operate anytime, day or night. You can work out of your home, or from your office. You might even want to add a separate workstation in your business office that's dedicated strictly to offshore interests. It all depends on your plans, your bank account, and your ambitions.

An integral part of proper systems management is written confirmation of everything. To help you in this area, here are three basic tips on written communications:

- Keep your writing simple. Experience has shown me that basic, straightforward letters and memos are the key to successful business writing.
- Make sure professional titles translate correctly. Since the same position may vary around the world, getting the right title is essential.
- Clarify all written items having to do with money amounts. Be sure that currency differences and rate exchanges are taken into account.

Step Five: Create the Right Image

In my opinion, your business image is one of the most important factors in the successful consummation of offshore ventures. Because I've worked and lived in Los Angeles, one of the media capitals of the world, I am repeatedly reminded of the value in projecting a strong, clear image, and the benefits of keeping that image in front of those you want to impress favorably.

For offshore investors the importance of image should direct everything from the design of your business cards to the wording of all printed material you use to outline your offerings, products, or services. Anything you produce to advance your financial activities should reflect the image you want to project.

You must establish your image before you go offshore. For example, your new offshore financial entity may offer banking services. Therefore, your bank will require a name, a logo, stationery, services brochure, and various types of banking forms. The image you want to project will direct all these specific choices.

You can create and promote a very serious, cautious, financially conservative image by working with basic muted colors (like gray and brown). By the same token, you can generate a more relaxed, contemporary, and slightly adventurous impression by using pastel colors (like sky blue and sand). It's up to you. Both have their benefits and drawbacks. Remember that no choice will appeal to every prospective customer in every nation. So, carefully think through your prime markets and direct your choices toward their concerns and priorities.

Going offshore is not like taking a vacation. Even for the most adventuresome at heart, it is not a time for playing things by ear. To be successful overseas—even if you never leave the United States—you need to learn something about the place where you're investing your money.

The key is careful coordination. Make sure all your printed material is coordinated in some way. This makes it easier for investors, depositors, shareholders, and customers to identify your service or product. Consistency is a must in business because it conveys stability.

Finally, some ideas about advertising. This will prove to be a critical decision when it comes to image making. Advertising is the direct approach to the people whose involvement you want. As such, it must send a message about your business image. This kind of intelligent advertising will help establish your offshore business, and, over time, will make it grow.

Let me quote from one of the masters of business advertising, Ted Nicholas: "It is not an oversimplification to say that nearly every ad, regardless of its degree of sophistication, follows the Attention-Interest-Desire-Action formula." That's exactly what you should keep in mind when you advertise. First, your ad must grab your potential client's attention, create interest, arouse a real desire to act, and then explain how to take that action.

Check with your consultant about all advertising, particularly about this attention-interest-desire-action formula. Will it produce results? Are there marketing experts who would be willing to review your materials and offer their professional criticism? You should be able to receive this kind of support and guidance from your adviser. Again, that's why you've commissioned his or her services. So, don't be shy about asking for help.

Step Six: Do Your Homework

Going offshore is not like taking a vacation. Even for the most adventuresome at heart, it is not a time for playing things by ear. To be successful overseas—even if you never leave the United States—you need to learn something about the place where you're investing your money.

To be realistic, the extent of your "homework" should be tied to your level of personal contact with the foreign locale. If your entire plan is to purchase stock at a brokerage firm that handles foreign investments, your information needs are clearly minimal. If, on the other hand, you plan to conduct business with South Korean textile manufacturers, you'd be smart to spend time learning what is and isn't acceptable behavior in their part of the world.

According to Stanford University's Richard Pascale, too many people think that a cocktail conversation with a few world travelers will prepare them for even the most in-depth offshore involvement. As he points out, "real effort is more like thirty hours of intensive study."

When it comes to this "homework" phase, I'm a firm believer in the value of small books and regular magazines. Clients who have been to my office often remark on my personal business library. They are sometimes amazed by my encyclopedia collections on various international business subjects as well as the scores of volumes on everything from international marketing to the history of world economic growth.

Of course, my work demands that I keep abreast of a wide range of international and global developments. You don't need to tackle that kind of reading load. Nevertheless, I do suggest that you consider building a basic collection that will help you understand the exciting changes that are constantly taking place in the offshore market.

Frankly, there are far too many books on the market that are just hype and do nothing more than feed existing fears and misconceptions. Don't be suckered into the belief that you must read everything that's published on the subject. Instead, take a fairly casual approach to building your library. After all, the offshore market will be around forever. You have time to become a master at it.

If you do decide to build a basic international investment bookshelf, the following tips may prove helpful:

General Reference Every investor should have at least one book on general investment. It should cover some of the essentials, like the do's and don'ts of personal financial planning. Make sure that any general reference books you buy were written after the tax reform of 1986 and the tax legislation passed into law in 1990 and 1993 because anything published before that is out of date. We now operate by completely different rules. You may also want to buy an investment vocabulary guide, such as the *Dictionary of Finance and Investment Terms* published by Barron's.

Books About Offshore Funds Offshore funds are investment funds based in tax havens or low-tax areas. As the *Financial Times* notes, "they are able to invest in a broader range of instruments than onshore domestic investment companies. It is this flexibility . . . which is their main attraction for investors." Because they are a cornerstone to offshore investment, I recommend that you get a basic background text about how they work. *Donoghue's Mutual Funds Almanac* is a good one. I also recommend that before you invest in any fund, you send for its prospectus and study it.

Books About Hard Assets With inflation always lurking around the corner, you may want to have a couple of books on real estate and gold. One well-recommended guide is Nicholas's *The Complete Book of Gold Investing*. Another is *Real Estate after Tax Reform.*

Step Seven: Know the Rules and Practices

Before you finalize the design of any international business plan, check out the legal requirements of your host country concerning local participation. It's no longer possible to just set up a business anywhere in the world, run it entirely with your own staff, and earn its full profit for yourself.

Growing nationalism and economic protectionism abroad have changed the nature of offshore ventures. Today, many foreign governments have strict laws governing the percentage of required native workforce and mandatory contributions to various national development goals. Don't be caught off guard: Know the laws of any country before you move beyond the thinking phase.

In short, other countries are raising the stakes for entrance into their economy. If the potential profit is substantial, it may be worth the price. But if foreign governments become too demanding, they can begin to extinguish the allure of any site.

Before getting involved in an offshore center, try to meet people who have done business in that country. If that's not possible, then try meeting people with other experiences in (and connections to) the area. If even that becomes difficult, I suggest that you keep trying until you find at least one person who's willing to offer limited social and professional support. Even if you dislike this sort of networking, you'll ultimately be glad to know someone you can call for advice on matters as minor as currency exchange or as major as government involvement in business operations.

These "mentors" can serve another essential purpose. They can provide you with names of people in the foreign location who, in turn, will refer you to others who will direct you to more contacts. And knowing people is the name of the game in international finance. Everyone likes a personal touch. That is especially true in other countries, where social values tend to emphasize personal associations and reputation.

As a second phase in this networking strategy, I urge you to hire a reliable representative in the foreign center where you plan to conduct business. In some countries this is a legal requirement. Even where it is not, experts

The best insurance against this problem is to know ahead of time exactly what the conditions are for transferring your involvement back into U.S. currency. How can your stocks be sold? How can your franchise or distributor agreement be signed over to another investor? Can you dissolve your local partnership at any time with the understanding that your share of the profits-to-date will be liquidated and made payable?

agree that you should pretend it is. The local representative should be native to the country.

Some people think they can just go out and place an ad in a foreign newspaper and they'll be deluged with resumes. But that's simply not the way it works. First of all, the cost of advertising is prohibitive. According to *East Asian Executive Reports,* "A small ad in a national Japanese-language newspaper can cost upwards of $20,000 per insertion . . ." Secondly, the demand for talent far exceeds the supply.

Once you do locate an agent, keep two things in mind. First, if you don't click with a prospective agent, move on right away. It will only become more difficult to make a change later on. If you do replace your representative, be careful not to offend him because his negative comments about you can have serious consequences. Second, don't count on your representative for everything. Few offshore operations can be initiated and successfully completed entirely by proxy. An agent can help, but at some point you will probably need to get directly involved.

Step Eight: Make Sure You Can Get Your Money Out

If you work with a professional financial consultant, you are unlikely to face this nightmare. However, if you try to handle an entire offshore venture alone, you can run into terrible trouble when it comes time to cash-out and return home. Some countries make it very easy to invest in, but very difficult to get out of their economy.

The best insurance against this problem is to know ahead of time exactly what the conditions are for transferring your involvement back into U.S. currency. How can your stocks be sold? How can your franchise or distributor agreement be signed over to another investor? Can you dissolve your local partnership at any time with the understanding that your share of the profits-to-date will be liquidated and made payable?

Have all conditions of transfer and dissolution formally agreed upon in writing. Keep one copy in your foreign business site and another here in the United States. That way, in the event of any problem, you will have a legally binding agreement to show the exact nature of your investment arrangement.

Know, too, that Uncle Sam will lay claim to his share of every dollar earned abroad and brought back to this country. So don't plan to repatriate funds unless you're willing to pay taxes on them.

PUTTING IT ALL TOGETHER

These eight basic steps are only a beginning. They can provide you with the minimum you will need to know for even the simplest international investment venture.

Perhaps the most important of all the suggestions is the value of a professional consultant. If you connect with the right person, he or she will help guide you through all the rest. Particularly in the beginning, when you are justifiably overwhelmed by most aspects of any offshore project, a seasoned expert can offer help and reassurance. As you become more experienced you may be able to initiate and implement some business deals without commissioning further expert advice.

International investment and business is a financial grab bag. Most of it is exciting. Much of it is lucrative. Some of it is risky. There are benefits and disadvantages to every kind of offshore venture. So it's your responsibility to know what your options are and to understand the perks and pitfalls that are attached to each. In the process, you will prepare yourself to reach for the offshore involvement that is best for you and your financial priorities.

Chapter 9

Offshore Money Havens: Where to Go (and Where Not to Go)

Never keep all your wealth in the country where you live because anything can happen—and usually does.

— Adam Smith

The secret numbered Swiss bank account is a remnant from the financial past. Using one in today's intensely competitive and highly unpredictable economy is like riding a bike on a superhighway. The vehicle we should use always depends on need. And while no one would take a bike on the freeway, too many investors rely on a Swiss account when a much more versatile option exists: offshore money havens.

People often ask me if they can *really* protect their money, earn a profit, and pay less taxes by using the offshore option. I always say yes—as long as they are careful in selecting their offshore business venue. International money havens actually do exist, and in light of the worsening U.S. economy and the tightening of U.S. tax rules, they are fast becoming the preferred choice for smart investors.

Several years ago, a study called *Service Banking* was prepared for the prestigious London-based Institute of Bankers. In reviewing it, I came across an insightful observation and jotted it down because it contained the essence of the offshore rationale:

> Like water finding its own level, entrepreneurial business, when constrained in one place, will emerge in another. When restrictions in one place become too burdensome, too discouraging and perhaps too punitive, the businessman will look elsewhere . . . as one door closes, another opens.

Over the years I've seen the truth of this observation borne out time after time in life as well as in business. If you don't like a situation, change it. Whether it's your relationship with your spouse, your employees, your dwelling, change it if it isn't working out. There is no reason to tolerate the current situation in Switzerland. As it has become subject to international agreements and its famous secrecy laws dissolve under international political pressure, other places pick up the slack. Some people now go to Austria, while others find Luxembourg useful. Many prefer the British Virgin Islands (BVI). The point is: Every investor can find what he needs, if he's just willing to look far enough.

One of the reasons I was compelled to write this book is that more and more of my clients have expressed alarm and concern over the uncertain economic situation in the United States. They also understand that in times of swift economic change, flexibility and liquidity are crucial requirements. When you factor in the bureaucratic red tape that has become part of all financial dealings within this country—as well as the low rates of return on investments, the heavy burden of taxation, and a general negative social environment—the offshore option is hard to overlook.

HOW THE OFFSHORE HAVENS CAME ABOUT

It's important to keep in mind that these offshore money havens were originally established by onshore banks and corporations. Why? Because they also felt hemmed in by archaic laws, regulations, and statutes. For example, Citicorp (one of the largest American-owned banks in the United States) was one of the first to set up offshore operations. It wasn't too long before 64 percent of its net income was being generated by offshore sources.

Some of the pioneering centers have evolved into first-class financial and economic headquarters. Since the early 1970s these centers have initiated policies deliberately designed to attract international trade by minimizing tax obligations and reducing (or entirely eliminating) other restrictions on business operations. The result is that economic activity within these centers is specifically geared to the special global needs of outside businesses and investors.

Typically, these centers are small states with tiny populations. To date, more than 200 of them exist throughout the world. Since 1985, the number has grown almost exponentially. Each one of them is a unique offshore haven deliberately intended to attract very particular investors

People often ask me if they can *really* protect their money, earn a profit, and pay less taxes by using the offshore option. I always say yes—as long as they are careful in selecting their offshore business venue. International money havens actually do exist, and in light of the worsening U.S. economy and the tightening of U.S. tax rules, they are fast becoming the preferred choice for smart investors.

with very specific needs. Singapore, for example, was designed to serve the Asian dollar market. Today, it's one of the most prosperous money havens in the world on a per capita basis. Bahrain was developed to process the Middle East's offshore financial needs, especially Saudi Arabia's.

International havens have become an established part of the international intermediate economy. They operate as "brokers" of a sort for global business and finance. It's important to keep in mind that all of this was initiated by large banks, corporations, and even government agencies from around the world. Keep in mind that every government in the world needs to obtain money on the international market. They, too, use money havens as convenient transaction points. The Bahamas became one of the biggest offshore havens because it serves the purposes of various government entities, from finance ministries to intelligence agencies.

Offshore havens are, today, an accepted financial fact. Even more important, they are seen as legitimate vehicles through which individual investors can take advantage of the offshore option. It's simply a matter of applying the basic financial principles of profit, tax protection, and privacy. They were developed over the centuries by Florentine merchants, royal treasurers, and brilliant bankers. These people are considered the first offshore bankers in history. They helped make Florence one of the world's most economically advanced centers. The mechanisms and strategies change continuously, but the goals always remain the same.

When I work with my clients I try to ensure that they are served by the money haven that is right for them. Based on their needs, I help them customize and tailor a program in an offshore haven that meets their personal criteria. As a consultant, I look forward to the discussions that help shape their final offshore money haven choice.

THE OFFSHORE INVESTOR'S GUIDE

The following guide is meant to serve not as a complete list of all offshore havens but, rather, as a list of the financial centers that I consider most important for today's U.S. investor. Again, I caution against using the list as an absolute measure of a location's desirability. It is always best to hire a professional consultant who can balance the benefits of a specific location against your very individual needs.

At minimum, you should look for an offshore center that offers the following: secrecy and privacy, reputation, quality of regulation, entry requirements, movement of funds, and jurisdictional ties to the United States.

- **Secrecy and Privacy** Your personal and business accounts should be completely confidential. Nobody but you and those you specifically designate should be able to learn anything about your investments or business activities. You need to shield your financial transactions from prying eyes. The eyes of Uncle Sam and his army of government bureaucrats seem to get keener instead of weaker with age. Make sure the laws of your chosen jurisdiction protect you from any unwarranted economic disclosures.
- **Easy Movement of Assets** You need to be able to transfer your investments and assets without incurring a tax liability or exchange charges.
- **Flexibility** You want to be able to plan your inheritance freely for family members and other beneficiaries. Not all international centers are set up to help in this area. Don't get involved with one that isn't.
- **Reputation, Entry Requirements, and Quality of Regulation** You need to be certain that your haven of choice enjoys an excellent reputation

in the offshore financial community. It should not be known for criminal activity, such as the laundering of drug money. In a respectable haven you can move your money in and out without undue problems or red tape. Finally, you want to be sure that there exists a legal recourse in the event of problems or disputes.

In addition, you'll want to look for a haven that offers government concessions, few or no taxes, easy access, smooth entry, political stability, absence of currency restrictions or controls, banking secrecy, a common language (preferably English), trained personnel, excellent telecommunications, and a positive attitude toward Americans. The following jurisdictions offer a full spectrum of some of the best-known centers based on the criteria I developed to rate money havens throughout the world.

Aruba

Aruba is English-speaking and a separate entity within the kingdom of the Netherlands. It is located in the Dutch Caribbean, less than twenty kilometers from the Venezuelan coast. Aruba is an island about twenty miles long and approximately five miles wide. It has a total population of 61,000 people and a delightful climate. Oranjestad is the capital. The island has an excellent educational system, and four languages are spoken: Dutch (the official language), English, Spanish, and Papamiento, the island's indigenous language. Telecommunications are first-rate. Automatic international communication provides access to any country in the world. A satellite ground station means that instant satellite communication as well as the latest data systems are operational.

The best way to utilize the features of Aruba is to establish a tax-exempted company there; Aruba does not

Offshore havens are, today, an accepted financial fact. Even more important, they are seen as legitimate vehicles through which individual investors can take advantage of the offshore option. It's simply a matter of applying the basic financial principles of profit, tax protection, and privacy.

require these companies to maintain bookkeeping or annual accounts. It allows companies to determine the value of shares upon the date of issue. Incorporators and shareholders need not be the same individuals or entities. Shareholders may meet anywhere in the world. Minutes are not mandatory. And no special licenses are needed.

The Aruban government is very flexible, and, since the early 1980s, has been concerned with developing alternative sources of revenue. For several decades it survived and prospered due to the presence of one of the world's largest oil refineries. When that refinery closed in 1985, the government decided to concentrate on tourism and international financial services.

Due to its longtime status as a center for oil, Aruba has a highly developed infrastructure. This, combined with government flexibility and a willingness to attract investors, makes Aruba a fine choice for anyone interested in establishing an offshore corporation in a friendly and strategically located center.

The Bahamas

The Bahamas constitute an independent state within the British Commonwealth. They comprise more than 700 islands and 2,000 keys scattered over 100,000 square miles of heavenly blue seas. With a total land area of about 4,000 square miles, the islands extend from sixty miles east of Florida to just north of Haiti. The population is around 250,000, with most people living on New Providence Island where the capital, Nassau, is located. English is the official language.

Long considered to be among the world's best offshore money havens, the Bahamas are a good choice for several reasons. It imposes absolutely no taxes. Since 1717, not a single penny has been paid in income, corporation, capital gains, remittance, estate, or inheritance tax. There is, however, growing concern that the no-tax advantages of the Bahamas may diminish because of a new and controversial business licensing law that mandates a fee on business operations.

Although the Bahamas are popular for establishing trusts, they are mainly known as an international banking center. Nevertheless, the bank market is fairly well saturated at this point. In fact, owning your own bank is nearly impossible because the government rarely issues a bank license to individuals or small companies. As a result, this may be a poor offshore site for the single investor or small consortium. I recommend the Bahamas to clients interested only in becoming offshore bank customers. It is now considered one of the best choices for International Business Companies (IBC) conducting international business and commerce.

Barbados

Political stability is a major benefit to anyone considering financial ventures in Barbados. Without racial friction, military rule, or serious labor problems, it operates as a parliamentary government located a few hundred miles off the northern coast of South America. It is twenty-one miles long, fourteen miles wide and, as of 1993, had nearly 300,000 residents. It is considered a

Political stability is a major benefit to anyone considering financial ventures in Barbados.

wonderful vacation spot due to the balmy trade winds that blow year-round and the sunshine that brightens every day.

Communication systems are top-of-the-line throughout Barbados. For example, it has an earth satellite that allows for international data transfer. It also offers the Caribbean's best roads and highways. As an added plus, the official and spoken language is English.

Barbados has recently embarked on a program to upgrade its image. It has simplified many of its regulations and incorporation procedures. It has also lowered its paid-in capital requirement for a bank license. It is truly on a course of improvement. This new attitude combined with its beauty make it one of the better places to conduct your offshore transactions. Barbados is popular with Canadians where I live. The Canada-Barbados tax treaty permits some amazing tax benefits to be gained (see Appendix 2 for more details).

Bermuda

Bermuda is the oldest self-governing state in the British Commonwealth. Located less than one thousand miles southeast of New York City and six hundred miles east from North Carolina, it is a small country consisting of 150 islands with a total area of less than twenty-five square miles. Communication and air facilities are excellent.

Bermuda is a true tax haven: There is no income tax, corporation tax, capital gains tax, or withholding tax

From almost every perspective, Bermuda is not a place to establish an offshore presence.

imposed by the local government. This makes it a hot spot for investors whose main concern is tax protection.

Nothing, of course, is perfect. When it comes to this island cluster, the major drawback is its stuffiness. Bermuda is only for the carriage trade because of local capital requirement laws. Bermuda will require substantial capital amounts to establish a corporation or insurance company, perhaps a major stumbling block for some investors. For instance, the minimum paid-in capital needed to form an insurance company is $125,000, and some Bermudan attorneys actually suggest a minimum of $250,000 to ensure incorporation. In addition, a proposal to introduce offshore banking was recently defeated by the houses of government.

Politically, Bermuda has been plagued by periodic unrest—including the assassination of a newly appointed governor in the 1970s. Tourism has traditionally accounted for a good part of the island's economy, but since the mid-1980s its popularity as a vacation spot has plummeted. The problem is primarily economic: The island's currency is pegged to the U.S. dollar and 85 percent of its tourists are U.S. citizens. However, most American vacationers are looking for getaways that offer a better exchange rate.

From almost every perspective, Bermuda is not a place to establish an offshore presence. Besides, Bermuda is quite dependent upon the U.S. economy. So if you want to avoid the economic negatives that affect the United States, it's best to go somewhere less vulnerable to the ups and downs of this financial arena.

British Virgin Islands (BVI)

Christopher Columbus is credited with the discovery of the Virgin Islands. Impressed by how many islands he found—60 in all—he tagged this Caribbean chain *Las Virgenes,* in honor of St. Ursula and her 11,000 virgins-in-waiting. During the sixteenth and seventeenth centuries, the volcanic rock islands were used as a base of operation by such notable buccaneers as Blackbeard and Sir Francis Drake.

Today, a new breed of adventurer has established a beachhead on the Virgin Islands. I'm referring, of course, to offshore investors—particularly U.S. companies that have set up subsidiary operations in the region.

The only language used in the BVI is English, which is certainly attractive to U.S. investors. Moreover, communications are excellent—with good telephone, cable, and fax service to the United States. On the downside, there are no direct international flights to Tortola, the main island. In order to reach the capital you first must fly to Puerto Rico, the U.S. Virgin Islands, or Antigua. From any of these three spots, you then can catch a plane to Tortola.

Many observers feel that the BVI are shaping up into a prime tax haven. In my opinion, with its new addition of a very user-friendly international business company ordinance, this is a very positive choice for your offshore business affairs. For the moment, I suggest that you keep a careful eye on what happens there. This may well become a great money haven for the late 1990s. I give the BVI thumbs-up for Americans.

Cayman Islands

The Caymans are a special place and an extremely popular money haven. Local government imposes no taxes of any kind on income, profits, capital, wealth, capital gains, property, sales, estate, or inheritance. Located five hundred miles south of Florida and about two hundred miles northwest of Jamaica, the Caymans are composed of three isles: Grand Cayman, Cayman Brac, and Little Cayman. The capital, George Town, is the area's financial and business center.

As you walk down George Town's main streets, you are immediately struck by the number of buildings that house banks, trusts, captive insurance companies, and various other offshore firms. However, before you rush headlong into a Cayman operation, you should know that nearly all those institutions are subsidiaries of the world's largest banks and corporations.

Offshore business in the Cayman Islands is a very big money game, and it's pretty much reserved for the globe's major players. To give you an idea of what constitutes a "major player," let me take you through an abbreviated who's who of the 18,000 companies and 550 banks now doing business in the Caymans: The Detroit Edison Company; Marine Midland Banks; Mellon Bank Company; United Energy Resources; Conagra; Kansas City Power and Light Company; McDonnell Douglas Corporation; Archer Daniels Midland Company; Amerada Hess Corporation; Houston Natural Gas Corporation; Wells Fargo; First Interstate Bancorp (to name just a few). As you can see, very large, public, and well-known companies are conducting offshore business in this region.

As a result, the Caymans are a first-class offshore center. Their infrastructure is excellent; communications are top-of-the-line. Direct flights to and from the United States are available. The official and spoken language is English, and the Cayman dollar is pegged to the U.S. dollar.

But there's one major obstacle, and it too is the result of the Cayman Islands' special involvement with big business. Bank charters and licenses are available

As a result, the Caymans are a first-class offshore center. Their infrastructure is excellent; communications are top-of-the-line. Direct flights to and from the United States are available. The official and spoken language is English, and the Cayman dollar is pegged to the U.S. dollar.

only to long-established companies and banks with a paid-in capital of at least $500,000. The small to medium investor is left out completely. Other than the government's closed-door policy toward individual investors, the Caymans would be a perfect offshore choice for bank accounts and offshore corporations.

Channel Islands

The Channel Islands are composed of the isles of Jersey, Guernsey, and Sark. The two main islands, Jersey and Guernsey, are longtime offshore centers with thriving economies. Situated in the Bay of St. Malo—closer to the French coast than to England, and yet only fifty minutes from London—the Channel Islands are one of the world's busiest tax havens. All three centers cater mostly to British and European companies and individuals. Nevertheless, they can provide a world-class financial environment for U.S. investors as well.

Like the Caymans, the Channel Islands have developed into a base of operations for major international banks and corporations. Chase Manhattan, Credit Suisse, Rothschild Bank, Hong Kong and Shanghai Banking Corporation are among the leading financial institutions based in Jersey or Guernsey. For individual investors, there is one special lure: a booming offshore fund market. Jersey alone is home base for some three hundred international funds. So if the fund market appeals to you, I'd recommend that you explore this option further with a professional consultant.

The official and spoken language is English. The transportation and communications services are top-of-the-line. Unfortunately, the Channel Islands are too far away to really serve the needs of most potential offshore investors from the United States. It's also worth mentioning that recent revelations of money laundering in Jersey may hurt the reputation of anyone involved with the islands. That's something no discreet investor ever desires.

Cook Islands

Out in the South Pacific are a group of islands whose climate is very similar to Hawaii's. These sixteen islands, called the Cook Islands, became an independent state in 1965. Located near New Zealand, Fiji, and Tahiti, the Cooks are a place of exceptional natural beauty with clear Pacific waters and stunning beaches. With a population of about 26,000 English-speaking people, it is a fabulous tourist spot. The atolls and volcanic islands feature low income and corporation taxes. In addition, for a variety of reasons, it is a fine location for an international bank.

The capital, Rarotonga, has an average annual temperature of 81 degrees and is one and a half hours behind Los Angeles in time. This makes it one of the few Pacific centers with the same business day as the United States. The islands boast full-service banks, insurance companies, accounting firms, and trust companies. Telephone communications are excellent, based on twenty satellite circuits. Fax communications are direct dial and fully automatic. The Cooks also have a fully operational international airport with service to the United States through Tahiti on Air New Zealand.

The Cooks have strong links to New Zealand and use the same currency (although its original currency was like a work of art with pagan gods riding canoes through the sea and Polynesian goddesses atop sharks over waves). In regards to offshore operations, its laws are extremely flexible, and they allow easy set up for international banks as well as other financial tools.

Liechtenstein

This tiny little state, wedged in a visually stunning mountain valley between Switzerland and Austria, covers about sixty-one square miles. It's located about seventy-five miles from Zurich, with a current population of 28,000. Due to its proximity to Switzerland, it has benefited from the strength of the Swiss franc. It is also one of the world's oldest and best tax havens, with extremely strict bank secrecy laws. One European financier told me that Liechtenstein is where the Swiss go when they want to protect their money. In fact, there are more "letterbox" corporations (40,000) than Liechtensteiners.

Unfortunately, for small- to midsize U.S. investors, this charming but minuscule principality has little to offer. Like some of the other money havens I've already covered, its users tend to be very wealthy individuals, large international corporations, and multinational banking institutions.

However, if you love forests or like to ski, and you have a lot of money to spend, this could be a viable option for you. As the *Washington Post* noted in a report, "Liechtenstein has everything a traveler needs for a European vacation—flowing rivers and dark forests, a bustling capital city and quaint farms, castles on the hills, mountains and lush valleys, good food, one superb hotel, Old Masters paintings, vineyards galore, fine wines, a benign prince, famous Winter Olympics competitors, friendly natives—all in an area the size of the District of Columbia."

To enjoy Liechtenstein, you need to like rubbing elbows with Europeans. Because Liechtenstein is located on the continent, it caters mostly to European business. One reflection of this orientation is the official language: German. So for most U.S. investors, the attractions are outweighed by practical drawbacks.

Luxembourg

This Grand Duchy is rapidly evolving into an appealing alternative to Switzerland. Its secrecy laws are wonderful, and it offers a host of tax benefits. Located in Central Europe, it is bounded by France, Germany, and Belgium. Covering approximately 1,000 square miles, it experienced an influx of foreign capital and investment in 1988 that far exceeded expectations. Most of this activity has resulted from a loss of confidence in Swiss secrecy laws. Germans, in particular, have been drawn by the financial discretion that is part and parcel of doing business in Luxembourg.

Europeans aren't the only ones being drawn to this little country. Crown Prince Henri himself flew into Japan recently with a large contingent of advisers and businesspeople to sell Luxembourg's status as a financial center. The big selling point: a plan that allows certain tax deferments on specific types of income. Never ones to pass up a good thing, nearly twenty Japanese insurance companies and a dozen banks have opened offices in that small land.

United States Banker reported in a recent issue that Luxembourg's "flexible legal framework, its generous accounting attitudes related to loan loss provisions, and the overall relaxed banking and exchange regulations" have helped its recent popularity. It also noted that "tax evasion (as distinct from tax fraud) isn't viewed as a crime" as it is in other locales. For the moment, this little state can offer real advantages.

For the average private investor, Luxembourg is best utilized as a banking resource. With over 120 banks crowding the Boulevard Royal—the Duchy's version of Wall Street—the banking business is enjoying a boom. I should add, however, that for the individual investor who wants to operate his own business or financial entity, Luxembourg is not appropriate.

To begin with, in terms of licensing, clear preference goes to large international companies. The official language is French, with German as the second language. Additionally, in 1992, the European Union freed all capital movements and exchange controls throughout western Europe. The effect will be to increase competition for banking customers and to clamp down on tax avoidance strategies by requiring banks to divulge details about their customers' accounts. Luxembourg was also the site of the Bank of Credit and Commerce International scandal. For all these reasons, I advise even my most privacy-conscious clients to stay closer to home, and to choose a money haven that operates in their own language.

Montserrat

Montserrat, one of the smallest islands in the Caribbean, is one of today's most erratic money havens. Located about fifteen hundred miles southeast of Miami, this forty-square-mile island has a population of approximately twelve thousand. Like the Cayman Islands, it is a British Crown Colony. Known as the "Emerald Isle," it boasts warm sulfur springs and lush mountain forests.

In my opinion, it is a vacationer's dream come true, but a bad choice for investors.

As a money haven, Montserrat offers some inducements that are overshadowed by official corruption in the past. Things got so bad there that Scotland Yard had to initiate a special criminal investigation. On top of that, it signed the U.S. Caribbean Basin Initiative. So this small island can be forced to lift its secrecy laws by U.S. government agencies. When all is said and done, Montserrat emerges as one of the worst international money havens for private American investors. A great place for a vacation, but I recommend you bypass it in terms of offshore banking.

Nauru

Perhaps one of the top money havens in the world is the tiny republic of Nauru, located in the middle of the west-central Pacific Ocean. Nauru's government consciously set out to create a center that would meet the financial needs of international investors. For starters, the nine-square-mile Nauru does not require public disclosure of any records for holding companies conducting financial transactions in the small island nation.

In addition, Nauru imposes no taxes on income or capital, which means that it is not party to any double taxation treaties. As of 1997, there is no provision for the exchange of information with other countries. With no taxes on inheritance, property, or real estate acquisition, it is truly a money haven. Its phosphate industry and overseas investment allow it to operate without taxes or duties of any kind.

Currently, there are about 9,000 Naurans. English is widely spoken and used for most government and commercial purposes. Because the government provides a

What interests me most about this story is what it says about the influence you can have when you make the kind of money that's there for the making in the offshore market. The fact is, this nation's highest tax policymakers were forced to retreat and to allow a money haven to remain intact, unencumbered by excessive government intrusion.

free education for every one of its citizens, Nauru has a 99 percent literacy rate. And with a per capita income of more than $20,000 (one of the highest in the world), it is fairly affluent. Its government was established in 1968 as a republic, and is now an associate member of the British Commonwealth.

Nauru has international phone links, telex service, and mail service that rank high on the money haven scale of amenities. Its national airline, Air Nauru, offers jet service between Nauru and Hong Kong, the Philippines, Australia, Japan, Guam, and Western Samoa. The Australian dollar is its currency. Nauru has no exchange control restrictions.

Based on my selection criteria, I give Nauru a clear thumbs-up as a base for your offshore operations.

Netherlands Antilles

There's an interesting story I'd like to tell you about the Netherlands Antilles because it illustrates the growing power and prominence of offshore business centers.

Called "Treasury's Blunder in Paradise" by the *New York Times,* the episode began in mid-1987, when the

U.S. Treasury decided to end a tax treaty that had prevailed for years between the United States and the Netherlands Antilles.

Keep in mind that a tax treaty between the United States and any other country usually ensures that certain profits, interest payments, and other investment income will not be double-taxed (in two different jurisdictions), or that if a double tax should occur it will be imposed at a reduced rate. With the U.S.-Netherlands treaty on the verge of dissolution, anyone heavily invested in the offshore center stood to suddenly incur a very heavy tax burden.

When the White House made a formal announcement concerning its plan, a firestorm of angry criticism came from some of this nation's biggest corporations, wealthiest private investors, and most influential financial institutions. It seems that, year in and year out, more foreign investment flows into the United States from the Netherlands Antilles than from Japan and Germany put together. By the mid-1980s, nearly $50 billion in investments and Eurobonds were held in this tiny island chain just north of Venezuela.

And who do you think constitutes that "foreign" investment flow? James A. Baker III, who was then the U.S. secretary of the treasury, found out in short order. No less than 30 percent of those investments were held by powerful American interests. These investors included major pension funds and banks such as First Boston Corporation, Harris Trust of Chicago, and big insurance companies like Travelers, Aetna, and Pacific Mutual of Newport Beach, California. You can bet that Secretary Baker heard from those folks! And their message to him must have been crystal clear: Reverse plans—Now!

As you might expect, after days of angry phone calls and increasing political pressure, the Treasury Department announced that the treaty with the Netherlands

Antilles would remain in effect—particularly the tax exemption for interest on Eurobonds and other investment vehicles.

What interests me most about this story is what it says about the influence you can have when you make the kind of money that's there for the making in the offshore market. The fact is, this nation's highest tax policymakers were forced to retreat and to allow a money haven to remain intact, unencumbered by excessive government intrusion.

The Antilles, as they are commonly known, offer vacationers a virtual paradise. Located at the crossroads of key shipping and airline routes, these South American islands combine wonderful, top-of-the-line international communications with trained personnel and easy access.

For the midsize private investor, however, the Antilles offer little in the way of true tax relief, profit potential, or financial privacy. The start-up required for companies, banks, and insurance firms is around $500,000, and the government prefers to work with multinational entities. My recommendation is to exercise caution in regard to using the Antilles as a base of operations or as an investment center.

Switzerland

Once considered the number one money haven in the world, Switzerland has now slipped to the second tier of offshore financial centers. Nearly 6.5 million people call the sixteen thousand square miles that comprise Switzerland their home. According to some estimates there is one bank for every fourteen hundred citizens in this visually stunning Alpine financial center.

Although its longtime reputation as a stable banking capital has helped it maintain a strong position in world finance, this country, known as the "heart of

Europe," is now more like the grand old dame of offshore finance. Her best days are behind her, but she still has 250 years of earned dignity.

There are reasons that Switzerland has its reputation for banking expertise. For one, the Swiss have served as Europe's bankers since as far back as the Middle Ages. More importantly, as one Swiss investor once told me at a conference in Geneva, "the single most important aspect that makes us different from other bankers is that we see the world without borders where money is concerned." In other words, as bankers and financiers, the Swiss were probably one of the first to see the value of the offshore concept.

Because Switzerland is bounded by so many large countries including France, Italy, and Germany, it has been forced to see the world in a certain way. The Swiss have also been able to turn a geographic circumstance into a prized asset. Their famous neutrality has made it possible for them to attract money in search of protection and privacy.

Today's offshore market owes a lot to the Swiss. However, like so much else, all things must pass. I think that their days as the number one offshore money haven have come and gone. Although they still play a key role in international finance, recent economic changes in the world and the emergence of new centers with stricter secrecy laws and an arm's-length relationship with the

Today's offshore market owes a lot to the Swiss. However, like so much else, all things must pass. I think that their days as the number one offshore money haven have come and gone.

U.S. have made Switzerland a haven only for those who are in no hurry to move their money.

You may want to put some small percentage of your assets into Swiss francs. Otherwise I recommend that you stay away from Switzerland as an offshore haven. Its ties to the U.S. government are too strong for anyone who wants to create a certain distance from Uncle Sam. Since so many of the big Swiss banks want to operate in the U.S., they must cooperate with American authorities. That effectively makes Switzerland an unsafe center.

Vanuatu

The nearly 100 South Pacific islands collectively known as the nation of Vanuatu have recently gained status in investment appeal. They are considered a desirable money haven, and have earned the confidence of investors throughout the world.

As Reuters News Service put it, "Normally sleepy Vanuatu, its islands fringed with coral and coconut palms, has no personal tax, no local exchange controls, no capital gains or profit tax, no company tax, and offers complete secrecy."

For seventeen years, Vanuatu worked to build its status as a financially beneficial tax and money haven. As one wire service reported, "Today over 1,200 companies, including major banks and law and accounting firms that represent billions of dollars, are incorporated in the small South Pacific island-state." Most of these companies are from Australia, New Zealand, Hong Kong, Taiwan, Singapore, and Indonesia.

Although located far in the Pacific, Vanuatu is developing into one of the most interesting money havens in the world. Because it's close to Australia and New Zealand, it is a place to consider when setting up your offshore involvement.

MAKING YOUR CHOICE

As you sit down to analyze your offshore options, it's important to clarify the financial benefits that mean most to you. It's just as essential to go about your research in a methodical way. If you're not the kind of person who wants to do that, then hire a professional consultant to do it for you. But do shop the various services and limitations that are associated with different foreign money havens. It's only when you can compare your needs with the benefits of several offshore sites that you can confidently select the spot that's right for you.

Does it sound like too much to hope for? It's not. Remember, you will be entering the international arena, where entire governments are organized around policies aimed at attracting foreign investment. They want your business, and they'll do a lot to get it. So start asking!

CHAPTER 10

INVESTORS ON FILE

Every man, as long as he does not violate the laws of justice, is perfectly free to pursue his own interest in his own way. . . .

— ADAM SMITH, *THE WEALTH OF NATIONS*

On average, I talk with twelve prospective international investors a week. That adds up to six hundred potential clients every year. I've been a consultant for more than twenty-five years. So, to date, I've talked with nearly twelve thousand people who are seriously interested in the offshore banking option.

Some of them are extremely well informed and convinced about the benefits of offshore banking even before we shake hands for the first time. In fact, I'm amazed by how aware many investors have become of offshore financial planning. Maybe their growing sophistication is still one more reflection of the dwindling profit opportunities available in the domestic marketplace.

Of course, many people contact me with only a hazy sense of what offshore involvement can offer. Occasionally, they tell me they've seen or skimmed through one of my books. Maybe they've heard about me from a friend or business associate.

Usually, they talk about the prospect of internationalizing their assets with a combination of anxiety and hope—anxiety over a leap into the unknown and hope for some level of economic freedom.

Not all these conversations end with a signed agreement. But I have established enough offshore banks for individuals, partnerships, small consortiums, and midsize companies to know that a lot of people are making a lot of money and avoiding a lot of taxes in complete privacy.

Too often, I think, people imagine all international investors to be glamorous kingpins of the underworld, famous Greek tycoons, or crowned royalty from Europe. Certainly there are offshore programs owned and operated by these types of characters. But the majority of my clients are much more down-to-earth. They live and work in virtually every part of the United States. Some come from wealthy families, from a financial support system in which creative investment is second nature. Others are self-made businesspeople and career professionals. There are doctors, politicians, university professors, and ministers. There are also used car dealers, building contractors, real estate agents, and plumbers.

And, in every case, it's lifestyle and personality that ultimately determine the specific nature of their offshore plan. For example, a professional couple in their mid-thirties may set very modest economic goals: a bigger home in a better part of the city, a guaranteed education for their two kids at one of the country's leading universities, and the assurance of a comfortable retirement. Offshore banking is tailor-made to meet those objectives.

Meanwhile, an aggressive and experienced businessman in his late 40s may approach the offshore arena as the best means to a diversified investment program that earns megaprofits in Asia, Europe, Latin America, and Canada—all at the same time. Private bank ownership can handle that assignment, too.

For me, the true enjoyment comes in knowing that I've helped someone enhance his or her life. That's my main motivation. I want to help people carry out their dreams. I want to show them the means toward realizing their aspirations. I understand their aspirations, because like everyone else, I'm moving towards my own dreams and goals. The empathy I have for my clients comes from my own life experiences.

When you read through the following client profiles, maybe you'll see a bit of yourself. If not, call me here in Vancouver, B.C. (see p. 241 for phone number). I'd like to hear from you because, just maybe, yours is the one offshore game plan that I still haven't heard!

THE BIG BONANZA

Imagine this: A man in his mid-forties—well-dressed in a navy blue suit, striped shirt buttoned all the way up and no tie, hair combed straight back and wearing dark glasses inside a hotel—walks up to me at one of my seminars with a check in his hand. He says a simple hello, and hands me the check. It's made out to my firm in the amount of $40,000. Clipped to it is a handwritten note: "I need a bank. You select the place. Call me when all the papers have been prepared." There was also a phone number on the note with a 212 area code: New York City.

This is a true story. The client's name is Donald Brenner, and in the years since that initial encounter I have become one his many admirers. Not, I might add, because of his personal charm. Don is *not* a charming guy. But he is a brilliant guy. And he typifies a new breed of offshore investor. They're lean and a little mean and they waste no time in getting down to business. What they lack in conversational savoir faire, they more than make up for in brains and gumption.

I'm amazed by how aware many investors have become of offshore financial planning. Maybe their growing sophistication is still one more reflection of the dwindling profit opportunities available in the domestic marketplace.

I was surprised to find out that Don was an attorney. He didn't have the air of a lawyer. He was fast-talking and a bit pushy. When I returned to my office after the seminar, I called him. I was not about to make the decisions he had asked me to make without knowing anything about his particular offshore concerns.

He did not seem happy to get the call. "I thought the note was clear enough," he said. "I don't know where to buy a bank. That's your business, isn't it? Pick the best spot and get me one." I pursued the matter a bit further by asking, in general, why he wanted the bank. "To make deals," he said. "To make a killing. Isn't that why everybody wants one?"

And that rock-bottom explanation of the offshore banking motive still tops my list for hitting the nail right on the head.

I selected Vanuatu for Don's offshore center. Simply titled The First Bank of Vanuatu, it has become one of the fastest-growing facilities in the area. Naturally, it offers all the basic services you'd find in any offshore facility. But that's only the start. Don most avidly utilizes the bank as a kind of intermediary between himself and a wide array of international investors looking for U.S. financial involvement.

Don himself may not be all that knowledgeable about cross-cultural, transnational business negotiations, but he has put together a team of people who are. Together, they nurture close and ongoing associations primarily with Japanese and Arabian investors who want to start, acquire, or merge with a U.S.-owned company.

Most of my clients use their offshore banks to get involved in global business opportunities. And they're well rewarded for their effort. Don likes to work the other way around. He uses his bank to structure deals with foreigners who are trying to get in the U.S. marketplace. He charges a hefty fee for making the proper introductions, handling the delicate stage of negotiations, and drawing up the final business contracts.

Even more important, though, The First Bank of Vanuatu aims to create a role for itself in the ongoing international partnerships that result from the initial deals. In a sense, the bank brings major global players together and makes itself a third member of the profitable business triads that get established.

Not many investors can wheel and deal like Don Brenner. Not many would want to try. He spends all his time running a very diversified investment program, and his profits show it. Last year alone, the bottom line surpassed $25 million. That means Don is playing a high-risk game, which is not to everyone's liking. But his enormous success bears out what I've been saying all along: When you're involved in offshore banking, the sky's your only limit.

A Silicon Valley Success

William Roesser was already a very successful man when I met him fifteen years ago. He was an established leader in high-technology research and industry development. He had worked for some of the biggest names in Silicon Valley, sometimes as a staff executive and other times as an independent consultant. He told me quite matter-of-factly that he charged handsomely for his time and still never had any of it to spare. In fact, our first meeting was over lunch in San Francisco. Bill invited me up there because a flight to my offices involved more downtime than he could afford.

As a private investor, Bill had also done quite well for himself. His computer savvy played a big role in that success. By feeding stock market information into his own software program design, he could predict with uncanny accuracy the companies that would do well over the coming months. His prerequisites for an attractive stock option were strict: a six-month forecast had to show at least a five-to-one profit advantage. And even then, he was skeptical. "But at that point," he says, "I will seriously consider it."

Halfway through that afternoon's appetizer, it became clear that offshore banking was not a new concept for Bill. For some time he had been researching it as an investment technique. First and foremost, he told me, he was drawn to its flexibility. A hard-core, high-tech whiz, Bill wanted the freedom to control a truly diversified international investment plan from his comfortable home study in Palo Alto.

He also liked the privacy guarantees that come with careful offshore finance. Again, his computer background had taught him the extent to which personal information is gathered, stored, and even exchanged between software data banks. His investments were entirely legitimate, but he liked the idea of circumventing what he considered excessive government and private industry investigation.

Five weeks to the day after our first meeting, Bill received formal title to Independent Commerce, his offshore bank in Vanuatu. In the beginning, he worked closely with an investment management firm that was based in Canada. With their help, he diversified his portfolio to include investments in the Far and Middle East, West Germany, Latin America, and Australia. Technically, of course, all these investments were owned and managed by Independent Commerce. So Bill's privacy was guaranteed.

I saw Bill later at one of my two-day seminars. He had come, he said, to explore the idea of expanding his offshore business. More than satisfied with the results of his international investment program, he had earned a two-year profit of just over $1 million. Now he was interested in attracting a wider spectrum of international depositors and borrowers.

My suggestion was that he keep Independent Commerce as his offshore investment arm and open a second foreign bank (perhaps in the Caribbean) to operate as a more active banking services facility. That way, he could keep faster track of where his profits were being generated. And he could spread out his financial independence, enjoying top-notch banking benefits at two foreign financial centers instead of just one.

He wanted to know what kind of profit he could expect on the second facility. Immediately, I remembered our initial meeting and his strict rule about a five-to-one profit advantage. "Better than five to one," I smiled. "Well, then," he replied, "I'll seriously consider it."

OFFSHORE MOUNTAIN MAN

One of the most intriguing clients I've had in a long time is Chuck Davis. My first contact with him came over the phone. He called me out of the blue, asking if he could

> **I pursued the matter a bit further by asking, in general, why he wanted the bank. "To make deals," he said. "To make a killing. Isn't that why everybody wants one?"**

come in to talk about a venture capital idea he had in the works. We settled on an appointment time for the next day.

When Chuck walked in, he looked like he had stepped right off a Marlboro Man billboard. He was tall and thin, and dressed top to bottom in faded denim. He wore boots and his beaded and bone wristbands were some of the most beautiful Indian artwork I'd ever seen. In every way, Chuck radiated masculinity. He was confident but fairly soft-spoken. He knew what he wanted from our meeting but was totally at ease in working through his agenda.

As it turned out, Chuck was only in town for a week. He lived and worked in Anchorage, Alaska. Originally trained as an engineer, he had been working for the past three years for a company owned and operated by the Inuits as a consultant on alternative energy development. Along with two other associates, he had been commissioned to design cost-effective solar-powered architectural plans for family residences and small business offices.

Together, the three partners were now interested in forming their own company, which would market very similar plans throughout the uppermost Northwest. The problem was simple and common: insufficient venture capital. They just didn't have enough cash on hand to commission a marketing firm and follow through on a professional promotional campaign. Interestingly, Chuck had heard about offshore banking from one of the tribal officials who had established a bank himself through my firm a number of years ago.

He suggested that Chuck use an offshore bank to generate part of the necessary money, and then use it to help borrow the rest from various international sources. Although Chuck's long-term aim was quite unique, his offshore banking plan was rather basic. He wanted to own a bank as a way of funding his own onshore business projects. The profits earned from depositors, borrowers, and assorted offshore business transactions would constitute the venture capital base that he needed to get them off the ground.

I suggested that, from the start, Chuck know what he wanted to do with his newly established Vanuatu Citizens' Bank. I suggested he work with an experienced international advertising consultant who could help select appropriate publications for ads to let potential depositors know about the facility's attractive interest rates and specialized international banking services.

In truth, there was nothing so amazing about Chuck's bank. It offered precisely the kind of customer-oriented amenities that have become closely associated with most offshore banks. But Chuck and his partners did something that most other banks don't do: They put some real time, effort, and money into a very professional advertising campaign.

The results were impressive. When I last talked with Chuck, it was by phone. He had been shut in by twelve feet of fresh snow, but he was as pleased as he could be. Citizens' Bank had on account deposits of more than $6 million, and his newly titled design firm (Solar Homes Unlimited) had already marketed over a hundred residential and office floor plans. With a little creativity and the confidence to try what other people might only dream about, he and his partners had made the first phase of their professional dream come true. Undoubtedly the profits they will continue to earn should help propel them into an exciting second phase.

A MAIL-ORDER MILLIONAIRE

One of the global market's great allures is its ability to turn small but solid business ideas into big success stories. Edith Metcalfe's story is a perfect example of this phenomenon.

A hard-driving but soft-spoken single mom with two teenage sons, Edith lives in Indianapolis. Shortly after divorcing her husband in 1992, she developed the idea for a small mail-order distribution company. At the time, she was desperately trying to think of some way to compensate for too little child support and too much grief at her mid-level management job within the auto industry. Edith's business concept was actually quite simple. She wanted to find and develop affordable items that would make everyday life a little easier for people. She assembled an eclectic product line—everything from hypoallergenic cosmetics to auto care gadgets—and she tried to interest direct-mail catalog distributors in promoting them.

Edith had a good idea, but she soon learned that the catalog business is a pretty closed industry. There are a few giants out there and they dominate the mail-order market while lots of tiny companies scurry around trying to get their toe in the door. Edith wanted (and needed) to make some real money and, despite her creativity and tenacity, she knew she was never going to earn it within the U.S. marketplace.

I met her at one of my seminars. Initially, she seemed almost embarrassed to tell me about her predicament, but after she'd finally described the whole scenario I was certain that an offshore game plan could help her. After several meetings and a fair amount of handholding, she was convinced too. The first step was a private bank license, which I secured for her in the British Virgin Islands. Edith took virtually every cent she had and transferred it into the bank. "This money was going to be a first year's college tuition for both my kids," she told me as we made arrangements for the transfer of funds. And I could tell that Edith was scared to death.

Things turned out well, though. Initially limited by Edith's relatively meager resources, The Freedom Bank of the British Virgin Islands didn't have much. But it had enough to get started. Using her bank as an official financial intermediary, Edith approached two well-established mail-order catalog publishers in western Europe. She offered them an appealing proposal. Would they be interested in creating a catalog for distribution throughout the nations of the former Eastern bloc? In exchange for including her products in their mailing, The Freedom Bank would be happy to cover partial publication costs on the premiere issue—enough to ensure that the mailer would be a beautifully designed, full-color home-shopping guide.

The publishers agreed to try one issue and within six months it was obvious that Edith's idea was golden. Finally free to investigate western goods, eastern European consumers were more than eager to buy. By the end of the first year, her bank was realizing a profit in the low six figures. This money allowed Edith to do two things. First, she could stop worrying about basic expenses. It no longer mattered so much whether her ex-husband made each month's support payment. She could take care of herself and her kids on her own. Second, Edith finally had a little bit of investment money; and, believe me, she didn't let much grass grow under her feet. She took a hefty percentage of that capital and established her own catalog company. By advertising in a number of international money magazines, she was able to solicit a wealth of products from manufacturers all over the world. By incurring the entire cost, Edith earned the entire profit. Business has been growing steadily for several years.

I got a Christmas card from Edith last year. In it was a One Number Card that allows me to call her toll-free at her Indiana home office. It was not just an ordinary telephone calling card. It had an elaborate modern art design printed on the front. Her greeting said: "Here's a new product in my line, a series of special-order fine-art telephone calling cards. We're marketing

Although Chuck's long-term aim was quite unique, his offshore banking plan was rather basic. He wanted to own a bank as a way of funding his own onshore business projects. The profits earned from depositors, borrowers, and assorted offshore business transactions would constitute the venture capital base that he needed to get them off the ground.

them as a promotional tool for small businesses and freelancers. They're selling like hotcakes." She also scribbled a P.S. at the bottom: "Aren't these offshore profits amazing?"

Edith is like many bright, deserving women entrepreneurs. For years, she bought into the notion that hard work and diligence would reap their just rewards. She found out the hard way that too often they do not. The global market is fast-paced. If you wait, if you hesitate for too long, you usually lose out to someone with the gumption to step forward first. That can be intimidating—especially for women who have been socialized to wait their turn. Edith is an example of just how well women can actually do offshore. All you need is the courage to try.

THE INVENTOR'S APPROACH

Clayton Louis Young did not fall quickly in love with the offshore option. Looking back, I think that's because it struck him as too clever a way around U.S. banking regulation. "You have to understand," he said, "African Americans have only just begun to gain financial entry into this country. Somehow, it doesn't feel right to walk out the back door of a banking system that funded my education for six years."

Basically, Clayton was an inventor. After receiving an MBA from Morehouse University in 1980, he had worked nearly three years for a New York–based import/export firm. The job never suited him, he told me, but it gave him the chance to monitor a steady flow of electronic imports. Fascinated by the idea of designing mimic products that could be produced less expensively right here in the United States, he eventually quit and opened his own business.

It was initially a small operation. His girlfriend ran the front office, and a crew of five women worked in back, assembling parts for his electronics line. He developed and marketed his inventions—products like a portable ionizer (designed to clean the air and generate negative ions within a six-foot radius), a handheld hologram camera (capable of producing three-dimensional images), and a digital thermometer.

When I met him, the business was four years old, and Clayton was doing well. Still, he had a major problem: aggressive competition. Almost every time he developed a new item, his company ran into legal trouble. He had been sued three times by manufacturers who claimed unfair product duplication. Other times, he had initiated legal action against competitors.

Regardless of who sued whom, Clayton said, he had been through one too many court battles in which access to his financial records was awarded to another manufacturer. "That means my entire business operation is laid bare for long and drawn-out legal review," he explained.

Although most rulings had been in his favor, Clayton was tired of fighting the war. He wanted an escape from constant regulatory intrusion, and knew he wasn't going to find it in the domestic banking scene.

We talked first about the benefits of maintaining bank accounts offshore in someone else's private foreign bank. I assured him that simply by transferring his company's checking account to an overseas facility, he would gain significant protection. Nevertheless, I encouraged him to consider a private purchase.

One of the great allures to offshore banking is "intellectual product" protection. In other words, for inventors like Clayton, the international arena offers a way around copyright red tape and bureaucracy. Each time Clayton sought to copyright a new formula or product, he had to disclose it to the U.S. Copyright Office. In the process, his million-dollar concepts were made part of the public domain, and became vulnerable to reformulation and subsequent competition.

By owning his own offshore bank, Clayton could convert his product designs into "financial information." Technically, they might be called "exhibits to an agreement between scientist and formula owner." Of course, each formula's owner would be the offshore bank, strategically located in a jurisdiction where bank secrecy laws prevent reporting to any foreign investigator including the U.S. court system.

It took almost three months, but Clay finally did call to say he was ready to proceed with a purchase. I could hear a level of resignation in his voice. I tried to reassure him that a bank in the Mariana Islands would offer him a level of professional privacy and product protection that he deserved. Then, without much more conversation, we hung up.

Much later, I had lunch with Clayton. I told him, as I had before, how different he seemed from the man who made that phone call two years ago. In that sense, he is a lot like many of my clients. They start out unsure of what internationalization can do, but they're willing to test the waters.

His bank, like theirs, has been the springboard to important introductions. In fact, his ionizer is now the rage in Germany—all because one of his bank's customers got to know him and decided to test market his electronic line in Berlin. "That should put an extra million in my pocket this year," he told me. And then he laughed, "Not bad for a kid from Harlem, is it?"

MR. ELEGANCE

My work introduces me to a lot of sophisticated people, but when it comes to sheer personal elegance they all take a back seat to Carson Slater. With his chiseled features and deep voice, he is the picture of old California gentry. He's suave and charming, and no matter what the circumstances he makes the right move. To my way of thinking, he is refinement personified.

Carson is not a self-made man. His family has been a respected part of Los Angeles's high society for several generations. His grandfather amassed a fortune in agribusiness. His father was a doctor. His mother was actively involved in various cultural and charitable institutions throughout the city.

A graduate of an Ivy League architectural school, Carson had run his life just as you might expect. He had married a woman from an equally respected family. They had two sons and a daughter, all of them grown and involved in their own lives. Years before I met him, he had left his own thriving architectural firm in order to devote all of his time to managing his and his wife's assets. He did, however, sit on the board of two major corporations.

Shortly after one of my firm's two-day seminars, Carson called the office to let me know that he had been there and had enjoyed the workshops. He was also interested in meeting privately about his own international options. Naturally I invited him to my office, but he suggested instead that we have lunch at his club. "You might enjoy a quick steam before," he said, "and this way, we can feel comfortable about talking as long as we like." The invitation was casual, like everything about Carson Slater, but I suspect he does quite a lot of serious business over these "casual" lunches at the club.

I enjoyed that first meeting. I especially enjoyed watching the ease with which Carson talked about investment diversification. It was a familiar subject for him, I could tell. Off the cuff, he mentioned regular columns and specific articles from a wide array of financial publications. He obviously read all the right newspapers and made it his business to stay abreast of the newest trends and profit-making strategies.

It was also clear that Carson was extremely well traveled. He talked about Japan as confidently as most people talk about their hometown. He was unshakably convinced that the Japanese market would continue to surge ahead and, as a result, wanted to pursue investment opportunities throughout the Far East. He was intrigued by the role a private offshore bank might play in that pursuit.

Although his interests were specifically geared at Japan, I urged him to consider Vanuatu as an appropriate foreign jurisdiction. I knew it would be easy to establish operations there. Furthermore, it is particularly respected by U.S. bankers, and I thought that would be

The global market is fast-paced. If you wait, if you hesitate for too long, you usually lose out to someone with the gumption to step forward first. That can be intimidating—especially for women who have been socialized to wait their turn. Edith is a example of just how well women can actually do offshore. All you need is the courage to try.

important to Carson, given his extensive network of contacts. Finally, Vanuatu is a fine vacation spot—perfect for someone who makes it a habit to mix business with pleasure.

Within a month, Fidelity International Bank and Trust had opened for business. At first, Carson ran the bank truly as a private institution. It handled only his financial transactions. His many checking and saving accounts were immediately transferred. And a number of stocks (domestic and international) were quickly purchased in the bank's name.

Unlike most of my clients, Carson decided to roll up his sleeves and hand-pick his own island representative. He ran a classified ad in one international publication and received enough responses to schedule six interviews. After meeting all the applicants, he chose a British gentleman who had been a London stockbroker for eighteen years. His knowledge of offshore banking was extensive. He himself now lived in Vanuatu and knew local officials on a first-name basis. He had replied to Carson's ad because he liked the idea of a low-key involvement in a diversified investment plan. The match was perfect.

Occasionally, I get a call from Carson. Always the gentleman, he typically mentions having read about me in this magazine or that. Usually he's calling for a referral. That's one of Carson's many strong points: He likes to keep up on who's who in every aspect of financial planning. He never boasts about the success of his offshore venture. In fact, I almost have to drag information out of him.

At last report, his portfolio had expanded to include a number of Asian market involvements. He had also added several friends, associates, and social connections to his client roster. A few of them were utilizing the bank for just checking and savings accounts. Most were taking advantage of the attractively low interest rates Fidelity can offer on business loans.

It's also interesting that Carson's interest has shifted somewhat away from Japan. Australia seems to intrigue him the most these days. In fact, he has recently used the bank to purchase a hefty percentage of two mineral resource plants deep in the outback. Maybe it's time for another bank purchase.

DRS. LASMAN AND LASMAN

When Judith Lasman graduated from orthodontic school in 1983, she could have joined any number of prestigious practices in Miami Beach. Instead, she joined her father in the small family dentistry practice he had established many years before.

From the way Dr. Bernard Lasman described his office, it was hardly the high-tech environment we now associate with medical care. It had two exam rooms, a waiting area, and the same receptionist he hired thirty-seven years ago. "But it's comfortable and it's familiar," he told me. "You have to remember, a lot of my patients have been coming to me since they were kids."

Judith had read my first book, she said, while she was still in school. By the time we first met, she had been in practice with her dad for two years. She had saved some money and had convinced him to save some, too. She was interested in talking about a bank purchase partnership. Essentially, she wanted two things from the venture. First, to liberate her own finances from excessive taxation. Like most medical and dental professionals in this country, she was in the 30 percent tax bracket, and needed relief. "My other concern is Dad's retirement," she said.

It seems Bernie had taken care of just about everyone but himself. He had spent a good deal of his career time treating low-income families for very low fees. He had also been offering volunteer services through the same synagogue for more than twenty years. His accounts were a mess. In fact, some of his patients had owed him money for untold lengths of time. In short, he had ignored the realities of financial planning and now found himself over sixty without the security he wanted. "I don't want a luxurious old age, mind you," he kept insisting, "but I think Judy's right. I need to take some action."

What intrigued me most about this client team was the fact that they had such different offshore objectives. Judith obviously planned on a lucrative career and wanted to protect a substantial income from the long reach of the IRS. Bernie just wanted to retire in a comfortable fashion. I remember thinking, after we concluded that first meeting, how ironic it was that they should need to move assets offshore in order to achieve those objectives. But, then, that is the economic reality of our time.

Before we shook hands good-bye, I suggested that they attend an upcoming seminar that I had scheduled for Miami. They did, and shortly afterward, they contacted me with a firm OK on the bank charter and license purchase. They chose Nauru as their offshore base. I helped locate a management firm to handle the

At last report, his portfolio had expanded to include a number of Asian market involvements. He had also added several friends, associates, and social connections to his client roster. A few of them were utilizing the bank for just checking and savings accounts. Most were taking advantage of the attractively low interest rates Fidelity can offer on business loans.

operational end of the business. They purchased a fax machine for their office, so they could rapidly send and receive pertinent information. The entire package cost them less than $35,000, and it formed the basis for a banking and investment plan that changed both their lives.

Drs. Lasman and Lasman started the International Bank of Nauru. And after six years of operation, Judith tells me that she has already earned close to $250,000—tax-free—through a series of investments.

She has focused most of her attention on commodities: gold bullion, silver, and various gems. When we last spoke, she was still instructing her management firm to handle most acquisitions and sales. But she had begun to dabble a bit in diamonds. In fact, she had taken a trip to South Africa just to meet a dealer who was offering a number of unusual cuts.

And how's Bernie? He's great! He's changed a lot, though. Like a lot of people who walk in the offshore door, he's glimpsed a different world on the other side. He's still in practice with his daughter, but their office has been transformed. They moved last year to a new building in downtown Miami. It's larger and has more state-of-the-art equipment. Bernie has cut his patient load almost in half. He sees only the people who have been coming to him for years. All new patients are referred to Judith, or to a third partner who joined their practice some years ago.

Bernie's offshore involvements have stayed fairly conservative. He has investments in Canada and Australia. He also joined Judith in the purchase of a Miami mini-mall—in the bank's name, of course. In short, Bernie's retirement is secure. Moreover, it will be a lot more comfortable than he ever imagined. And what about his volunteer work? "Oh, I still do that," he chuckles. "We rich guys have to do what we can, you know."

TWO AND TWO EQUALS THREE

If one offshore bank can make you rich, can two offshore banks make you even richer? They can if you're like Jake Hayes. In just six years, Jake has personally earned close to $3 million as the sole owner of First American Bank in Montserrat and American International Bank in Nauru. Here's how he did it.

First, Jake entered the offshore market with a genuine passion for money. He liked talking about it. He liked learning about how it works in the domestic and international scene. Most of all, he liked having it. That may strike you as a given for anyone who even considers moving assets outside the United States. But I have found that some people really are more fascinated by money than others. In fact, I have even come to the conclusion that some people actually don't like money. They're not comfortable with it, and so—no matter how much they think they'd like to get rich—they position themselves for failure when it comes to making profits for a sustained period of time.

Secondly, Jake had a definite plan for how he would use his banks. That, too, is more of a rarity than you might imagine. A large percentage of my clients purchase their first charter and license without a clear vision of what it is or how to use it. It's a testament to the power of offshore banking that, even for them, the venture is an intelligent move. Still, when someone contacts me with a well-defined strategy that has been thought through down to every detail, I always know I'm talking with a winner. International banking, like any other undertaking, works best when it's approached methodically.

Thirdly, Jake had found a way to connect his onshore professional life with his offshore banking program. A disenchanted CPA and tax attorney, he had chucked the Chicago business scene for a thriving desktop publishing

I saw Jake recently at a tax seminar. We had lunch together and he reported that things were going extremely well. Both First American and American International are gaining roughly twenty new customers a month. It's no wonder: Both banks are paying 13 percent, compounded daily, for a regular savings account and up to 21 percent for five-year term accounts. One- through three-year term certificates offer rates in between.

business that allowed him to tell the truth to people who wanted to hear it. He published two newsletters, and both of them focused on tax avoidance strategies.

One catered to a professional readership: doctors, dentists, lawyers, and scholars. The other was directed at successful business executives, private investors, and entrepreneurs. He ran his business out of a small office near Chicago's lakefront, and he liked the freedom of being his own boss.

Jake knew from the start that he wanted two banks. He planned to use each one as a discreet offshore resource for the respective readerships of his two newsletters. By running articles about private international banking that outlined the opportunities available outside the U.S. financial scene, and by including a regular column that described his personal experience as a private banker, Jake stimulated an almost immediate reader interest in the subject.

Within six months, he had received over 100 telephone calls from readers wanting to do business with his bank. It cost him nothing to solicit their interest because his promotional expenses were covered by the subscription fee that people paid to get the newsletter. And, because he was attracting customers through a paid-circulation newsletter rather than a direct advertising solicitation to the general public, Jake avoided entanglement with U.S. bank regulators.

I saw Jake recently at a tax seminar. We had lunch together and he reported that things were going extremely well. Both First American and American International are gaining roughly twenty new customers a month. It's no wonder: Both banks are paying 13 percent, compounded daily, for a regular savings account and up to 21 percent for five-year term accounts. One- through three-year term certificates offer rates in between.

Because both facilities are small and private, they can work quickly to take advantage of investment deals that would require subcommittee, committee, and board approval in domestic banks. And because they're based outside this country, they are free of the restrictions that bind U.S. financial institutions. They can get involved in everything from factoring to leasing, wholesaling, manufacturing, or even offshore publishing. As Jake says in the brochures he has produced for each bank, "That gives us a tremendous advantage over other bankers who are locked into lending and a few other paper-shuffling endeavors."

And guess who profits from that advantage? Everyone: the bank's customers and, most especially, its owner.

THE POWER OF EXPERIENCE

I can tell story after story about my clients, people who have caught sight of an economic opening and walked right into it. I can describe all their idiosyncrasies, the personal traits and tendencies that motivated them toward assertive international investment. I can do that because I've made it my business to know my clients.

They form the basis of my business, and I admire almost all of them. For me, they are the pioneers, the global adventurers who are making tomorrow's world a reality today. They are the people who will be interviewed and profiled in economic journals twenty years from now for having taken a daring plunge at the right time.

There is only one thing that distinguishes these people from you: making the first move toward protecting assets, avoiding unnecessary taxes, and securing privacy. As you've learned, it wasn't easy for all of them to make that move. It may not be easy for you. But I truly believe that unless you do it, you'll never know what it is to be financially free.

CHAPTER 11

GETTING STARTED THE EASY WAY

Even the longest journey begins with a single step.

— ANCIENT CHINESE PROVERB

I would like to repeat once again that only decisive action stands between you and lucrative offshore opportunity. If you've taken the time to read this book, then you must be fairly serious about entering the international market. If you're like most readers, you've probably moved from one chapter to the next, calculating the investment profits you could earn outside the United States. You're undoubtedly attracted to the idea of genuine financial privacy. Like everyone, you'd like to reduce your tax burden.

Still, there's a definite difference between admiring the concept of offshore financial activity and actually taking part in it. Don't get me wrong: Offshore "fans" have their place. In fact, over the past several years, they have become a major force in the growth of global banking and business. They buy books, subscribe to newsletters, attend workshops, and, in general, contribute to the popularity of a burgeoning offshore world.

It's the offshore participants, however, who transform enthusiasm into profit. There's nothing magical about making money offshore. You simply need to take the proper steps. As I've argued in previous chapters, you must separate yourself from your assets and then strategically place funds in the foreign markets most likely to generate a sizable return. Then, as international financial dynamics change, you can move your money around, always making sure that it works for you in the most profitable places.

My major aim in writing this book is to help you decide what's right for you. Will you be happiest pledging your allegiance to the offshore fan club? Or would you prefer to take the plunge into an actual international involvement? I've tried to give you the facts you'll need to make that decision. I've also tried to acknowledge the psychological considerations that come into play when you consider a personal role in global finance.

Ultimately, though, it is up to you. Taking into account all that I've said, and tossing in whatever you may have picked up from other reliable sources along the way, you must decide the next move for yourself. If you think it through and decide that foreign moneymaking doesn't suit you, I hope you'll consider this book a worthwhile investment in your financial education.

There's nothing magical about making money offshore. You simply need to take the proper steps. As I've argued in previous chapters, you must separate yourself from your assets and then strategically place funds in the foreign markets most likely to generate a sizable return.

If, however, you feel that you're ready to get started, then the rest of this chapter is meant to point you in the right direction.

REVIEWING YOUR OPTIONS

In presenting my argument for offshore investment, I've covered a number of different offshore options. There are lots of ways to make and save money within the domestic economy. That goes double when you're operating internationally. In fact, it's hard to conceive of a profit-making venture that could not be legal and feasibly implemented somewhere in the world.

The point is, there are various ways to operate beyond your country's borders. I suggest that you learn a bit about the ones that really interest you. I would not encourage you to become an expert on every conceivable offshore investment option. You'll only exhaust yourself by trying, and still not get the job done.

To help you outline some of your choices, let's review the seven most popular ways in which Americans get financially involved offshore. Consider the benefits as well as the drawbacks associated with each of these investment strategies, and then begin developing a game plan that complements you and your portfolio objectives.

Option Number One: Foreign Trusts

Until the late 1970s, foreign trusts were an extremely popular form of offshore financial involvement. Before the federal government implemented the Tax Reform Act of 1976, they offered a creative form of tax avoidance and simultaneously allowed people to take long-term care of their heirs. Unfortunately, foreign trusts have run into a lot of trouble over the past several years, and no longer provide the wide range of benefits that once attracted so many people to them.

Under the old law, a U.S. citizen could create an irrevocable foreign trust that was taxed in basically the same manner as a nonresident alien would be. To put it simply, American investors could use foreign trusts to indefinitely defer taxes on their assets—until distributions were actually made to their beneficiaries. And even when the distributions were made, they were taxed without any interest or penalty to offset the advantages of many years of tax-free accumulation.

But even in the old days foreign trusts were imperfect. For example, the grantor of the trust had to place all trust property beyond his control for his entire lifetime. Furthermore, neither the grantor nor the grantor's spouse could be a beneficiary. Still, these offshore "wills" were an appealing option for investors with substantial assets and a concern for the welfare of family members after their death.

Today, even those fundamental benefits have been scaled back in certain circumstances. As part of the Tax Reform Act, Congress enacted several provisions designed to penalize the use of foreign trusts. Under them:

- The grantor of a such a trust (with more than one U.S. beneficiary) continues to be taxed on the foreign trust's income for the rest of the grantor's lifetime, as though he or she still owned all the trust's assets.
- Upon distribution of those assets, a nondeductible 6 percent per year interest charge is imposed on taxes due under "throwback" rules. If there has been a lengthy accumulation period, the tax plus the interest can sometimes wipe out the entire amount originally envisioned as a gift to the beneficiaries.

- If the trust is ultimately distributed to U.S. beneficiaries, then all accumulated capital gain is converted into ordinary income, and is sometimes taxed at a higher rate than the beneficiaries' income tax bracket would suggest.

As a result of these legal changes, most Americans no longer stand to derive significant tax benefits from transferring property to a foreign trust. Trusts are still fairly popular, but I would say that in today's market, given their limited benefit standing alone, they should be avoided. They have no economic purpose, and with the possibility of even more restrictive tax legislation down the line, it just doesn't seem worth the bother. In a sense, the foreign trust concept is just another example of how Uncle Sam makes it his business to get you, one way or another.

Option Number Two: Foreign Annuities and Endowments

Annuities and endowment policies are most easily understood as special types of savings deposits with some specific features guaranteed by the issuing insurance company. Foreign annuities can be either lump sum or periodic savings deposits, and they guarantee an income for the rest of the depositor's (or named beneficiary's) lifetime. The income level will vary based on the owner's age, deposit size and frequency, and when the income payments begin. They're a fairly common approach to offshore investment, and for good reason. If the international currency exchange rate is in your favor, they can allow you to make a handsome profit.

Swiss banks have become particularly well known for handling these foreign annuities, and during times when the Swiss franc exchanges favorably with the U.S. dollar, a guarantee-level franc annuity income can produce increasing dollar income. For example, if you had purchased a single payment, immediate-income Swiss franc annuity worth $10,000 in 1970, it would have been worth more than $17,000 by 1976.

Americans are investing in these insurance annuities for the following reasons:

- To protect their purchasing power against the falling U.S. dollar.
- To partake of the safety and security of Swiss insurance companies.
- To protect themselves against possible future government attacks on retirement plans as well as the potential failure of pension plans.
- To assure themselves of the liquidity and offshore protection in the event of a market collapse or financial panic in the United States.
- To seize the opportunity of investing globally.

Endowment policies add life insurance protection and dividends to annuities, and are also available in single deposit, periodic deposit, and increasing deposit forms. An example of the single deposit form might go like this: For a forty-five-year-old man making a single 100,000 Swiss franc deposit payment, the cash account value would grow to 252,107 francs by age sixty-five. The immediate death benefit to his beneficiary would be 159,058 francs at age forty-five, and would rise to equal the cash value by the time he reached age sixty-five.

The drawbacks to foreign annuities and endowments are, I think, obvious. First, their appeal is inseparably tied to international currency exchange rates. So long as the dollar compares negatively with the currency in which you happen to hold your annuity, you're safe. But as the exchange balance fluctuates, you are vulnerable to profit loss and, perhaps, even capital devaluation.

Another problem with annuities is that they make their profit so very slowly. In the case illustrated above, it took six years for $10,000 to grow to $17,000! That's very sluggish activity when you begin to compare that with the return on other investments. This same criticism applies to endowments.

Again, the example above shows a 4.75 percent annual rate of dividend compounding. Most other offshore ventures offer much more impressive profit potential. However, if you know what you're doing, have a good consultant work with you, and take the time to monitor the market for impending adjustments in the international currency exchange rates, I think that annuities and endowments can be reliable investments. They're a conservative choice, and as such, they don't involve a great deal of risk.

Option Number Three: A Foreign Bank Account

You can move toward faster and larger profits by opening a checking or savings account with a foreign bank. For

You can move toward faster and larger profits by opening a checking or savings account with a foreign bank. For starters, an offshore account allows you to rest assured that your money is being held by a financially stronger and better managed institution than you could ever find here in the United States. In part, that's because your offshore bank must maintain a higher ratio of liquid assets to accumulated debts.

starters, an offshore account allows you to rest assured that your money is being held by a financially stronger and better managed institution than you could ever find here in the United States. In part, that's because your offshore bank must maintain a higher ratio of liquid assets to accumulated debts.

An offshore account will also let you avoid the high service costs that have become part and parcel of domestic banking. And you'll benefit from the international banking environment, where regulations are kept to a minimum and customer service is made the top priority. We have already covered the specific benefits that come with an offshore bank account. Just for review, here they are again.

- Foreign banks offer a very attractive interest rate—typically several points above what you could find onshore. Remember, too, that the longer you keep the money on deposit, the more interest you earn.
- Checks written from a foreign account allow you to enjoy "float time," usually three or four weeks between the writing of a check and its arrival at the offshore bank for clearing. During that period, you will continue to earn interest on the money in your account.
- "Twin accounts" let you combine the benefits of a current checking account with the profits of a high-interest deposit account. You keep most of your money in the bank for high-interest earnings, but maintain a small balance for everyday withdrawal.
- Offshore banks also offer fiduciary accounts that allow you to direct the bank to make proxy investments for you. The record shows that your bank acted on its own behalf, but all profits earned on the investment are paid to you. However, they're

not tax-free because they were earned outside the United States.

Are there problems with having one (or more) of these offshore accounts? No, but there are limitations to what they can do for you.

I should also mention offshore debit cards. Yes, just like the ones you use here in North America when you shop at the grocery store. You know how they operate. The merchant puts your debit card (a regular-sized plastic card) through his electronic verifier, and if your account is approved he imprints the debit cards and gives you a sales voucher to sign.

Your bank account is immediately debited by the amount you have purchased or withdrawn. The beauty of the card is that it is convenient and very popular with banks. Also, it allows a certain level of freedom since these cards can be used throughout the world. The new Maestro card issued by MasterCard is a global debit card and will probably overtake Visa as the number one card for global transactions. As one financial analyst put it, "No money in your account, no transaction." This up-and-coming tool can be issued by your offshore bank. All purchases will be debited to your offshore bank account (for more detailed information on foreign accounts, refer to Appendix 1).

Option Number Four: Private International Corporations

If you like the idea of actually running a foreign business, you might want to own your own private international corporation. Maybe you'd want to establish a manufacturing business, and make your million-dollar invention concept a reality. Believe me, it's been done by people no more experienced at international business than you.

If you're less confident about what you'd like to do with your business, you can finalize the incorporation and allow the corporation to function simply as your broker in the international marketplace. It can invest in stocks, commodities, CDs, real estate, and foreign currencies. It can import and export, and serve as a holding company to protect patents and trademarks.

You can also choose a professional offshore management firm to operate your new corporation. If you don't know how to identify such a firm, talk with any reputable offshore consultant. He's likely to refer you to a number of Hong Kong and Vancouver firms—any one of which will impress you with a wide range of investment and administrative services.

There's not a lot to be said against the private international corporation concept. Particularly if you can manage to buy a company that's already been licensed and approved for operation, it can be an affordable way to establish an offshore involvement. These prepackaged, "turnkey," situations are not easy to find, but they're worth pursuing. A good financial consultant can sometimes help you locate a business that's named and ready to go.

One of the keys to a successful foreign trust is the selection of a friendly host country. By that I mean you should establish your trust in an offshore jurisdiction that, first and foremost, maintains stringent laws against enforcing foreign judgments. It's also critical that your preferred foreign site have nothing equivalent to the U.S. "statute of frauds."

Option Number Five: Offshore Asset Protection Trusts

In Chapter 7, I explained at great length the nature of offshore asset protection trusts (APT). This type of trust is so important that I want to briefly revisit it again. First of all, it is one of the best asset protection strategies. This single offshore venture can provide you with an unparalleled level of tax protection and financial invisibility. The very purpose of an APT is to place both legal and physical obstacles in the way of creditors. It puts your assets substantially beyond the reach of any U.S. court, and severely limits anyone's ability to enforce a money judgment against you.

One of the keys to a successful foreign trust is the selection of a friendly host country. By that I mean you should establish your trust in an offshore jurisdiction that, first and foremost, maintains stringent laws against enforcing foreign judgments. It's also critical that your preferred foreign site have nothing equivalent to the U.S. "statute of frauds." In other words, you want to be sure that if you were to physically transfer your assets to the offshore center and then place them in trust there, courts and creditors here in the United States would be unable to claim fraudulent intent. Why? Because the laws that govern the creation of trusts in your chosen offshore center do not recognize such fraud.

A basic offshore APT can be set up with anyone as the direct beneficiary—including you as the creator of the trust. However, for maximum protection, it's better to choose someone else for that role. (Otherwise you could be seen to have too much of a beneficial interest in the trust and its activities.) Just like domestic trusts, all offshore APTs have a "trustee," someone to administer the trust and hold its assets for the benefit of the beneficiaries.

Establishing an offshore APT is not a terribly complex or lengthy undertaking, but it does require expert legal advice from a trust attorney. There are a number of special features that should be included in the trust agreement. One is an anti-duress provision. This allows the offshore trustee to simply disregard a U.S. Court order stipulating that the creator of the APT or the trustee turn over the trust's assets to your creditors. Another important clause is called "transfer of situs." This clause allows the APT's trustees to change the legal locale of the trust. For example, if some type of action is to be taken against the creator of the trust, the APT trustees can move the trust and its assets from the British Virgin Islands to a bank in the Bahamas. This forces the creditor back to square one. And this can be done again and again.

Finally, because it is generally required that you transfer title or ownership to the property of the offshore jurisdiction *before* you actually establish a trust there, the offshore APT is usually best for holding liquid assets: cash, stocks, bonds, and certificates of deposit. In addition, assets transferred to a simple APT should generally be those not needed for your daily living or business needs. As always, I recommend that you work with an experienced adviser or consultant in designing and setting the terms of your offshore APT.

Option Number Six: Private Offshore Bank Ownership

If you want the benefits associated with all five options outlined above, and several more, then consider the establishment of your own offshore bank. In my opinion, it is the single most complete and profitable move you can make into the offshore arena.

For starters, your own offshore bank will provide all the advantages of a foreign checking and savings account at no charge, because you'll be your own customer. All

Offshore banks offer you as much investment flexibility as you desire. If you tend to be cautious in your portfolio management, you can use your private bank as a discreet international broker. Essentially, it can be a one-person operation. Using its name rather than your own, you can purchase low-risk stocks and commodities from around the world and watch your profits gradually build without tax. If you're a more adventurous investor, you can use the bank to structure high-stakes business partnerships and ventures on virtually every continent. You can turn your bank into a full-scale operation, with an experienced staff of employees to monitor your numerous international involvements.

your transactions can be handled in the bank's name, so your financial privacy is guaranteed.

Like all businesses, your offshore bank will aim to make an impressive profit. So, it will probably advertise in various international publications for customers. As the deposits come in, they will figuratively pass through a revolving door and become money with which your bank offers loans to international borrowers. Within a matter of months, the interest generated by those loans will form the basis of a handsome bottom line.

Your bank can increase its profit by expanding services. For example, once you get enough depositors, you can begin issuing letters of credit and financial guarantees. You can offer back-to-back loans. You can also provide venture capital loans at whatever interest rate the free market will allow—sometimes as much as 10 percentage points above the comparable domestic rate.

Offshore banks offer you as much investment flexibility as you desire. If you tend to be cautious in your portfolio management, you can use your private bank as a discreet international broker. Essentially, it can be a one-person operation. Using its name rather than your own, you can purchase low-risk stocks and commodities from around the world and watch your profits gradually build without tax. If you're a more adventurous investor, you can use the bank to structure high-stakes business partnerships and ventures on virtually every continent. You can turn your bank into a full-scale operation, with an experienced staff of employees to monitor your numerous international involvements.

Option Number Seven: Foreign Residency

Americans can take advantage of a tax benefit known as the foreign-earned-income exclusion. It allows for U.S. citizens who live and work outside the country to exclude from gross income up to $70,000 of foreign-earned income. In addition, an employer-provided housing allowance can be excluded from income. There are other tax breaks available: Each member of a married couple working overseas, for example, can exclude salary of up to $70,000. That's a total of $140,000 plus housing allowances.

It is important to note that this is not a deduction, credit, or deferral. It is an outright exclusion of the money from gross income.

Naturally, to get these benefits you have to meet certain requirements: You must establish a tax home in a foreign country; you must qualify for either the "foreign-residence test" or the "physical-presence test"; and you must have foreign-earned income. In the IRS view of the world, your tax home is the location of your regular or principal place of business. That is, the tax home is where you work, not where you live.

The definition goes further for the foreign-earned-income exclusion. The problem is that many Americans overseas think they are earning tax-free income. If you work overseas and maintain a principal place of residence in the United States, your tax home is not outside the United States. To qualify, you have to establish both your principal place of business *and* your residence outside the United States.

After establishing your tax home, you must pass one of two additional tests. The more straightforward of the two concerns your "physical presence." You must be outside of the United States for 330 days out of any twelve consecutive months. The days, of course, do not have to be consecutive. That sounds very simple, but there are a number of smaller rules that can complicate it. Few people begin their foreign assignments on January 1 and end them on December 31. For most people, therefore, the first and last twelve months of their overseas stay will occupy two tax years. This requires them to prorate their income and the $70,000 exclusion for those tax years.

Foreign residency is the U.S. tax privilege that I have here in Vancouver, British Columbia, Canada. It works very well for someone who really does live and work in a foreign country.

Option Number Eight: Expatriation—The Ultimate Offshore Option

Let me begin by offering a definition.

> Expatriation: To leave one's home country, and often renounce one's citizenship, to reside in another country.

It sounds serious because it is serious. Expatriation is not for the fainthearted. Each year a few hundred Americans take this serious and ultimate step into the

It sounds serious because it is serious. Expatriation is not for the fainthearted. Each year a few hundred Americans take this serious and ultimate step into the offshore world.

offshore world. Like Floyd Sutcliff (that client of mine whom I profile in my introduction), many Americans get tired of the taxes and the economic mess. They look around and realize that the Cold War is over. The Evil Empire has been defeated. Satellite communications means that they can be in touch with anyone, anywhere in the world, in an instant. And many offshore jurisdictions are quite comfortable and secure places to live (see Chapter 9).

Expatriation is the ultimate offshore option, and in many ways its time has come. Every year more and more Americans consider taking the plunge. It means renouncing your U.S. citizenship, taking up residence in another country, and obtaining a new citizenship. One tax planner calls it "the ultimate estate plan" because you can reduce your taxes considerably.

Years ago, the actor William Holden made international headlines when he changed his legal residence or domicile from the United States to Kenya. Many wealthy Chinese Americans are making the switch back to Chinese citizenship for the simple reason that they can gain significant savings every year on income, gift, and estate taxes.

A recent expatriate is the billionaire Kenneth Dart, member of the family whose company makes more than half of all the polystyrene cups sold in America. He gave up his U.S. citizenship and became a citizen of the Central American country of Belize. He doesn't live there, though. He's domiciled in the Cayman Islands, a very comfortable island paradise. Other U.S. expatriates are headed to Ireland, Israel, Costa Rica, Canada, Portugal, Monaco, and any number of Caribbean money havens.

Expatriation is a complex process. I advise prudence and patience because a lot of careful legal and financial planning is involved if expatriation is to really work.

First of all, before you renounce your current citizenship, you should have already lined up a dependable citizenship with all appropriate documents in your new home country. Always remember that once you have renounced your citizenship, you immediately lose your passport. And renunciation involves signing an Oath of Renunciation with the U.S. State Department in a foreign country, not in the United States. In other words, renouncing your citizenship, obtaining your new citizenship, and setting up a legal residence in a new country must occur almost simultaneously.

Secondly, be sure that the benefits outweigh the disadvantages. Once you're no longer a citizen you can stay in the United States for no more than 182 days. Any more than that and you will be considered a resident for tax purposes. On the plus side, once you've renounced your citizenship and set up a legal residence somewhere else, you will be seen as a nonresident alien and be forced to pay estate taxes *only* on property actually located in the United States. And you can avoid further U.S. estate taxes by simply transferring all real U.S. property to a foreign corporation.

In terms of income tax, expatriation means that you will be taxed on U.S.-source income only—that is, income from assets geographically located in the United States. But it's important to know that there are special tax provisions intended to trap what the IRS calls "tax expatriates." Bottom line: Be very careful, and work with an experienced financial planner.

DON'T DO IT YOURSELF

Most people will decide that expatriation is too complex for them, which brings them back to the bank ownership option. If you decide that the offshore bank concept is for you, then you immediately face a critically important choice. Do you want to try to handle the entire transaction on your own? Or would you prefer to work with a company that can manage the process for you?

Frankly, most people are intimidated by the prospect of so much research and so many international business maneuvers. I think they're wise to feel that intimidation. There's nothing more foolish than biting off more than you can chew, especially when there are qualified professional teams that can help you.

You need months just to research the various offshore jurisdictions and their particular strengths as well as weaknesses. Even if you feel certain that you've identified the right place, several overseas visits will also be required in order to meet with island officials and process the necessary paperwork.

As you consider all this, remember that if you spend a lot of time setting up your offshore bank, you will pay a price in lost investment opportunity. They say that time is money, and I certainly agree. When you're looking at offshore profit strategies, every minute counts.

To ensure that your bank's legal framework is well conceived, I would suggest that you work with a reputable

As your consultant, I can eliminate the risk of offshore operation in disadvantageous jurisdictions and secure private banking facilities in island environments supportive of private bank operation.

attorney based in your preferred offshore center. This way, you can sidestep involvement with any U.S. officials or agents, but also rest assured that someone with appropriate expertise is looking out for your interests.

If you don't know anyone who can refer you to a good lawyer in the area, you'll need to conduct still another phase of meticulous research. I suggest that you thoroughly check professional references because, on occasion, U.S. investors find themselves faced with a costly legal bill and no offshore bank charter or license to show for it. The legal acquisition of an offshore bank is not an extremely complicated matter, but it does require specific knowledge and skill.

Be prepared for a lengthy application process. For example, under your guidance, the attorney can begin drafting your bank charter. That process alone is likely to take several weeks. After all, these articles of incorporation and banking bylaws constitute the backbone of your facility. The charter should literally spell out the reasons why you have decided to establish the bank, and it must specify all the financial activities that you intend to conduct.

Since you're establishing a new bank, your lawyer will also need to run a check on the bank's proposed name. Far more often than you might think, investors choose a name only to discover that someone else is operating under the same title. In that case, the entire procedure must begin again, but with another name.

Usually, the host government approves a well-drafted charter, but you must submit it for official review. This, too, takes time. If your foreign attorney is well connected within his jurisdiction, you can expect legal authorization within several weeks. If not, the process could take several months.

It is not uncommon for an independent investor to be sent back to the drawing board. In other words, a foreign government may demand that you recast your entire charter. It's possible, in fact, that you may be denied an operating license altogether. At that point, you're back to square one, and you must look for another offshore jurisdiction.

The bottom line: Don't do it yourself. There is, however, another way to go, a safer way.

THE SCHNEIDER APPROACH

For those of you who want to avoid the hassle of doing all the work yourself as well as avoiding the pitfalls of going out on your own, here is good news. You can hire a qualified consultant or attorney to do all the work for you. You need someone with the expertise to cover all the steps I mentioned above. For sources, you can contact your local bar association or my office in Vancouver, B.C. (see page 241). I am always ready to give referrals.

Although I have reduced my consulting time as far as offshore banking is concerned, I do accept a limited number of new clients. What I usually do is help my clients cut down on the months of research and legwork required to establish a bank. I also arrange for an international bank management firm to handle the specific operations of your offshore program.

Frankly, I put a strong emphasis on the availability of such international management because few things can have a greater impact on the ultimate success of a bank than a quality management service. Most of my clients have no firsthand international banking experience. So my recommendation is that they hire a top-notch management team upon whom they can rely for key administrative functions and skilled investment advice. Your management company can also give you foreign exchange privileges and access to wholesale capital markets.

So think about it, but don't think too long. Every day, the government closes a few more doors to international profit potential. My advice is to get out there and get started while the laws still allow you to discreetly make a lot of nontaxable money. When I look at the people who have read my books and the clients who have explored investment in the offshore arena, I can tell you that they are all markedly better off today than they were before we met.

As your consultant, I can eliminate the risk of offshore operation in disadvantageous jurisdictions and secure private banking facilities in island environments supportive of private bank operation. My clients can select from jurisdictions that:

- Impose no income tax, no capital gains tax, no death tax, no stamp duty, no estate duty, and no gift duty.
- Require no previous banking experience on the part of the controlling owner.
- Offer, on a case-by-case basis, an exemption from customary paid-in capital requirements (often totaling $300,000 or more).
- Charge an extremely low annual license renewal fee (sometimes as low as $1,500).
- Allow for bank ownership by nominees or in the form of bearer shares owned by a holding company. Such arrangements help preserve the total anonymity of the actual bank owner.
- Guarantee the strictest bank secrecy law, including a guarantee that information pertaining to past or present banking transactions will never be disclosed; and maintain excellent banking legislation.

SHALL WE MEET?

This has been a book about the profit, privacy, and tax protection available to you through offshore money havens. In this edition of my book I have tried to review the current state of the U.S. economy and have offered a bit of insight into the global economy—those mysterious dynamics by which even countries with opposing political orientations rely on one another financially and face a future of escalating interdependence.

I hope I've managed to fully warn you about the poor financial outlook for our domestic economy. Our national debt keeps growing, while those who owe us money find themselves increasingly unable to meet their commitments. Inflation looms over us as a constant threat. Even our biggest corporations are often unable to compete effectively with their foreign counterparts. In short, the future is bleak for U.S. investors who confine their financial activity to domestic ventures.

By contrast, I hope I've succeeded in showing you that an offshore involvement will offer benefits that will brighten your economic future. There's more money to be made today than there has ever been. And it's there for a song. But you have to know the tune. Offshore involvement is part of tomorrow's most successful investment strategy. It's the vision of a bright economic future. Best of all, it's legally and affordably available to you today.

So think about it, but don't think too long. Every day, the government closes a few more doors to international profit potential. My advice is to get out there and get started while the laws still allow you to discreetly make a lot of nontaxable money. When I look at the people who have read my books and the clients who have explored investment in the offshore arena, I can tell you that they are all markedly better off today than they were before we met.

When you're ready to get started, let me hear from you. I'd like to be involved in developing your offshore game plan. I think my experience will allow me to offer some worthwhile pointers. I know I could learn from you, by watching you create the international investment package that best suits you and your priorities. So give me a call. Let's get together because who knows: It could be the start of a great friendship. You can contact me at:

Jerome Schneider
Premier Corporate Services, Ltd.
Box 12099-Harbour Centre
Suite 700-555 West Hastings Street
Vancouver, B.C., Canada V6B 4N5
Telephone: 604-682-4000
Fax: 604-682-7700
E-mail: taxhavens@aol.com
Web site: http://www.offshorewealth.com

Appendix 1

How to Open a Foreign Bank Account

Suggest to the average American that he or she might benefit by owning a foreign bank account and you'll more than likely get a questioning look and a response such as, "Why on earth would I want to do that?"

Americans, in my opinion, tend to have an extremely parochial attitude when it comes to their money—and they also tend to have an almost unnatural suspicion of foreign banking activities. After all, the media has exposed them to an unending series of foreign banking tales involving political shenanigans, financial fiascoes, and criminal capers.

Yet, the simple fact is that most Americans could benefit by owning a foreign bank account. Already, foreign banking—or, as it is more popularly known today, "offshore banking"—has become an important tool for thousands of legitimate and highly successful businesses and individuals.

In practice, a foreign bank account gives the prudent investor the opportunity to synchronize the benefits of various banking activities and blend them into a unique profit-making and tax-saving financial strategy. For the careful and conscientious investor, it is one of the most practical ways of expanding the realm of financial opportunity, because it is one of the most creative ways to diversify assets.

Accounts held in offshore banks are rarely subject to our state and federal laws and regulations. Offshore banks can also offer a wide range of services well beyond the legal ability of domestic banks. Through aggressive use of these services, investors can increase their profits, reduce their tax burdens, and raise capital at lower interest rates—all without the restrictive maze of red tape often encountered in the United States.

SECTION 1: WHY OPEN A FOREIGN BANK ACCOUNT?

There are a number of legitimate reasons for opening a personal bank account in a foreign country; foremost among them is the fact that maintaining a foreign bank account carries a greater degree of freedom, security, and opportunity than would be possible in the United States. Depending on the depth of one's portfolio, a penchant for adventurous investing, or strategic financial needs, a foreign bank account can provide a varying degree of advantages and conveniences.

Following are some of the principal reasons why an ever-increasing number of savvy U.S. investors are opening one or more foreign bank accounts for themselves. (These are by no means all the reasons, and you may well find additional personal motivations for banking offshore).

Privacy

Americans who have accumulated any kind of retained wealth are finding it more and more difficult to hold on to their assets. Other people, as well as the federal and state governments, are becoming increasingly nosy about the financial affairs of individual Americans—and the courts are helping them.

The best solution to this ever-increasing assault on your financial well-being is to do your banking in a country safe from the prying eyes of government agents, creditors, competitors, relatives, ex-spouses, and others who might want to appropriate your wealth. In a hyperlitigious society in which anyone will sue at the drop of a hat—it's nice to know that your money is in a country where your enemies can't touch it.

Many countries specialize in guaranteeing bank secrecy. Some offshore havens have bank secrecy laws so strict that it is a crime for a bank employee to disclose any information about a bank account to any person other than the owner of the account.

Unfortunately, as some countries have strengthened their secrecy laws, the U.S. has virtually eliminated bank secrecy. Any transaction involving more than $10,000 must be reported to the Treasury. Records of transactions involving less than this amount can be subpoenaed by the IRS, litigants in a lawsuit, or anyone else with a real or imagined need to pierce your secrecy.

Thus, if you want to maintain real financial privacy, you have little choice but to look offshore, where your bank accounts are protected, rather than opened by the governments and the courts.

Currency Controls

Despite the fact that more than 80 percent of the nations of the world impose some form of currency control, few U.S. citizens have actually experienced the discomfort of living in a country that severely restricts their ability to move their money outside their own borders. However, with annual budget deficits running at $200 billion and with trade imbalances growing steadily larger, the U.S. may be the next country to clamp a lid on the outward movement of dollars. In fact, we may have already seen the beginning of a trend—under current law, Americans must now complete a customs declaration when taking more than $10,000 overseas.

Thus, it only makes good financial sense to move at least a portion of your assets into a foreign country while you still can. Such a move also protects you against the possibility that the U.S. government, at some point in the future, may confiscate a portion of the wealth of its citizens—most likely under the guise of combating drug trafficking or dealing with the underground economy. Citizens living under totalitarian regimes in Latin America and the Middle East have already experienced the trauma such actions can bring—and they would be the first to advise you to move at least a portion of your assets offshore.

Higher Return on Investment

If a foreign bank will give you a better interest rate on your invested money than a U.S. bank, there is little reason to keep your money here. Many foreign banks can offer better interest rates because they're unregulated and can make more lucrative investments with their depositors' funds. In addition, many foreign banks operate in countries that don't place a premium on lavish offices, high rents, and excessive executive salaries. Thus, they are able to pass these savings on to you in the form of higher deposit rates.

Taxes are often an important consideration as well. By maintaining assets in an offshore jurisdiction, the prudent American investor gains tremendous opportunities to realize capital gains—and, by keeping those gains offshore, he or she can also avoid paying taxes on the profits. Many foreign financial centers have earned an international reputation as legal tax havens—and many investors find that the tax benefits of offshore investment activity greatly enhance their financial performance.

Diversification

You would never put all your assets into one investment—it's inherently too risky. Yet, most people do all their banking in one country. No one knows what the future will bring. If you hope to hedge your financial security against the unforeseen, it's best to hold your assets in bank accounts in more than one nation.

Have Fun While You Earn

Wouldn't it be nice to vacation in a tropical paradise while doing your banking? Many Americans do. Many of the world's offshore banking centers are also located in the world's best vacation spots.

SECTION 2: DIFFERENT TYPES OF FOREIGN BANK ACCOUNTS

There can be no doubt of the advantages of banking in a foreign country—advantages such as privacy, freedom, diversification, and enhanced investment opportunities. In addition, the American who banks in an offshore locale also enjoys more flexibility in the selection of accounts that can be maintained. Here are just a few of the types of accounts that are offered by most foreign banks:

A Current Account

This is the most common type of foreign bank account—and the one that gives you the most flexibility in managing your funds. It allows you to withdraw all or part of your account balance at any time. Most current accounts pay interest on your balance, though some do not. Many current accounts can be maintained in U.S. dollars, or they can be held in a host of foreign currencies; some offer "multi-currency" privileges, meaning you can deposit or withdraw funds in your choice of currencies.

Most current accounts provide you with checking privileges, and some foreign banks will provide you with a check card (the most popular of which is the "Eurocard"), which will permit you to write checks anywhere up to a certain amount. You will probably receive a statement of your account's activity semiannually.

Regardless of the complexity of your international business, you should have at least one current account.

Deposit Account

A deposit account is a savings account in a foreign country. The account will pay you interest, but the rate of interest will vary according to the currency in which the account is denominated and the length of time for which the money is deposited. Generally, the longer the money is deposited, the higher the interest rate. Most deposit accounts require a minimum deposit of $5,000 or more.

Deposit accounts are not as liquid as current accounts, and you may be prevented from withdrawing your money for a period of time. As with a current account, you will receive a semiannual statement of the account's activity.

Numbered Account

Switzerland, Belgium, Luxembourg, and Mexico all provide numbered accounts. A numbered account is an account identified by a number, rather than by a name. To that extent, it provides a certain amount of protection and privacy, especially if bank records or passbooks are lost, stolen, or obtained under duress.

It's important to remember what a numbered account is not: A numbered account doesn't mean that no one at the bank knows who the real owner of the account is. It just means that the junior people at the bank, who handle the transactions, don't know your identity.

Safekeeping Accounts

A safekeeping account is one in which you deposit such things as bonds, stocks, and other valuables. The bank will clip the coupons, redeem the bonds, and do whatever needs to be done with the valuables entrusted to them. The bank will charge you for the service, something in the range of 0.015 percent of the market value of the securities or other assets they are safekeeping.

Commodities Account

Some of the larger foreign banks have geared themselves up to trade in commodities on your behalf. (This is a prime example of the freedom foreign banks have to operate, as contrasted to the restrictions imposed on U.S. banks.) They're set up to give you the latest commodities prices, and to let you buy and sell commodities over the phone.

Managed Accounts

Many of the larger foreign banks also offer a variety of managed accounts, wherein you entrust your money to the bank's investment advisers and they choose the types of investments, based on your objectives and investment goals. Managed accounts are offered for stocks, currencies, debt instruments, commodities, or combinations. Again, the bank charges for this service, with fees usually based on a percentage of the funds under management.

The foregoing list represents only the tip of the iceberg. There are countless types of accounts and services—including such familiar American-style amenities as automated tellers, and Visa and MasterCard accounts—that foreign banks can provide for you. And, the number of such services is growing annually.

SECTION 3: HOW TO OPEN A FOREIGN BANK ACCOUNT

Before you can actually open one of the accounts we've just discussed, you must take some time to select both a foreign country and a foreign bank for your account. (An evaluation of some of the major offshore financial centers is featured in Section 7 (page 259), and a list of many of the leading overseas banks is provided in Appendix 3.)

If you plan to visit the country in which you'll be banking, you should check out a number of banks. Insist on meeting with a director of each bank you visit. If they won't meet with you, don't give them your business. Whether you visit or can only correspond by mail, here are some of the criteria you should consider when selecting a bank:

- Does it provide the banking services you require? For example, if you need to earn interest on your current account, and also require a check card, keep searching until you find a bank that will provide both services. One of the best sources of leads is the *Rand McNally International Banker's Directory*.

- How large is the bank? There are trade-offs here. A larger, more established bank may offer greater security than a smaller bank, but at a price—the larger bank may pay a lower interest rate and charge you higher fees for its services.
- How secure is your investment? Deposit insurance is not nearly as prevalent overseas as it is in the United States. If you require that your account be insured, you should inquire specifically as to the types of accounts that are insured and the investment limitations. Local insurance regulations can be confusing. For example, most Swiss banks do not provide insurance, but some Swiss cantonal (i.e., regional) banks do. Be aware, too, that the absence of deposit insurance can actually be an advantage since banks must employ prudent investment and business practices in order to successfully compete and remain in business. In the United States, banks can be inefficient and poorly managed and can follow imprudent investment strategies because they know their mistakes will be rectified by the government.
- How easily will you be able to communicate with your bank? There's no problem here if you plan on doing all your overseas banking in person. However, if you'll need to communicate with bank officials by mail, it's important to establish whether the officials will communicate with you in English. Even if they do, some offshore banking centers are so remote that mail, courier, and even telephone communications are tenuous. There's

nothing more frustrating than needing to conduct a banking transaction and not being able to get through to your bank.

Once you've narrowed down the possibilities, the next step (assuming you won't be visiting the bank) is to send each bank a *short, typed letter.* The letter should state that you are interested in opening a certain type of account. You should ask about the following:

- The fees that the bank charges—both to open and to maintain an account.
- The minimum balance required to maintain an account.
- The currencies in which an account can be maintained, and the ease or difficulty of switching from one currency to another.
- The extent to which the account will be insured, and who will insure it.

Ask about how the bank will communicate with you, and you with it. Some banks will provide you with a telex code, which will allow you to give the bank instructions and conduct normal banking business without revealing your identity. The use of the code also assures the bank that it is dealing with you and not someone who wants your money.

You also may wish to ask about any other services the bank provides, such as a check card, credit cards, safe deposit boxes, etc.

The first thing you'll receive from most banks in response to your letter is an account application form (see page 343) and signature cards, similar to the forms needed to open an account in the United States. Some banks may also require letters of reference. Be wary of this—the more information you have to reveal, the lower your level of confidentiality. If you plan on opening a corporate account (one whose owner is a corporation), you may have to provide proof that the corporation is in existence and minutes of resolutions from the board of directors authorizing the account.

You may wish to consider keeping an account in a fictitious name. Before you do, you should inquire into the laws of the country in which you'll be banking. Many countries prohibit accounts with fictitious names, even those countries with strong bank secrecy laws.

You may also wish to open an account for a minor. Before you do, check with the bank to determine their local rules regarding an adult maintaining an account for a minor.

Since almost every bank requires a minimum deposit to open an account, you'll have to send money with the application form and the signature cards. The guidance for the initial deposit is the same for any subsequent transmittal of funds. Wire transfers are the best way to do it—they are more secure than sending checks or money orders through the mail, and there is a minimal loss of interest (your local bank will, however, charge you for the wire). The overseas bank should provide you with wire transfer instructions.

If you use the mail to send checks, have the checks made out to you, endorsed: "For deposit only at Bank for the account of ______." Whenever you mail funds, the mail should be preceded by a fax transmission, alerting the bank that a deposit is in the mail, and stating the amount of the deposit and any further instructions you deem helpful to the bank's personnel. (Note: If you send more than $10,000 overseas, your bank is required under the Bank Secrecy Act to report the transaction to the U.S. Treasury. Under current law, they are not required to report a wire transfer, regardless of the amount.)

If you are opening a managed account of any kind, the bank may also require you to grant it a power of attorney over the assets in the account. If so, make sure the power of attorney is specific and offers protections for both you and the bank (a sample power of attorney form can be found on page 341).

SECTION 4: SOME SUGGESTIONS ON HANDLING YOUR ACCOUNT

There are as many different particular investment needs as there are investors, so it is impossible to tell you exactly how to handle your foreign bank account. However, here are some general tips that should apply in almost every instance:

- **Start Conservative** If you've never had an overseas bank account, start out by being a conservative investor. I suggest starting out with an account denominated in U.S. dollars. Place only a fraction of the amount you have available for savings in an overseas account until you ascertain you are comfortable with the concept, the country, and the bank. If, after six months or so, you're comfortable, you can add to the account or open a different account. I advise against such activities as commodities accounts until you have your feet on the ground and are comfortable with your overseas banker.
- **Diversify** Once you're comfortable overseas, you should consider diversifying your overseas holdings. This may result in your spreading out the countries in which you do your banking, or at least diversifying the currencies in which you invest. There is one downside to diversification—the more you have in any account, the higher the rate of interest you'll usually earn, and diversifying obviously reduces your account size. Thus, it's important to diversify in such a way that your effective rate of interest is reduced as little as possible.

- **Consider a Managed Account** If you are unfamiliar with the foreign investment markets and unaccustomed to dealing in foreign currencies, you may want to consider opening a managed, or discretionary, account—one where your banker is given the authority to invest your funds on your behalf. Of course, your banker will charge you for the service, but you will get the benefit of his expertise.

You should *never* open a discretionary account by mail. It is essential that you get to know your funds manager and that he get to know you. Only after you're comfortable with his investment philosophy and background should you entrust any funds to him.

If your investment philosophy is conservative in nature, a Swiss managed account may be for you. The Swiss reputation for conservatism is well earned (though recent changes in Swiss attitudes toward secrecy have diminished the appeal of Swiss bank accounts).

SECTION 5: TRANSFERRING MONEY ANONYMOUSLY: THREE METHODS

Moving money around the world anonymously can be a boon to privacy and convenience. There are many ways to do it, but there are three ways *not* to do it. Over the years, each of these notorious methods has acquired its own special name.

1. The Richard Nixon Method

Former U.S. President Richard M. Nixon's re-election effort (CREEP) actually encouraged various large American businesses to use offshore companies to donate anonymous cash for the campaign.

CREEP's fund-raising was headed by U.S. Commerce Secretary Maurice Stans and Attorney General John Mitchell. Stans and Mitchell naturally preferred cash-in-hand contributions because there could be no processed checks to connect the campaign to its sometimes highly suspect sponsors. Anonymous cash also concealed the near blackmail efforts CREEP used to solicit donations.

For example, CREEP put the squeeze on George Spater, then chair and CEO of American Airlines, for $100,000 in cash. Spater was then faced with the task of finding a way to divert corporate funds without alerting the company's internal auditors. So he simply arranged to have a Lebanese corporation called Amarco submit a phony invoice for a commission allegedly earned on the sale of airplane parts to a Mideast airline.

American Airlines paid the invoice. Amarco deposited the money in its Swiss bank account, and then wired it to its U.S. dollar account in New York. After it arrived, Amarco's agent withdrew the $100,000 in cash, handed it to Spater, who dutifully handed it over to Stans and Mitchell.

American Airlines' auditors never questioned the transaction. And if the whole tawdry story of the Nixon fund-raising effort had not come out in the aftermath of Watergate, the true nature of this transaction would have remained a secret to this day.

2. The Oliver North Method

In the mid-80s, the Reagan administration wanted to support the Nicaraguan "Contra" rebels who were fighting a jungle insurgency against the country's leftist Sandinista government. But an amendment passed by the U.S. Congress specifically outlawed sending any U.S. government funds to aid the Contras.

Stripped to its essentials, the administration's problem was identical to the one faced by George Spater: How to move money from here to there in such a way that its origins could not be traced? The solution: They used a Panamanian offshore company called Lake Resources.

The architect of this particular scheme was Marine Lt. Col. Oliver North, then a National Security aide to the Reagan White House. With his partners—Air Force Gen. Richard Secord and businessman Albert Hakim—North bought 2,000 high-tech American antitank missiles from the U.S. Central Intelligence Agency (CIA) for $12 million. North then sold these missiles to Iran for $30 million. (North considered the sale as harmless to U.S. interests because he knew the missiles would be used in Iran's ongoing war with Iraq.)

Iran paid the money into Lake Resources's Swiss bank account, which sent the profits on to the Contras. Because the offshore company was not subject to U.S. tax scrutiny, this transaction would also never have come to light had it not been uncovered by politically motivated snooping.

3. The CIA Method

In 1947, U.S. President Harry Truman signed the National Security Act that created the Central Intelligence Agency. It wasn't long before a pressing need arose to transfer funds from here to there in a way that could not be traced.

In 1953, the United States sought to overthrow Iran's Mossadegh regime, and put the Shah back on the Peacock Throne. But the Eisenhower administration could scarcely ask Congress to appropriate money for such a venture. To secretly funnel U.S. funds anywhere in the world, the CIA eventually created a vast network of private offshore corporations—many of which are controlled by former military and ex-Agency personnel.

Such companies helped obscure the origins of the funds used in President Kennedy's well-documented attempts to assassinate Cuba's Fidel Castro, and Ronald Reagan's attempts to get rid of Libya's Mu'ammar Qaddafi.

The most famous of the CIA's clandestine offshore ventures was Air America, the Southeast Asian airline that functioned as front for all manner of intelligence-related matters during the Vietnam War era.

Nor is the U.S. government alone in its use of offshore banks and companies. Most other governments do the same thing for the same reasons. Especially during the Cold War, governments on both sides of the Iron Curtain used hundreds of offshore banks and companies for just this reason.

As you can see from the three methods I've outlined, I cannot recommend a way to transfer money anonymously. Whatever you do, you must always follow reporting requirements.

SECTION 6: REPORTING REQUIREMENTS

You may have noticed on your Form 1040 personal income tax return the following question: "Did you have at any time during the taxable year a financial interest in or signature authority over a bank, securities, or other financial account in a foreign country?"

If the answer is yes, and you have more than $5,000 in a foreign account, you must file Form 90-22.1 by June 30 of the year following any year in which you had the account (a copy of the form is attached). There is a stiff fine—and the possibility of criminal prosecution—for failure to file this form. The form cannot be obtained from the IRS by your creditors or by opponents in a lawsuit.

If you physically transport more than $10,000 outside of the United States, you'll have to fill out an appropriate customs declaration. There is nothing, in and of itself, illegal about moving money outside of the United

States—you violate the law only if you fail to declare it. The declaration requirement applies if you mail, ship, or carry bearer securities, traveler's checks, or cash.

SECTION 7: A BRIEF REVIEW OF OVERSEAS BANKING CENTERS

Here is a checklist of some countries that want to do business with foreigners. Each of these countries has done something to make itself attractive to overseas investors. The list is by no means complete, and changes rapidly.

Anguilla

Anguilla is a small British colony located at the northernmost end of the Leeward Islands in the Caribbean. It has a very stable government, and no taxes are imposed on the profits of foreign bank account holders or foreign bank profits—which can improve your investment performance. Though the financial industry here is fairly young, there are a number of banks with proven track records—though you should still exercise extra care in choosing a bank for your account. Strict bank secrecy laws are in place, and the island features a good communications system, an adequate mail service, and the advantage of close proximity to the United States. It is also a pleasant, if somewhat quiet vacation spot.

Austria

Located in central Europe, Austria has a reputation as one of the most politically and financially stable countries in Europe. Austrian bank accounts are freely convertible from one currency to another, which makes them attractive. Austrian bankers also have a strong commitment to privacy, yet Austrian bank accounts are seldom viewed with the same suspicion that might be engendered by an account in other jurisdictions. Austria's bank secrecy law is very strict in that it is a crime for any Austrian bank official to reveal information on an account without authority. However, they will reveal information to a foreign government in the context of a criminal investigation or an investigation regarding tax evasion.

The Bahamas

Now an independent nation in the northern Caribbean, the Bahamas has made itself into one of the premier offshore banking centers of the world. Bahamian banks are modern and efficient, and communications with the United States and the rest of the world are excellent. The country is also a tax haven and attracts all aspects of international business as well as banking. Adjuncts of all kinds are available, in any currency. There are no foreign exchange controls. The Bahamas has a strong bank secrecy law. However, it is newly independent and has a vocal left-wing minority, and cannot be considered as politically stable as other countries.

Bermuda

Of all the tax and banking havens in close proximity to the United States, Bermuda is the oldest and has the best reputation. Located 570 miles southeast of Cape Hatteras, it is conveniently located for most U.S. investors, and it boasts excellent banking and communications facilities. Bermuda has no exchange controls;

accounts may be kept in any currency; and no taxes are imposed on interest earned by nonresidents.

Cayman Islands

Located due south of Cuba, these three little islands have one major industry—international banking. This is no fluke; the government does everything it can to nurture the industry. Funds may be transported out of the Caymans free of any reporting requirement, and accounts can be maintained in any currency. Travel, hotel, and communications services are excellent. The Caymans also have what may be the strongest bank secrecy law in the world. However, even the Caymans have recently had to knuckle under to pressure from the U.S. government, and local banks will cooperate with U.S. criminal and tax investigations. It is relatively easy for a nonresident to form a bank in the Caymans. Consequently, you should exercise extra caution when choosing a bank located in the Caymans.

The Channel Islands

The Channel Islands are eight small islands in the English Channel—the most important of which are Jersey and Guernsey. Except for defense and foreign policy, the Channel Islands are independent from Great Britain. Over the years, Channel Islands banks have developed an excellent reputation for secrecy and probity in the handling of offshore investors' business. As a result, it is the principal offshore financial center for British citizens. There is no taxation of interest paid to foreigners and no exchange controls, and accounts may be maintained in any currency.

Hong Kong

Hong Kong has, for many years, been the world's leading international banking center. However, its future is clouded because the colony will come under rule by the People's Republic of China in 1997. For now, however, it continues to flourish. Hong Kong takes bank secrecy seriously, but its bankers will cooperate with foreign criminal investigations. Unlike many offshore centers, Hong Kong imposes a 15 percent tax on foreign bank account earnings.

Singapore

Singapore is an island nation on the eastern edge of the Malay Peninsula. It has been independent since 1965, and it is politically and economically stable, as well as being one of the busiest ports in the Pacific. The government has worked hard to make Singapore an international banking center. Communications are excellent. There are no taxes on interest earned by nonresidents, and it is relatively easy to open an account in any currency.

There are approximately forty-five other jurisdictions around the world that bill themselves as offshore financial centers or banking havens. However, many of these centers are remote, lack adequate support facilities, or have flaws in their banking or tax laws that could affect your privacy or your rate of investment return. That does not necessarily mean you should avoid banks in these jurisdictions when shopping for a location for your foreign bank account. However, it does mean that you should exercise additional caution, making sure the bank is well managed and offers the services, experience, and security you are seeking.

APPENDIX 2

HOW TO USE TAX HAVENS LEGALLY FROM CANADA

On a recent visit to Canada, a manufacturer told me it was impossible for him to be profitable in his business at current Canadian tax rates—and that the situation was getting worse. His concern—and that of so many other businesspeople—is that the tax bite leaves insufficient cash for reinvestment. I've heard similar tales of concern before, and all too often they end up with a comment such as: "If only we could use tax havens like the Americans in your book do."

The truth is that Canadians *can* use tax havens legally and profitably, so I've prepared this appendix to show exactly how it can be done, including facts on the exciting potential that exists to save on taxes. Here and there, the details may get a little legalistic and boring, but with this report you'll have all the technical information you need to be assured that tax havens do work for Canadians; in my book you'll learn about the many exciting ways to put these legalistic details into fun and profitable practice.

In just one case, creating a foreign sales and marketing subsidiary for your Canadian company can reduce the tax rate from 45 percent to 2.5 percent! On a profit of $750,000, after paying the tax haven country only $18,750 in taxes, there is $731,250 profit that can be remitted to Canada—without paying any Canadian taxes.

Once available exclusively for the very rich—if not the famous—the use of foreign nations as personal tax havens (also known as "offshore" tax shelters) now has a broadening appeal for many overtaxed Canadians.

For a variety of reasons, Canadians now earning $100,000 or more annually can profit greatly by creating foreign-based tax-reduction devices: sophisticated legal arrangements that can also double as successful asset-protection mechanisms. The bigger tax bite means those whose income places them in the upper reaches of Canada's middle class—lawyers, doctors, dentists, airline pilots, professionals in general—should seriously consider "going offshore" as a means of generating immediate tax savings. Reductions of as much as one half of an individual's total annual income-tax bill are possible!

IS TAX "AVOIDANCE" LEGAL?

To the uninitiated, the exotic phrase "tax haven" may evoke a mental picture of some far off corner of the world, populated with secretive millionaires who spend their days sipping daiquiris on the beach, their cash secure in numbered Swiss bank accounts. Not so. As we have seen, tax havens are no longer the exclusive playground of only the Canadian ultrarich. People of a bit more than average means ($100,000-plus in annual income) can now at least partially escape the clutches of Revenue Canada by joining the modern financial jet set.

As federal government powers continue to expand, swallowing individual human rights, the national deficit and income taxes grow apace. Intelligent individuals seek protection for their hard-earned income and assets. While the tabloid media love to tattle about celebrity "tax evaders," a very important point is ignored: Tax evasion is illegal. Tax avoidance is not.

This is a crucial distinction lost on many people.

Because of the potential for tax avoidance, tax havens should be of great interest to the international investor—yet too few Canadians of wealth understand and use them properly. Some disregard tax havens as hiding holes for dirty money—which is certainly not a legitimate use. Others think tax havens are only for banking money after you have earned it. Not true either. Canada's wealthiest families and largest corporations have been using tax havens profitably for a long time—and you can too.

Your money grows much faster if you include a tax haven in your planning, and almost any international investor can create an opportunity to use one. It is the purely domestic investor, confined by uninformed choice to one country, who fails to benefit from the many available international tax savings.

Most often, people tend to make the move offshore one step at a time. They open an offshore bank or brokerage account, then consider an offshore trust, and finally begin thinking about engaging in offshore business activities. A better approach for most wealthy individuals is to look at an overall offshore strategy—one that employs trusts, bank accounts, business operations, and/or other activities to provide real protection for personal assets, as well as both corporate and individual tax savings. To give you an idea of the possibilities, the remainder of this appendix will provide an overview of the various types of offshore structures available for use by Canadians.

OWNING YOUR OWN OFFSHORE BANK

Suppose you don't want to simply open a foreign bank account. Suppose you want to bank offshore, but you want some more control of your money. One option is ownership of an offshore bank.

Owning a bank is a lot easier in many countries than it is in Canada. Some countries cater to individual foreigners who want to own banks, streamlining chartering rules and making the cost affordable (approximately $20,000). Joining the world of international finance, such a privately owned bank can take deposits, make loans, issue letters of credit, and invest money—just like the major players.

And, here's the best part for Canadian taxpayers: Offshore banking income is not presently taxed until it is paid to the owners. If you set up the bank in the right country, your taxes will be low in your home country. Careful investing and use of tax treaties should eliminate or reduce taxes from other countries.

To qualify for the income-tax exception, however, your bank must conduct real business. This means you have to solicit business from independent parties. You have to get deposits and make loans. If the parties involved are not independent of the bank's owners, Revenue Canada likely will say it is simply an offshore investment corporation and not a bank, and will tax the shareholders on the corporation's income.

To start a foreign bank properly, you need professional advice to select the right country for incorporation and to find six employees who will work for your bank full-time, which is required under Canadian tax law. One of the real advantages of an offshore bank is that you do not need a walk-in retail operation, such as your neighborhood bank. Most offshore banking transactions are done through modern electronic communications. The occasional client who wants to visit the bank will be satisfied with an office that looks like any other professional office.

If you are serious about operating an offshore bank—and if you seek help from someone who is fully informed on the international banking situation—you might find that your own private offshore bank is the ultimate opportunity.

The Tax Bite

Upper-income Canadians are driven to seek new tax-reduction methods because of a constantly increasing tax bite on individual income (in excess of 50 percent in some cases), and on corporations (now as high as 45 percent). The effective combined federal/provincial personal tax rate in Ontario, for example, is 52.35 percent this year. The elimination of the $100,000 capital-gains tax exemption, which took effect with the 1995 federal budget, spurred thousands more beleaguered upper-income taxpayers to consider ways and means to escape what rapidly became confiscation, rather than just mere taxation.

Still another incentive for moving business abroad is the possibility of the reimposition of federal or provincial estate taxes. Although the federal estate tax was abolished in 1971, several provinces continued these taxes until the last was repealed by Quebec in 1986. Now, however, there is talk of imposing new death taxes—especially in Ontario.

ATTRACTIONS ABROAD

As if one needed more reason to be disturbed about the trend of government, just compare the outrageously high Canadian income taxes with those imposed in many foreign countries, where rates for the same income and corporate taxes are in the low single digits. Prudent Canadians can take advantage of this wide international tax disparity by establishing an offshore tax shelter that can easily double disposable after-tax income. This feat can be accomplished in full compliance with federal law and the tax code so that Revenue Canada (RC) cannot mount a successful challenge—although, based on recent history, RC may well go after anything it considers to be an "overly aggressive tax strategy."

In addition, various proposals for further tax-law changes are pending, although it is interesting to note that changes proposed in February 1994 were revised again in June 1994, before even being presented to Parliament. What is clear from these new proposals, however, is that future Canadian law will tend to follow American law, with the use of tax havens for individuals being limited, but no restrictions being imposed to prevent corporations from using tax havens for their legitimate business. Thus, whatever form the law finally takes when adopted, opportunities will continue to exist for offshore business-related activity.

TO PROTECT WHAT YOU HAVE

Another reason Canadian taxpayers are eyeing other parts of the world is the increasing problem of individual personal asset protection.

Professional malpractice suits, nasty divorce proceedings, legislative and judicial imposition of no-fault personal liability on corporate officers and directors—these are now common occurrences of everyday life. Any active business or professional person can suddenly find himself or herself held responsible for unforeseen obligations flowing from a company's environmental pollution, bank failures, dissatisfied clients, or just a disgruntled employee. Premiums for professional malpractice insurance have gone through the roof.

In this unpredictable climate, astute people are forced to find new ways to protect their personal assets. Legal offshore mechanisms, called asset-protection trusts, are available to do just that. (Note: The proposed new changes in Canadian tax law will not affect asset-protection trusts for individuals, as they are generally tax neutral.)

A Need for Caution

The objective of an offshore tax haven is the legal reduction of your tax obligations.

Keep in mind: It will do you no good to suffer the bother of extensively restructuring your personal economic life only to find yourself embroiled in years of complex and expensive court battles with Revenue Canada—or worse, finding yourself facing criminal charges for tax evasion or a variety of other possible tax crimes.

Reasonable caution places a premium on pursuing the path you choose the right way—from the very beginning and with the assistance of competent expert advice. Cutting corners can only mean you and your financial advisers could be headed for deep trouble.

For example, one of the easiest methods to avoid taxes is to transfer your cash to a bank in the United States, then simply fail to declare the interest paid to you when you file your income tax forms. There is only one major problem with this: It is against the law. Of course, since U.S. banks issue no tax receipts to nonresident alien account holders, it is all but impossible for Canadian authorities to discover your nice little scheme. But, if they do—watch out. They usually do find out because an underpaid secretary or a spouse in a divorce case decides to tell them.

DON'T DO ILLEGALLY WHAT YOU CAN DO LEGALLY

The most dangerous attitude one can adopt when dealing with the establishment of offshore business arrangements is the cavalier approach, the idea that white-collar crimes are somehow less serious than violent crimes, such as bank robbery, or the notion that the federal government is less concerned about tax or financial offenses than other civil wrongs. The truth is, the chances of getting away with fudging on Canadian domestic tax laws—even as they apply offshore—are minimal at best. There are many court cases to prove this point.

And don't think geographic distance offers sure protection for those who want to bend the law by going offshore. During the last fifteen years, Canada has rapidly expanded its tax-treaty relations—bilateral and multilateral—aimed at stifling both tax avoidance and tax evasion. Canada now has more than sixty mutual tax agreements in force (or under negotiation) with foreign governments. Canadian courts display a stiff attitude toward tax scofflaws, and the judicial long arm reaches across oceans. For example, the Canadian Supreme Court has held (in *Robert Spencer v. R,* 85 DTC 5446) that the former manager of the Freeport branch of the Canadian Royal Bank could be forced to give testimony at a tax-evasion trial in Canada, even though doing so would be a breach of Bahamian bank secrecy laws.

The federal government and Revenue Canada's vigorous international tax enforcement efforts have been aided by new and powerful laws aimed at tax avoidance practices. For example:

- Laws were changed to extend the statute of limitations on government questioning of certain offshore tax transactions from three to six years.
- RC was given greatly increased powers to obtain "foreign-based information or documents" about a Canadian citizen's business activities abroad.
- Elaborate, detailed annual corporate reporting requirements were imposed on "intercompany transactions" between Canadians and any offshore affiliated entities. Failure to report or false statements concerning such transactions can result in fines of up to $24,000.

Revenue Canada keeps an eagle eye on the tax-shelter industry and tracks the offshore business activity of individual Canadians as best it can. RC spokesperson Luce Morin means it when she says: "This department is concerned about any kind of tax shelter."

Whether RC, employing its own informational sources, finds out about offshore activity or not, reporting requirements concerning foreign investments place personal responsibility squarely on taxpayers to reveal what they are doing abroad, or suffer the legal consequences if they get caught.

In spite of these tough federal tax-enforcement policies and an array of laws with sharp teeth, there are still many lawful opportunities for offshore financial activities designed to minimize the impact of Canada's high tax rates. Offshore tax havens are legal; and, in selective circumstances, there are useful ways in which nonresident-owned international investment and business structures can serve you by substantially reducing your exposure to Canada's high taxes.

THE CANADIAN TAX SYSTEM

The tax system of Canada is comprehensive and, as I have pointed out, imposes burdensome tax rates on the income of individuals (over 50 percent) and corporations (up to 45 percent).

Canada taxes the worldwide income of its residents—citizens and resident aliens alike—who are resident in Canada at any time during the year. Residents include individuals, corporations, and trusts. Nonresidents are also taxed on income from employment, business, and certain capital assets located in Canada. Canadian citizens employed abroad, even for extended periods of time, have been held liable for domestic income taxes, though double taxation credits are permitted when taxes are paid abroad. Any person who spends 183 days or more in Canada in a year is deemed to be a resident for income tax purposes.

TAX SHELTERS UNDER SIEGE

Parliament, even when under Conservative control, has had a record in recent years of cracking down on tax shelters, particularly those operating domestically. Its actions include the 1988 adoption of the infamous "General Anti-Avoidance Rule."

This radical rule gives Revenue Canada the discretionary retroactive power to revisit and recharacterize for increased taxation purposes any business transaction that RC interprets as having no "bona fide purpose," other than to effect a tax savings. This places squarely on business the burden of demonstrating a "bona fide purpose" (other than tax savings) in order to obtain that savings. And, as you might imagine, there have been more than a few court cases contesting the rule's application, scope, and still unsettled meaning. That this Draconian rule even exists should give you an accurate idea of the essence—and the direction—of federal tax policy.

Strangely enough, the federal anti-tax shelter attitude generally has not extended to offshore tax entities, still governed for the most part by the Foreign Affiliate System statute, which has been law since 1972. As you will see, this law allows plenty of room for legitimate international tax planning designed to minimize domestic taxes by using Canadian-foreign affiliate company profit sharing and dividend distributions.

Is There an Offshore Tax Shelter for You?

No one, probably including even Revenue Canada, knows for sure how many Canadians now have established—or are in the process of setting up—some form of offshore tax shelter.

However, there is definitely a rush of offshore-bound taxpayers, as indicated by booming attendance at tax-haven seminars, sales of books on the subject, and the number of foreign bankers suddenly arriving here seeking Canadian business. Every increase in the tax rates means another layer of upper-income taxpayers finds it affordable to recoup their tax losses by setting up an offshore tax-savings mechanism. Where that should be done, as we will discuss, is a matter of choice. There are several excellent foreign locations to consider.

Among the foreign jurisdictions that are popular tax-shelter destinations for Canadians are Barbados, the Cayman Islands, and the Turks and Caicos—all Caribbean favorites. European choices include Ireland, the Netherlands, and the Channel Islands. All of these foreign bailiwicks have exceptionally low tax rates on corporate and personal income earned by foreign nationals, as well as other attractions to make them economically feasible for offshore Canadian operations.

One thing should be understood: Going offshore is not cheap. Start-up and annual operating costs can be considerable, depending on the form of shelter employed. Before you decide, these costs must be realistically calculated against tax savings and other expenses—including the possible need to defend your tax shelter against attack by Revenue Canada. However, if you can cut your taxes by half, that should finance much of your initial cost; after that, the net results will be like receiving an annual bonus. So this isn't something to measure in absolute dollars spent, but in percentage of savings—at which point it becomes extremely profitable.

TAX HAVEN OR "SHAM"?

Before you start planning how to spend the increased income that will start rolling in from your offshore tax haven, you should know about four very basic rules of the game laid down by Canadian law—and strictly enforced by Revenue Canada. These rules apply to all offshore tax shelters—both corporations and trusts—and are aimed at abuse of such operations.

1. **Residence** A corporation or a trust, even though created in a foreign country under that country's laws, whose effective management is in Canada, will be taxed on its entire income and capital gains as if it were a resident of Canada.

This means actual control and management must be located within the foreign country, and all legal formalities must be observed. You are not prevented as a Canadian citizen from being a shareholder, officer, or director of an offshore company, but proving foreign control, on paper and in fact, is essential.

2. **Artificiality** There must be a demonstrably credible reason for the operations of the corporation or trust in the foreign country, other than mere tax avoidance. Otherwise Revenue Canada will hold it to be a sham and tax it as a Canadian resident. This means there must be a legitimate purpose, a functioning business, a board of directors, an office and staff, and all the other trappings of corporate life.

When there is a legitimate business purpose, there will be no Canadian taxes on any income from a corporation based in a tax-haven country until it is actually paid to the Canadian resident in the form of salary or dividends. There is no penalty for accumulation of capital in the foreign company, and no rules that require capital distribution.

This means that until the Canadian owner needs money for his or her use, or until they sell the foreign business, taxes on these earnings can be deferred indefinitely, even for decades. Owners who want the money right away can be paid dividends, on which the Canadian tax is 36 percent, well below the income tax rate of 50 percent plus.

It is worth underscoring that if a Canadian corporation has a foreign affiliate company in a country where Canada has a reciprocal tax agreement (nearly sixty nations are now listed by RC), any dividends paid out of the affiliate's exempt surplus (essentially meaning profits from current income) will be tax-free if paid in Canada to a corporate shareholder.

For example, an Irish foreign affiliate manufacturing for export to the United Kingdom and enjoying a tax holiday under liberal Irish business-incentive laws, or a Barbadian, Cypriot, or Jamaican foreign affiliate qualifying under the domestic tax-incentive laws of those nations, can easily generate surplus dividends not taxable in Canada to a Canadian corporate shareholder. This is a major and very profitable tax savings in many instances.

Dividends paid by a tax-haven affiliate company to a Canadian corporate shareholder are treated as exempt surplus and are tax-free to the Canadian company—a major boon for tax planning and tax reduction. Interest and royalties paid between two such affiliated companies are also tax-free. For example, loan interest paid by a U.S. affiliate to a Canadian company is subject to a 15 percent gross tax, but the same U.S. payment routed through a Netherlands affiliate corporation to its Canadian affiliate company would be tax-free. It is worth noting that Canada does not tax foreign affiliates that are, in fact, holding companies.

3. **Foreign Accrual Property Income** In order to regulate offshore financial activity by individual Canadians, the federal government in 1976 promulgated the Foreign Accrual Property Income—known fondly to Revenue Canada and accountants as "FAPI." The FAPI bottom line requires reporting on income tax forms any "foreign accrual property income," especially "passive" income from offshore investments of any kind. This is so even if the income is not transferred back to Canada, even if the money only accumulates abroad in a foreign trust or corporate account. Depending on the applicable provision of law, such foreign income may or may not be taxable; but regardless of any tax liability, every dollar of it must be reported.

Personal foreign accrual property income not only must be reported, but certain types of FAPI (as defined by law) from a Canadian-controlled foreign corporate affiliate, and from certain specified foreign trusts, is currently taxable to Canadian shareholders or trust beneficiaries, whether or not that income is actually remitted to Canada. This covers Canadian investors, regardless of how many shares they own, who have passive interests in offshore investment corporations. While the entire actual net profit of the offshore investment company is not taxed proportionally to each shareholder, there is a complicated RC formula that apportions annual tax liability. Together with annual FAPI reporting requirements, this annual offshore investment tax has dampened Canadian enthusiasm for foreign ventures devoted solely to producing investment income.

4. **Inter-Company Pricing** There can be no overpricing charged by a foreign parent company—for example, for exporting goods from a Canadian subsidiary for international sales. (Tax-haven companies created solely for importing into Canada were subjected to full Canadian taxes beginning in 1972.) Overpricing has been a popular, but illegal, tactic used in an attempt to shift capital from parent companies in high-tax Canada to the low-tax offshore affiliate. RC has gone to court repeatedly to challenge such schemes, albeit with mixed results.

In cases of offshore trading in which a Canadian-affiliated tax-haven company transfers goods between two other countries, RC authorities always watch very closely, and often conduct annual audits. Even if the tax-haven company survives the RC residency and sham tests, it may fail the inter-company pricing regulations, especially if Canada is involved as one leg of the shipping triangle as an importer or exporter. Of course, when Canada is "out of the loop," as when an affiliate in the Channel Islands is shipping Scottish woolens to Europe, such pricing regulations don't apply and neither do the taxes.

All this may sound discouraging, but it can be done! Here's how.

Using Foreign Tax Havens—Legitimately

Simply stated, a tax haven is any country whose laws, regulations, traditions, and (usually) international treaty arrangements make it possible for any person or corporation, domestic or foreign, to reduce their overall tax burden. This general definition, however, covers many types of tax havens, and it is important to understand the differences.

"No-Tax" Havens These are countries with no personal or corporate income, capital-gains or wealth (capital) taxes, where you can easily incorporate and/or form a trust. The governments of these countries do earn some revenue from corporations and they may impose small fees on documents of incorporation, a charge on the value of corporate shares, and annual registration fees. Primary examples are Caribbean countries such as Bermuda, the Bahamas, and the Cayman Islands.

Consider, for example, the Cayman Island tax structure. There are no taxes levied except stamp taxes on certain transactions and import duties. Nonresidents who form exempted corporations automatically qualify for and receive a government guarantee of no taxes for twenty years; trusts are given a fifty-year, no-tax guarantee.

The process of incorporation is quick, easy, simple, and relatively inexpensive. It can be done in a matter of hours at the office of the Registrar of Companies in George Town, the capital city located on Grand Cayman Island, only 475 air miles from Miami International Airport. There is a registration fee and an annual operating fee thereafter. Start-up costs can run as low as $2,500, with a yearly operating cost of about $1,000. Establishing a trust can cost as little as $2,000. The Cayman Islands' corporation and trust statutes allow a wide range of business activities, stock issues, and great flexibility in actual operation.

The Cayman Islands are noted for laws strongly protecting corporate and bank privacy, with stiff penalties—including fines and/or prison—for anyone, including government officials, who violates the law.

In every respect, experience shows the Cayman Islands are superior because of future no-tax security, low costs, easy incorporation and operation, flexibility of business structure, privacy, immigration, and proximity to North and South American business markets.

It is obvious why the Caymans are a favorite location for Canadians to establish offshore trusts and investment corporations. The problem is, most Canadians getting involved in the Cayman Islands, or any other no-tax haven touting secrecy, don't get professional advice. Instead they fly to the islands and buy into a scheme based on secrecy and lies. Then if their newfound Cayman friends overcharge or make unexplained withdrawals from their capital, there is always the blackmailer's threat of "you can't sue us, because then your secret corporation will be revealed on court records, and you'll go to jail in Canada for tax fraud." Trusting strangers to keep your secrets is a very foolhardy way to proceed, especially when everything can be done legally and profitably with proper professional advice.

Here's how you could use a financial base in the Caymans: Let's say you have $3 million you wish to invest. Being a reasonable person, you want to avoid Canadian taxes on the income produced by your investment, and also avoid the application of the infamous FAPI rules.

First, you need a nonresident friend or relative to act as manager of your offshore investment corporation, which will be registered in George Town. You can't do it yourself or it might be called a sham. You transfer the $3 million to an offshore Cayman-registered trust, also administered by your friend, probably in the same George Town office. That money is invested in Canadian Treasury bills or public company stocks, and the interest income this produces can be paid to your children tax-free. At current interest rates, that translates into a savings of about $100,000 a year.

Given such savings potential, this tax-haven structure—a Cayman corporation and a trust—is worth a try. However, it may be expensive to establish and will probably be challenged by Revenue Canada because it wasn't set up with professional advice using an interplay of Canadian law and double-taxation treaties with appropriate haven countries (such treaties do exist with Ireland, the Netherlands, and Barbados, three of the most useful tax havens for Canadians). Besides, it's not really necessary. By using treaties and professional advice, one can create a completely legitimate tax-haven structure that does not require dishonesty and secrecy for its functioning.

"No-Tax-on-Foreign-Income" Havens These countries do impose income taxes, both on individuals and corporations, but only on income earned within the country, not abroad. The laws here exempt from tax any income earned from foreign sources involving no local business activities, apart from simple "housekeeping" matters. For example, there is often no tax on income derived from the export of local manufactured goods.

The no-tax-on-foreign-income havens break down into two groups, those that:

1. Allow a corporation to do business both internally and externally, taxing only the income coming from internal sources.
2. Require a company to choose at incorporation whether it will do business locally, with consequent tax liabilities, or whether it will do only foreign business, and thus be exempt from taxation.

Primary examples in these two categories are Panama, Liberia, Jersey, Guernsey, the Isle of Man, and Gibraltar.

"Low-Tax" Havens These countries impose some taxes on all corporate income, wherever earned worldwide. However, most have international double-taxation agreements with high-tax countries such as Canada that may reduce the withholding tax imposed on income earned in the high-tax countries by the local corporations. Cyprus is a primary example. Barbados, about which we'll have more later, is another low-tax (2.5 percent on corporate income) country popular with Canadian businesspeople.

"Special Tax" Havens These countries impose all or most of the usual taxes, but either allow valuable tax concessions, write-offs, or "holidays" to special types of companies they wish to encourage (such as a total tax exemption for shipping companies, movie-production companies, or financial institutions), or they allow special types of corporate organization, such as the flexible corporate arrangements offered by Liechtenstein. The Netherlands and Ireland are particularly good examples of nations that offer major tax concessions to selected foreign businesses.

Ireland—Special Opportunities for Canadians Just as with Barbados, the Republic of Ireland can also be used as the location of an offshore corporate affiliate, giving you commercial access to the 340 million people who live within the boundaries of the European Union. Ireland has many useful features, especially for manufacturing subsidiaries, but also sometimes for holding companies to collect royalties and interest under various tax-saving treaty arrangements.

Using Ireland as an affiliate base is one way to lock in low labor costs and a twenty-year tax holiday in the process. In some cases, you can even get free government money to fund your start-up costs. Irish labor costs are only 60 percent to 70 percent of Canadian wage levels; there is a 10 percent ceiling on corporate taxes, and cash grants are available to lure foreign business investors.

Since the 1970s, the Irish government has pursued an aggressive foreign investment program. To encourage foreign entrepreneurs to set up businesses, the government created the Irish Development Authority (IDA). To qualify for IDA incentives, a company must be engaged either in manufacturing or in international services. The latter category includes computer or software services, offices for insurance companies, and financial and other primary services.

Recently, the Irish parliament passed a law extending, through the year 2010, the maximum corporate tax rate of 10 percent on foreign investments. Thus, Canadian companies investing now can look forward to fifteen years of tax relief. The government cash grants can take the form either of reimbursement for the entire first year's payroll for a labor-intensive business, such as software development, or capital grants for factories or other more capital-intensive operations.

In addition to the IDA package, Ireland offers other programs. One of them is the Shannon Free Zone program. Incentives are similar to those of the IDA, with taxes held to 10 percent and capital grants available. Companies are required to locate near Shannon Airport. The Shannon Free Zone operation is administered separately from the IDA.

Ireland offers many advantages compared to rival centers such as Luxembourg and the Channel Islands, including lower wage and housing costs, a skilled and abundant labor force, and good communications with other European business centers.

Another Irish program is the International Financial Services Center (IFSC), a special zone in Dublin for financial services companies such as mutual funds, insurance companies, and banks. One of the IFSC's attractions has been the possibility for cash-rich firms to place their surplus cash in investment funds, which are then managed in Dublin by specialist companies. Profits are taxed at the 10 percent rate and can be repatriated without further tax liabilities due to Ireland's double-taxation treaties.

The Barbados Offshore Corporation A simpler approach than the Irish manufacturing subsidiary is to create an offshore corporation in a tax haven such as Barbados. Done properly, this can be one of the most effective tax-saving devices for a Canadian business.

The offshore corporation is best suited to the needs of Canadian business owners who wish to do good business, as well as lower their taxes and increase profits.

But foreign corporations—as we have seen, and as Revenue Canada demands—must be more than a mere “sham.” A full-scale company, complete with working offices, staff, international fax and telecommunications facilities, bank accounts, a registered agent, board of directors, a local attorney, and an accountant, is expensive. However, it will be more than worth it when weighed against the easily measurable tax savings.

Members of your board of directors—usually associates of the local tax specialists who help you form the company—will be paid about $2,500 a year. There will be annual taxes to pay and reports to be filed with the local government and with Canada.

As the Canadian owner, you will want to visit your company offices once or twice a year, a pleasant enough activity if you locate your business in one of the tropical venues specializing in such corporate arrangements. January is an excellent month to visit.

How Will It Work? Let’s say you are a Canadian manufacturer exporting $5 million in products around the world each year. Because you are a legitimate business with established foreign transactions, your Canadian company can incorporate an offshore affiliate in, say, Barbados. Like Canada, Barbados is a member of the Commonwealth and, very unlike Canada, is a place where international companies pay only 2.5 percent corporate income tax.

There are fewer than three quarters of a million people living on this pleasant, tropical 166-square-mile island, where the mean temperature hovers between 76 and 80 degrees Fahrenheit year-round.

Your adviser can set up your affiliate with offices in the capital, Bridgetown (population 8,000), a city with eight major international banks, including branches of the Royal Bank of Canada and the Canadian Imperial Bank of Commerce, as well as Chase Manhattan and Barclays. Regular air service is offered by Air Canada, British Airways, and American Airlines, among others.

Your Bridgetown affiliate will handle all foreign sales and international marketing for your Canadian company, charging for its services a 15-percent markup on the value of the goods it sells, or about $750,000 a year, at your current export levels.

What you have done is legally transfer your Canada profits to your offshore affiliate where taxes are much lower—2.5 percent versus 45 percent! After gladly paying only $18,750 in Barbados local corporate income taxes, the rest of the money, $731,250, can be sent back to Canada as a dividend from exempt surplus income and paid to the parent company tax-free!

Until the parent company shareholders need the money for their own use, or until they sell the business, Canadian taxes on the income can be deferred indefinitely. If the shareholders want payment immediately, it can be paid out as dividends—and taxed by Canada at the rate of 36 percent, well below the personal income tax rate of 50 percent-plus.

Investment Potential The Barbados affiliate could also serve as an investment arm for your parent company, actively making international investments.

All the earned income from such investments—dividends, interest, and capital gains—will go to your Bridgetown affiliate, and be taxed at the 2.5 percent rate. Investment profits can also be sent to the parent company, tax-free. In order to follow this course successfully, meeting the requirements laid down by Revenue Canada, all corporate investment decisions must originate with your Bridgetown money manager, who runs your affiliate on a daily basis; it cannot be you dictating every move by phone from Montreal or Ottawa. As an added consideration, those with experience say that in order to be successful in using foreign affiliates for investment purposes, a minimum of $1 million in initial capital is needed to start, although many have been profitable and successful on less.

In theory this all sounds grand, but there are practical problems associated with an offshore corporation. First of all, just as in establishing a domestic corporation, legal formalities must be strictly observed when you incorporate abroad; Revenue Canada will check this carefully. You will need a local legal counsel who knows the law and understands your business and tax objectives. Corporations anywhere are rule-bound creatures requiring separate books and records, meetings, minutes, and corporate authorizing resolutions that make them less flexible than many other arrangements. However, you can pay for a whole lot of record keeping with the tax money you can save.

In the right circumstances, Barbados can also become a base for your private offshore bank or other financial corporation, since rendering a financial service is just as much a product under the tax code as is a physical manufacturing operation.

ASSET PROTECTION TRUSTS: A VALUABLE STRATEGY FOR INDIVIDUALS

Although most tax-haven plans involve business corporations, the asset-protection trust is one strategy that every individual with assets should be using.

When tax havens are mentioned, knowledgeable people think of foreign offshore trusts. There is good reason. The trust is an established and proven fixture in the use of tax havens and offshore financial planning. One way to place your assets beyond the reach of potential litigation plaintiffs, creditors, and their lawyers is the creation of an offshore asset-protection trust located in a foreign country where the law favors such goals.

Even though an offshore trust, especially under Revenue Canada's FAPI rules, may not mean greatly reduced taxes these days, some of the biggest benefits of offshore trusts are the nontax benefits. To many Canadians, these benefits are far more valuable than any potential tax savings. Nontax benefits of offshore trusts include not only the protection of assets from creditors, but privacy, estate planning, and international investing and diversification benefits as well.

Many wealthy Canadians today have at least one financial foe they fear more than Revenue Canada: a plaintiff's lawyer. Business and professional people see a legal system out of control and courts willing to give others' assets to a sympathetic plaintiff. One mistake, or even one unfortunate accident, can take away the fruits of life's labors. And insurance companies often cannot or will not cover an entire claim.

Because of this, many successful professionals and business owners are putting a higher priority on asset preservation than on tax avoidance. A foreign trust is one key to preserving assets from creditors.

Fair-Weather Financial Planning

One of the most important considerations about foreign asset-protection trusts is anticipation of future problems. In order to avoid allegations of fraud, tax planners insist such trusts should be established well before problems with creditors, an irate spouse, or a court judgment develop—at least two years prior is recommended. This arrangement will only work if it is planned and created at a time of financial calm, not in a personal asset crisis.

If the foreign asset-protection trust is established only days or weeks before you are sued or forced into bankruptcy (or especially afterwards), the act of transferring your assets to a foreign trust will subject you and your assets to strict fraudulent-conveyance laws, which strongly favor creditors. In such an instance, a court can declare the trust an illegal sham designed to conceal or remove assets from creditors and, therefore, void. If your assets are still within the court's jurisdiction, conveying title to a foreign trustee won't protect them from domestic attachment.

Financial Privacy

The country in which the trust and trustee are located should be one with strong financial-privacy laws. The ideal countries for asset-preservation trusts are usually tax havens such as the Cayman Islands, Jersey, the Channel Islands, and the Cook Islands, among others. In these places, trustees are not required to divulge information about assets held by the trust, and cannot be forced by Canadian courts to turn over those assets to Canadian creditors unless and until those creditors go through the host country's judicial system.

You generally should transfer only cash and intangible assets (bonds, stocks, etc.) to the trust. Portable assets, such as gold coins or diamonds, can also be used. You should not transfer title to real estate or a business located in Canada. This does nothing to keep the assets away from Canadian creditors, and could make the trust subject to the jurisdiction of a Canadian court, i.e., by holding title to assets within the country, the trust would be deemed to be doing business in Canada.

An offshore asset-protection trust will not affect your tax return. You will be the grantor who creates the trust by transferring your selected assets to it. The beneficiaries likely will include your family members, but will not include yourself. The foreign trustee will follow your instructions on how trust assets should be invested and disbursed. You will notice very little difference in how you operate—unless you suddenly are faced with creditors who want your assets.

Under FAPI rules, you must disclose the existence of the trust on your federal tax return, but creditors must get a court to order you to reveal your tax return—and that takes time. If they do discover the trust's offshore location and file a collection suit in that country, foreign laws are likely to be hostile to nonresident creditors, and the trustee can shift the trust and its assets to another country and another trustee. Then creditors must begin the process all over again. Many of these foreign jurisdictions do not recognize Canadian or any nondomestic court orders, and a creditor must retry completely the original claim that gave rise to a Canadian judgment. It won't be long before the creditor will want to talk with you directly about settling the dispute.

Unlike a corporate charter and bylaws, the actual language of a trust agreement is not registered with government authorities in most countries. However, some tax-haven countries require registering trust agreements, so you must consider whether this is helpful or harmful in choosing a locale for your trust. In most cases, the terms of the agreement are between you and the trustee unless a dispute forces one of you to bring the trust agreement into court. Many beneficiaries have never even seen the trust agreements.

The Trust Advantage

This gives trusts a distinct privacy advantage over corporations.

In every country at least one person involved in organizing the corporation must be listed on the public record, along with the name and address of the corporation. In most countries, the directors must also be listed. In a few maximum-privacy tax-haven countries, only the organizing lawyer is listed—but even that reference gives privacy invaders a starting point from which to work against you.

With a trust, however, you are usually required to register nothing but its existence—and often not even that fact. The trust agreement and the parties involved do not have to be disclosed, and there is little or nothing on the public record. In privacy-conscious countries, the trustee is allowed to reveal information about the trust only in very limited circumstances.

The country chosen for such a trust must have local trust experts who understand fully and can assist you in your objectives. The foreign local attorney who creates your trust unquestionably must know the applicable law and tax consequences.

Once established, the offshore asset-protection trust in its basic form can consist of as little as a trust account in an international bank located in the foreign country. Many well-established multinational Canadian banks can provide trustees for such arrangements and are experienced in such matters—but you might want to consider using a non-Canadian bank. With today's instant communications and international banking facilities, it is as convenient to hold assets and accounts overseas as it is in another Canadian city. Most international banks offer Canadian and U.S. dollar-denominated accounts, which often offer better interest rates than Canadian institutions.

Asset-Protection Trust Costs

Because a foreign jurisdiction is its situs, the cost of creating an asset protection trust abroad usually is more than $15,000 initially, plus several thousand dollars in annual maintenance fees. As a rule, unless the assets you seek to shield are worth more than $2 million, the trust may not be a practical device—although *Business Week* magazine estimated in 1990 that "a net worth of $500,000" or more could be enough to justify a foreign asset-protection trust.

Depending on the country of choice, the settlor of a foreign asset-protection trust can gain many advantages, including the exercise of far greater control over assets and income from the trust than permitted under domestic law.

The trust can provide privacy, confidentiality, and reduced domestic reporting requirements in Canada; avoidance of domestic taxes and probate in case death taxes are reimposed; and increased flexibility in conducting affairs in case of disability, in transferring assets, in international investing, or in avoiding possible domestic currency controls. A foreign asset-protection trust can also substitute for or supplement costly professional liability insurance or even a prenuptial agreement as protection for your heirs and their inheritance.

Trust Creation Abroad

The structure of foreign asset-protection trusts is not very different from that of a Canadian trust. The settlor creates the trust and transfers title to his assets to the trust, to be administered by a trustee according to the terms of the trust declaration. Usually the trustee is a bank in the offshore jurisdiction chosen. Beneficiaries can vary according to the settlor's estate-planning objectives, and the settlor himself may be a beneficiary, although not the primary one.

Many foreign jurisdictions also permit appointment of a trust "protector" who, as the title indicates, oversees the operation of the trust to ensure its objectives are being met and the local law is followed. A protector does not manage the trust, but can veto actions in some few cases.

The greatest worry about a foreign asset-protection trust often is the distance between you, your assets, and the people who manage them. While your assets do not have to be transferred physically to the foreign country in which the trust exists, circumstances may dictate such a precautionary transfer. Without such a physical transfer, a Canadian court could decide to disregard the trust and take possession of the assets.

If you are considering a foreign asset-protection trust, you should find out whether the foreign jurisdiction's laws are favorable, clear, and truly do offer the protection you seek. Examine the economic and political stability of the country, the reputation of its judicial system, local tax laws, the business climate, language barriers, and available communication and financial facilities.

Several offshore financial centers have developed legislation hospitable to foreign-owned asset-protection trusts, among them the Caribbean-area nations of the Cayman Islands, the Bahamas, Belize, and the Turks and Caicos Islands; the Cook Islands near New Zealand; and Cyprus and Gibraltar in the Mediterranean.

Most of these countries have laws preventing foreign creditors from attacking trust assets as long as two years have passed since the date of the trust creation, so there is a good reason to set up your trust as soon as possible.

GET STARTED NOW

Tax havens are a very complex subject, but the hours you spend studying their use will probably pay you more per hour than the hours you spend directly earning an income—an unfortunate commentary on the confiscatory taxation policies of most governments.

Just stop and think for a moment how much faster your money can grow if you are not paying out an average of 40 percent to a taxing government somewhere. And, the sooner you start, the sooner you begin saving that money. With proper professional advice, you can enjoy these benefits almost immediately.

APPENDIX 3

OFFSHORE BANKS

ARUBA

ABN AMRO BANK N.V.
Caya G F Betico, Croes 89
P.O. Box 391
Oranjestad, Aruba
Telephone: 297-8-21515
Fax: 297-8-21856
Telex: 5032 ABNAR AW
World Wide Web Page: http://www.abnamro.nl/
Branch of bank in Amsterdam, Netherlands. One of top 20 banks worldwide. Manager: R. R. Harmson

ARUBA BANK, LTD.
Caya G F Betico, Croes 41
P.O. Box 192
Oranjestad, Aruba
Telephone: 297-8-21550

Fax: 297-8-19152
Telex: 5040 ABANK
Established: 1925. Member: Aruba Bankers Association. Ownership: Foundation John G. Eman

FIRST NATIONAL BANK OF ARUBA
Caya G F (Betico) Croes 67
P.O. Box 184
Oranjestad, Aruba
Telephone: 297-8-33221/4
Fax: 297-8-21756
Telex: 5034 FNBAR AW
Type of bank: Commercial. Established: 1987. Ownership: Citco Commercial Bank Banking Corp (76%), JR Croes (24%).
Managing Director: C. Rund

INTERBANK ARUBA N.V.
Caya G F (Betico) Croes 38
P.O. Box 96
Oranjestad, Aruba
Telephone: 297-8-31080
Fax: 297-8-24058
Telex: 5224 INTER AW
Type of bank: Commercial and Retail. Ownership: Mansur Trading Company, N.V., Oranjestad (100%).
Managing Director: Carlo R. Mansur

AUSTRIA

BANK AUSTRIA AG
Private Banking
Am Hof 2
A-1010 Vienna, Austria
Telephone: 43-71191/ext. 6512, 6521

Fax: 43-71191/ext. 6544
Telex: 115561
Established: 1880
Member: Haupt Verband der Osterreichischen, Sparkassen; Verband Osterreichischer Banken and Bankiers, Vienna; ABECOR–Brussels. Ownership: AVZ (45.6%), Republic of Austria (20.35%), institutional investors (23.7%), widespread stockholders (10.3%). Moody's Rating (1995): bank deposits:Aaaa/P-1; financial strength rating—C+
Services: Broad spectrum of retail banking services such as savings, credit cards, loans, financial planning, international banking, electronic banking.

BANK FOR ARBEIT AND WIRTSCHAFT AKTIENGESELLSCHAFT
Seitzergasse 2-4, P.O. Box 171
A1011—Vienna, Austria
Telephone: 43-1-534530
Fax: 43-1-53453 /2840
Telex: 115311
Type of Bank: Joint Stock and Commercial. Established 1947; Member: Vergand Osterreichischer Banken und Bankiers—Vienna. Ownership: Austrian Federation of Trade Unions (67.7%); Konsum Osterreich (30.7%), Others (1.6%). Management Chairman: Walter Flotti. Principal Correspondents: Frankfurt Am Main—Bank Fur Gemeinsirtschaft Ag; London—Barclays Bank PIC; New York—Chase Manhattan Bank.
Services: Commercial business loans, mortgage lending, investments, lending to other banks, leasing services, insurance.

CENTRO INTERNATIONALE HANDELSBANK AKTIENGESELLSCHAFT
Tegetthoffstrasse 1, P.O. Box 272
A-1015 Vienna, Austria

Telephone: 43-1-515200
Fax: 43-1-5134396
Telex: 136990 CENT A
Type of Bank: Commercial and Merchant. Established: 1973; Member: Austrian Bankers Association—Vienna.
Management Executive: Dr. Gerhard Vogt.

CITIBANK (AUSTRIA) AG
Lothringerstrasse 7, P.O. Box 90
A-1015 Vienna, Austria
Telephone: 43-1-717170
Fax: 43-1-7139206
Telex: 112105
Type of Bank: Commercial. Established: 1959; Member: Vergand Osterreichischer Banken and Bankiers—Vienna. Holding Company: Citibank Overseas Investment Corporation—Wilmington, DE, US (100%). Principal Correspondents: Frankfurt Am Main—Citibank, NA; Johannesburg- Citibank, NA.

CREDITANSTALT BANKVEREIN
Schottengasse 6, P.O. Box 72
A-1011 Vienna, Austria
Telephone: 43-2-531310
Fax: 43-2-53131/7566
Telex: 133 030 CAWF
Type of bank: Joint Stock Company. Established 1855, with an emphasis on providing banking, finance and services for Austria's trade industries.
Services: Commercial and investment banking services to clients in Austria and abroad.

DIE ERSTE OSTERREICHISCHE SPAR-CASSE BANK (FIRST AUSTRIAN BANK)
Graben 21, P.O. Box 162
A-1011 Vienna, Austria

Telephone: 43-1-53100
Fax: 43-1-5339528
Telex: 114012 ESPKWW
Type of Bank: Commercial, Joint Stock Company. Established: 1819; Member: Hauptverband der Osterreichischen Sparkassen—Vienna. Management Chairman: Konrad Fuchs. Moody's rating (1995): bank deposits—A1/P-1; financial strength—B+.
Services: Full range of domestic and international banking services such as retail, commercial, and investment banking.

ROYAL TRUST BANK (AUSTRIA) AG
Rathausstrasse 20, P.O. Box 306
A-1011 Vienna, Austria
Telephone: 43-1-436161
Fax: 43-1-428142
Telex: 114911 RTB A
Type of Bank: Joint Stock. Established: 1890; Member: Austrian Bankers Association; Forex Club—Austria; Vienna Stock Exchange—Vienna. Ownership: Royal Trust Co. Ltd.—Toronto, Ontario, Canada (100%).

BAHAMAS

BANKAMERICA TRUST AND BANKING CORPORATION (BAHAMAS)
BankAmerica House
East Bay Street, P.O. Box N-9100
Nassau, Bahamas
Telephone: 809-393-7411
Fax: 809-393-3030
Telex: 20-159
Type of Bank: Trust and Banking Company. Subsidiary of BankAmerica Corporation—San Francisco, CA, US.

BANKERS TRUST COMPANY
Claughton House
P.O. Box N-3234
Nassau, Bahamas
Telephone: 809-325-4107
Telex: 20262
World Wide Web Page: http://www.bankerstrust.com
Branch of New York (Manhattan), NY, US. Holding Company: Bankers Trust New York Corporation—New York City (Manhattan) NY, US.

BANK OF BAHAMAS, LTD.
50 Shirley Street, P.O. Box N-7118
Nassau, Bahamas
Telephone: 809-326-2560
Fax: 809-325-2762
Telex: 20141 BBL
Type of bank: Private Stock. Established: 1970. Ownership: Bahamian Government.
Services: Commercial banking services.

BANK OF BOSTON TRUST COMPANY
(BAHAMAS), LTD.
Charlotte House
P.O. Box N-3930
Nassau, Bahamas
Telephone: 809-322-8531
Telex: 20189 BOSTRUST
Branch bank. Holding Company: Bank of Boston Corporation—Boston, MA, US.

BANK OF NOVA SCOTIA
Box N-7545 Bay Street
Nassau, Bahamas
Telephone: 809-322-4631
Fax: 809-328-8473
E-mail: 19163288473@faxsav.com

Branch of Bank of Nova Scotia—Toronto, Ontario, Canada.

BARCLAYS BANK
Box N-3045 Bay Street
Nassau, Bahamas
Telephone: 809-322-4921
Fax: 809-328-7979
Telex: 20149 BARCLADOM BS
E-mail: 19163287979@faxsav.com
Branch of bank in London, UK.

CITITRUST BAHAMAS
Thompson Boulevard, P.O. Box N-1576
Nassau, Bahamas
Telephone: 809-322-4240
Fax: 809-325-6147
Telex: 20420
Type of Bank: Joint Stock. Subsidiary of Citibank N.A., New York City (Manhattan), NY, US.

LLOYDS BANK INTERNATIONAL (BAHAMAS), LTD.
Bolam House
King and George Streets P.O. Box N-1292
Nassau, Bahamas
Telephone: 809-322-8711
Telex: 20107 BOLAM
Type of bank: Joint Stock. Ownership: Lloyds Bank PIC—London, UK. Principal Correspondents: London Lloyds Bank PIC, New York Irving Trust Company.

OFFSHORE TRUST BANKING CORPORATION, LTD.
West Bay Road, P.O. Box N-7197
Nassau, Bahamas
Telephone: 809-322-4585
Telex: 20111

Type of bank: Offshore. Established: 1981. Member: Association of International Banks and Trust Companies in the Bahamas.

ROYAL BANK OF SCOTLAND (NASSAU), LTD.
Box N-3045, 50 Shirley Street
Nassau, Bahamas
Telephone: 809-322-4643
Fax: 809-326-7558
E-mail: 19163267558@faxsav.com
International private bank established in 1950.

BARBADOS

BARCLAYS BANK PIC
Broad Street, P.O. Box 301
Bridgetown, Barbados
Telephone: 809-429-5151
Fax: 809-436-7957
Telex: 2348 BARCLADOM WB
Branch of London, UK. Manager: K.L. Lewis.

THE CHASE MANHATTAN BANK, NA
Neil and Broad Streets, P.O. Box 699
Bridgetown, Barbados
Telephone: 809-6-1100
Telex: WB269 CHASEBANK
Branch of New York (Manhattan), NY, US. Manager: David Da Costa.

THE ROYAL BANK OF CANADA
(BARBADOS) LIMITED
Royal Bank House, Bush Hill, The Garrison
P.O. Bag Service 1022
St. Michael, Barbados

Telephone: 809-431-6682
Fax: 809-436-9675
Type of bank: Offshore. Established: 1981. Subsidiary of RBC Bahamas Limited—Nassau, Bahamas. Ownership: The Royal Bank of Canada—Montreal, Quebec, Canada.
Principal Correspondents: Montreal—Royal Bank of Canada; New York—Manufacturers Hanover Trust Company.

SCOTIABANK
P.O. Box 202
Bridgetown, Barbados
Telephone: 809-431-3000
Fax: 809-426-0969
Telex: 2223
Branch of Bank of Nova Scotia—Toronto, Ontario, Canada. Area Manager: A.C. Allen.

BERMUDA

BANK OF BERMUDA, LTD.
Bank of Bermuda Building
6 Front Street, P.O. Box HM 1020
Hamilton HM AX, Bermuda
Telephone: 809-295-4000
Fax: 809-295-7093
Telex: BA 3212
Type of bank: Commercial. Established and incorporated in 1890. Member: American Bankers Association. As of June 30, 1996, total assets exceeded $8 billion.
President and CEO: Charles Vaughan-Johnson
Services: Full service banking including ATMs.

THE BANK OF N.T. BUTTERFIELD and SON, LTD.
Bank of Butterfield Building
65 Front Street, P.O. Box HM 195
Hamilton HM AX, Bermuda
Telephone: 809-295-1111
Fax: 809-949-7004
Telex: 4263 BFIELD EP
E-mail: Bntb@ilb.bm
Established in 1858 and incorporated in 1904. As of June 30, 1996, total assets were just over $4 billion. Member: American Bankers Association—Washington, D.C. US; Bank Marketing Association—Chicago, IL US.
Acting President and CEO: Scott MacDonald
Services: Full service banking including ATMs, banking by computer/modem.

BERMUDA COMMERCIAL BANK, LTD.
Bermuda Commercial Bank Building
44 Church Street, P.O. Box HM1748,
Hamilton HM GX, Bermuda
Telephone: 809-295-5678
Fax: 809-295-8091
Telex: 3336 COMBK BA
E-mail: 18092958091@faxsav.com
Incorporated in 1969 as Bermuda Provident Bank, Ltd. Name changed in 1984. Acquired by First Curacao International Bank (FCIB) in May 1993. Along with Merrill Lynch, established BCB Merrill Lynch Asset Management. Received a B/TBW-1 rating in 1995 by Thomson Bank Watch of New York.

STANDARD CHARTERED TRUST COMPANY, LTD.
P.O. Box HM 1735
Hamilton HM GX, Bermuda
Telephone: 809-295-1111
Fax: 809-295-1258
Telex: BERMUDA 3211

Type of Bank: Trust Company. Ownership: Bank of NT Butterfield and Sons, Ltd. (60%); Standard Chartered Trust Groups Holdings, Ltd. (40%).

BRITISH VIRGIN ISLANDS

VP BANK (BVI), LTD.
P.O. Box 3463, 65 Main Street, Road Town
Tortola, British Virgin Islands
Telephone: 809-494-1100
Fax: 809-494-1199
E-mail: vpbank@caribsurf.com
World Wide Web Page: http://www.vpbankbvi.com/
Wholly owned subsidiary of the VP Bank and ATU Group–Liechtenstein.
Services: Complete financial services including customized banking, accounts in all major convertible currencies, call and time deposits, money market funds and investment, foreign exchange trading, securities and precious metal trading, loans, custodian bank services, investment management services.

CAYMAN ISLANDS

ALEXANDRIA BANCORP, LTD.
P.O. Box 2064
George Town, Grand Cayman
Cayman Islands, British West Indies
Telephone: 809-945-1111
Fax: 809-945-1122
E-mail: Bancorp@CandW.KY
Subsidiaries in Tortola, St. Thomas, and Curacao. Contact: David Dobson—Trust Manager.

Services: Private banking, multi-currency accounts, trust administration, company formation and management, mutual and pension fund administration, investment management.

ALTAJIR BANK
P.O. Box 691
George Town, Grand Cayman
Cayman Islands, British West Indies
Telephone: 809-949-5628; 809-949-8562
Fax: 809-949-6339
A small private stock bank established in 1979. Contact: Rosaleen Corbin-Manager; Lillian Burger-Deputy Manager, Services. Member: Cayman Island Bankers Association. Ownership: Altajir Establishment—Liechtenstein.
Services: Personally tailored banking programs. A deposit taker for U.S. Dollar, Sterling, and Canadian Dollar accounts. Small accounts welcome.

ANSBACHER (CAYMAN) LTD.
P.O. Box 887
George Town, Grand Cayman,
Cayman Islands, British West Indies
Telephone: 809-949-8655
Fax: 809-949-7940
Telex: CP 4305
E-mail: 18099497940@faxsav.com
Contact: S. Fraser Jennings—Chief Executive; J. Bryan Bothwell-Director, Services.
Services: Private banking, trust and corporate services.

BANCO BILBAO VIZCAYA
P.O. Box 1115
George Town, Grand Cayman
Cayman Islands, British West Indies
Telephone: 809-949-7790
Fax: 809-949-9086

Telex: 4264 BRADESCO
Branch bank of a major banking/financial services provider in Spain. Contact: Enrique Arranz-Central Manager; Elias Beniflah-Deputy General Manager, Services.
Services: Full range of banking services available.

BANCO BRADESCO, S.A.
Caledonia House, 3rd Floor, Mary Street
P.O. Box 30327 SMB
George Town, Grand Cayman
Cayman Islands, British West Indies
Telephone: 809-945-1200
Fax: 809-945-1430
Telex: 4264 BIIADESCO CP
Branch office of a Brazilian bank. Contact: Joao Albino Winkelmann—Manager.
Services:
Promoting and providing support to international trade related financing.

BANCO DO ESTADO DE SAO PAULO, S.A.
The Clarion Grand Pavilion Hotel, 2nd Floor, West Bay Road
P.O. Box 1811
George Town, Grand Cayman
Cayman Islands, British West Indies
Telephone: 809-947-5144
Fax: 809-947-5153
Telex: 4296 BANESGC CP
Incorporated in Brazil, limited liability. Contact: Dorival Soares de Mello—General Manager; Odiwaldo T. Sancinetti-Manager.

BANCO DO ESTADO DO RIO GRAND DO SUL, S.A.
British American Centre, First Home Tower
P.O. Box 31499 SMB
George Town, Grand Cayman

Cayman Islands, British West Indies
Telephone: 809-949-6604
Fax: 809-949-4834
Contact: Alexandre Pedro Ronzi—General Manager.
Services: Private banking, international trade-related transactions, asset management.

BANCO ECONOMICO, S.A.
British American Centre, Building 3, 2nd Floor, Dr. Roy's Drive
P.O. Box 1112
George Town, Grand Cayman
Cayman Islands, British West Indies
Telephone: 809-945-1027
Fax: 809-949-6455
Telex: 4223 BESA CP
Contact: Andre Neeser-Manager.
Services: Deposit accounts, private banking, investment management/advisory services, trade financing, letters of credit.

BANCO PORTUGUES DO ATLANTICO
Scotia Building, 4th Floor, Cardinal Avenue
P.O. Box 30124 SMB
George Town, Grand Cayman
Cayman Islands, British West Indies
Telephone: 809-949-8322
Fax: 809-949-7743
Telex: 4283 ILEK
Local branch of largest commercial and international bank in Portugal. Contact: Alvaro Cortes—Managing Director; Valdemar B. Lopes—Deputy General Manager.
Services: Comprehensive range of corporate services and private banking services, agency representation to international banks, company incorporation and registered office services.

BANCO REAL, S.A.
Genesis Building, 3rd Floor
P.O. Box 473
George Town, Grand Cayman
Cayman Islands, British West Indies
Telephone: 809-949-8633
Fax: 809-949-8742
Established: 1974. Branch of a Brazilian bank headquartered in Sao Paulo, Brazil.
Contact: Luis Flavio Nogueira Da Silva—General Manager.
Services: Providing support for international trade financing and investments for corporate clients.

BANKAMERICA TRUST AND BANKING (CAYMAN), LTD.
Fort Street
P.O. Box 1092
George Town, Grand Cayman
Cayman Islands, British West Indies
Telephone: 809-949-7888
Fax: 809-949-7883
Telex: CP4234 BATCAYL
E-mail:18099497883@faxsav.com
Contact: Daniel Haase—Managing Director.
Services: Deposits, payments, loans, personal trust services for tax and estate planning corporate services, investment programs and management, safe custody.

BANK BALI
Micro Commerce Centre #203A, North South Road
P.O. Box 31241 SMB
George Town, Grand Cayman
Cayman Islands, British West Indies
Telephone: 809-945-2921
Fax: 809-949-6532
E-mail: 18099496532@faxsav.com

Contact: Hadi Lesmon—Vice President.
Services: Corporate finance, treasury services, commercial and syndication loans, investment fund management, guarantees.

BANK OF BERMUDA (CAYMAN), LTD.
British American Tower, 3rd Floor, Dr. Roy's Drive
P.O. Box 513
George Town, Grand Cayman
Cayman Islands, British West Indies
Telephone: 809-949-9898
Fax: 809-949-7959
Contact: Stanley G. Wright—Manager, Corporate Banking.
Services: Full range of banking services, including corporate banking services, cash management, checking accounts, computer/modem access to accounts.

BANK OF BUTTERFIELD INTERNATIONAL (CAYMAN), LTD.
Butterfield House, Fort Street
P.O. Box 705
George Town, Grand Cayman
Cayman Islands, British West Indies
Telephone: 809-949-7055
Fax: 809-949-7004
Telex: 4263 BFIELD CP
One of six clearing banks on the Cayman Islands. Branch of Bank of N.T. Butterfield and Sons, Ltd.—Bermuda. Contact: Nicholas I. Duggan, FCIB-Managing Director.
Services: Comprehensive range of personal and confidential services including trust, corporate and private banking; investment management.

BANK OF CREDIT AND COMMERCE
Int. Guiness Mahon Building
P.O. Box 1359

George Town, Grand Cayman
Cayman Islands, British West Indies
Telephone: 809-94722

THE BANK OF NOVA SCOTIA
Cardinal Avenue and Airport Industrial Park
P.O. Box 689
George Town, Grand Cayman
Cayman Islands, British West Indies
Telephone: 809-949-7666
Fax: 809-949-0020
Serving Cayman for more than 25 years. Local branch of one of North America's largest financial institutions; parent bank operates in 44 countries through 1,400 branches and offices. Contact: Colin McKie—Vice President and Manager.
Services: Complete range of personal, commercial, corporate banking services for local and international clients.

BARCLAYS BANK PLC
Cardinal Avenue
P.O. Box 68
George Town, Grand Cayman
Cayman Islands, British West Indies
Telephone: 809-949-7300
Fax: 809-949-7179
Telex: CP4219
Part of Barclays PLC Group. Contact: Clive W. Black—Managing Director.
Services: Private banking, investment management, corporate management, trusts, registered office and bank agencies.

CALEDONIA BANK AND TRUST, LTD.
Caledonian House, Ground Floor, Mary Street
P.O. Box 1043
George Town, Grand Cayman

Cayman Islands, British West Indies
Telephone: 809-949-0050
Fax: 809-949-8062
Category "A" licensed bank and trust company; licensed mutual fund administrator and insurance manager. Contact: David S. Sargison—Managing Director.
Services: Corporate, trust, and mutual fund administrative services; accounting services; registered office services.

CAYMAN INTERNATIONAL TRUST COMPANY, LTD.
Cayman International Trust Bldg., Albert Panton Street
P.O. Box 887
George Town, Grand Cayman
Cayman Islands, British West Indies
Telephone: 809-949-8655
Fax: 809-949-7946
Bank and trust company established in 1971. Ownership: Ansbacher International Trust Group. Member: Cayman Island Bankers Association.

CAYMAN NATIONAL BANK, LTD.
West Wind Building, Fort Street and Harbor Boulevard
P.O. Box 1097
George Town, Grand Cayman
Cayman Islands, British West Indies
Telephone: 809-949-4655
Fax: 809-949-7506
Commercial bank established in 1973. Ownership: Cayman National Corporation, Ltd.

CIBC BANK AND TRUST COMPANY
(CAYMAN), LTD.
Edward Street
P.O. Box 695
George Town, Grand Cayman

Cayman Islands, British West Indies
Telephone: 809-949-8666
Fax: 809-949-7904
Telex: 4222 CP
Contact: Peter H. Larder—Managing Director.
Services: Representation/management of offshore banks; fiduciary services for managed banks. Full retail banking such as term deposits, letters of credit, foreign exchange, checking and savings accounts. International trade; project finance.

DELTA BANK AND TRUST COMPANY
Genesis Building, 2nd Floor, Jennett Street
P.O. Box 706
George Town, Grand Cayman
Cayman Islands, British West Indies
Telephone: 809-949-0437
Fax: 809-949-9327
Contact: I. Henrique D. Campos, General Manager.
Services: International private banking services, money market accounts, investment portfolio management.

DEUTSCH-SÜDAMERIKANISCHE BANK AG
Anderson Square Building
P.O. Box 714
George Town, Grand Cayman
Cayman Islands, British West Indies
Telephone: 809-949-8888
Fax: 809-949-8899
Contact: Guenter Backer, Manager.
Services: Trust services, investment management services, company formation and registration.

DEXTRA BANK AND TRUST CO., LTD.
P.O. Box 2004
George Town, Grand Cayman

Cayman Islands, British West Indies
Telephone: 809-949-7844
Fax: 809-949-2795
Discount bank and trust company incorporated in Switzerland. Contact: Peter Blackman, Managing Director
Services: Investment and private banking, trustee services, estate planning/administration, company formation and administration.

FIRST CAYMAN BANK, LTD.
Thompson Building, West Bay Road
P.O. Box 1113
George Town, Grand Cayman
Cayman Islands, British West Indies
Telephone: 809-949-5266
Fax: 809-949-5398
Telex: CF4347
Contact: C.G. Watt, Manager.
Services: Personal and corporate banking, investment advisory services. Consumer, commercial, and mortgage loans. Accepts time deposits (in internationally traded currencies) at competitive rates of interest.

GUARDIAN BANK AND TRUST (CAYMAN), LTD.
Elizabethan Square, 4th Floor
P.O. Box 490
George Town, Grand Cayman
Cayman Islands, British West Indies
Telephone: 809-949-7533
Fax: 809-949-8419
Telex: 0293 4516 GUARDBK CP
Private bank. Member: Cayman Island Bankers Association, American Bankers Association.
Services: Complete private banking services for international investors.

IBT SCHRODER BANK AND TRUST COMPANY
West Wind Building, 3rd Floor
P.O. Box 1040
George Town, Grand Cayman
Cayman Islands, British West Indies
Telephone: 809-949-5566
Fax: 809-949-5409
Telex: 0293-4274
A subsidiary of the Industrial Bank of Japan–New York City, NY, US. Affiliated with the Schroder Group. Contact: Rory Heary, General Manager.
Services: Cash management services, U.S. dollar clearing, interbank deposits.

ITAU BANK, LTD.
Ansbacher House, 3rd Floor, Jennett Square
P.O. Box 1379
George Town, Grand Cayman
Cayman Islands, British West Indies
Telephone: 809-947-4175
Fax: 809-947-4185
Telex: 4284
Incorporated in the Caymans in 1992 under class "B" unrestricted banking and trust license. A wholly owned subsidiary of Banco ITAU S.A.–Brazil. Contact: Antonio Carlos Genoveze, General Manager.
Services: Offshore commercial banking services.

LLOYDS BANK INTERNATIONAL (CAYMAN), LTD.
CIBC Building, 3rd Floor
P.O. Box 857
George Town, Grand Cayman
Cayman Islands, British West Indies
Telephone: 809-949-7854
Fax: 809-949-0090

Services: Full range of international trust and private banking services; investment portfolio management; company incorporation.

MERCURY BANK AND TRUST, LTD.
Caledonian House, 3rd Floor, Mary Street
P.O. Box 2424
George Town, Grand Cayman
Cayman Islands, British West Indies
Telephone: 809-949-0800
Fax: 809-949-0295
Telex: 4331 MERCURY CP
Contact: Volker Mergenthaler, Resident Manager.
Services: Trusts, mutual fund administration, banking services, company formation.

MORGAN GREFELL (CAYMAN), LTD.
Elizabethan Square
P.O. Box 1984
George Town, Grand Cayman
Cayman Islands, British West Indies
Telephone: 809-949-8244
Fax: 809-949-8178
A wholly owned subsidiary of the Deutsche Bank Group. Contact: Andrew R. Collins, Manager.
Services: Offshore administrative services for mutual funds, banking services for international corporate clients.

MUTUAL SECURITY BANK (CAYMAN), LTD.
Caledonian House, 3rd Floor, Mary Street
P.O. Box 31120 SMB
Grand Cayman
Cayman Islands, British West Indies
Telephone: 809-949-8002
Fax: 809-949-4006
Telex: 4278 MSB

Contact: Karen Pachman.
Services: Private banking services to international private and corporate clients; formation and management of companies. Small accounts welcome.

ROYAL BANK OF CANADA
Cardinal Avenue
P.O. Box 245
George Town, Grand Cayman
Cayman Islands, British West Indies
Telephone: 809-949-4600
Fax: 809-949-7396
Telex: 4279 QBTC CP
A local branch of Canada's largest bank. Contact: H. C. Chisholm, Manager.
Services: Personal and commercial banking, trust, and investment services.

SCOTIABANK
P.O. Box 689
George Town, Grand Cayman
Cayman Islands, British West Indies
Telephone: 809-949-7666
Fax: 809-949-0020
Telex: 4330
Branch of Bank of Nova Scotia–Toronto, Ontario, Canada.

UNITED STATES TRUST COMPANY OF NEW YORK
P.O. Box 694
George Town, Grand Cayman
Cayman Islands, British West Indies
Telephone: 809-949-2126
Telex: CP254
Branch of New York City, NY, US. Branch Management: Douglas B. Gearhart. Holding Company: US Trust Corporation, New York City, NY, US.

CHANNEL ISLANDS

ANZ BANK (GUERNSEY), LTD.
Frances House, Sir Williams Place
P.O. Box 153
St. Peter Port, Guernsey, Channel Islands
Telephone: 44-1481-726148
Fax: 44-1481-714533
Telex: 4191362
World Wide Web Page: http://www.anz.com/australia/international/Guernsey/default.html
Type of bank: Joint Stock. Member: Association of Guernsey Banks; International Bankers Association of Guernsey, St. Peter Port. Ownership: Australia and New Zealand Banking Group Ltd.–Melbourne, Victoria, Australia. Management Chairman: D.G. Creasey.

BANCO BILBAO VIZCAYA
20 Grenville Street
St. Helier, Jersey, Channel Islands
Telephone: 44-1534-75148
Fax: 44-1534-34649
Telex: 4192042
Branch bank of a major banking/financial services provider in Spain.
Services: Full range of banking services available.

BANKAMERICA TRUST COMPANY (JERSEY), LTD.
Union House
Union Street, P.O. Box 120
St. Helier, Jersey, Channel Islands
Telephone: 44-534-74431
Fax: 44-534-78546
Telex: 4192017
Type of Bank: Joint Stock. Subsidiary of Bank of America National Trust and Savings Association–San Francisco, CA, US. Managing Director: Anthony M. Robinson.

BANKERS TRUST COMPANY
West House, Peter Street
St. Helier, Jersey, Channel Islands
Telephone: 44-534-22500
Telex: 4192364 BTCJERC
Branch of New York City (Manhattan), NY, US. Holding Company: Bankers Trust New York Corporation–New York City (Manhattan), NY, US.

BARCLAY'S BANK PLC (GUERNSEY), LTD.
P.O. Box 41
Le Marchant House, Le Truchot
St. Peter Port, Guernsey GY1 3BE Channel Islands
Telephone: 44 1481-723176
Local branch of Barclay's Bank–London, UK. Contact: Gordon Rhodes, Senior Manager, Offshore Corporate; Chris Bunton, Personal Sector Manager, Personal Banking International; Kay Parnell, Premier Banking Manager.
Services: Full range of services including offshore banking services, multi-currency banking, international payment service, letters of credit, cash management, trade and international services, checking. Ability to order checkbooks, statements, and other information via e-mail.

BARCLAY'S BANK PLC (JERSEY), LTD.
P.O. Box 296
29/31 The Esplanade, Victoria Road
Georgetown, Jersey JE4 Channel Islands
Telephone: 44-1534-813577
Local branch of Barclay's Bank, London, UK. Contact: Mike McQuaid, Senior Manager, Personal Banking International.
Services: See description for Barclays Bank PLC (Guernsey), Ltd.

BARCLAY'S BANK PLC (JERSEY), LTD.
P.O. Box 784
Victoria Road
Georgetown, Jersey JE4 8ZS Channel Islands
Telephone: 44-1534-812594
Local branch of Barclay's Bank–London, UK. Contact: Mike McQuaid, Senior Manager, Personal Banking International.
Services: See description for Barclays Bank PLC (Guernsey), Ltd.

BARCLAY'S BANK PLC (JERSEY), LTD.
P.O. Box 8
13 Library Place
St. Helier, Jersey JE4 8NE Channel Islands
Telephone: 44-1534-878511
Local branch of Barclay's Bank–London, UK. Contact: Graham Christmas, Director, Offshore Corporate.
Services: See description for Barclays Bank PLC (Guernsey), Ltd.

THE BRITISH BANK OF THE MIDDLE EAST
1 Grenville Street
St. Helier, Jersey, Channel Islands
Telephone: 44-1534-606511
Fax: 44-1534-606149

CHASE BANK AND TRUST COMPANY (C.I.), LTD.
Chase House
Grenville Street, P.O. Box 127
St. Helier, Jersey, JE4 8QB Channel Islands
Telephone: 44-1534-25561
Fax: 44-1534-35301
Type of bank: Joint Stock. Established: 1966; Member: Jersey Bankers Association, St. Helier. Holding Company: Chase Manhattan Overseas Banking Corporation–New York City, NY, US (100%). Management Chairman: David Gibson-Moore

CITIBANK (C.I.), LTD.
P.O. Box 104
St. Helier, Jersey, JE4 8QB Channel Islands
Telephone: 44-1534-608000
Fax: 44-1534-608290
Type of bank: Joint Stock. Established: 1968. Holding Company: Citibank NA–New York City (Manhattan), NY, US. Management Director: R.L. Mitchell.

LLOYDS BANK TRUST COMPANY (C.I.), LTD.
Waterloo House
Don Street, P.O. Box 195
St. Helier, Jersey JE4 8WZ Channel Islands
Telephone: 44-1534-22271
Fax: 44-1534-27380
Type of bank: Joint Stock. Established: 1947. Subsidiary of Lloyds Bank PIC–London, UK. Management Chairman: W.P. Plummer. Principal Correspondent: London Lloyds Bank PIC.

MIDLAND BANK INTERNATIONAL
FINANCE CORPORATION, LTD.
28/34 Hill Street
P.O. Box 26
St. Helier, Jersey JE4 8NR Channel Islands
Telephone: 534-606000
Fax: 534-606016
Telex: 4192098
Type of bank: Trust company, commercial and merchant bank. Ownership: Midland Bank PIC–London, UK. Management Chairman: S. Toker.

NATIONAL WESTMINISTER BANK
FINANCE (C.I.), LTD.
23-25 Broad Street, P.O. Box 125
St. Helier, Jersey JE4 8QG Channel Islands
Telephone: 44-534-282000
Fax: 44-534-282100

Deposit taking and mortgage finance company. Ownership: Ultimate Holding, Company, National Westminister Bank PIC, Coutts and Company Trust Holdings, Ltd.

ROYAL BANK OF CANADA (C.I.), LTD.
P.O. Box 194
19-21 Broad Street
St. Helier, Jersey, JE4 8RR Channel Islands
Telephone: 44-1534-27441
Fax: 44-1534-32513
E-mail: Info@royalbankci.com
World Wide Web Page: http://www.royalbankci.com/
Offshore trust and merchant bank. A local branch of Canada's largest bank. Ownership: Royal Trustco, Ltd.,–Toronto, Ontario, Canada (100%).
Services: Banking and deposit services, trust and company management, investment management, insurance services.

TSB BANK CHANNEL ISLANDS, LTD.
P.O. Box 597
St. Helier, Jersey JE4 8XW Channel Islands
Telephone: 44-1534-503909
Fax: 44-1534-503211
E-mail: tsbci@itl.net
World Wide Web Page: http://www.itl.net/business/ofw/Jersey/adverts/tsb/tsbc.html
Contact: John Hutchins (Banking Services); Liz Wiscombe (Investment Services).
Services: Offshore checking accounts, fixed deposit accounts, investment accounts, credit cards, personal loans.

COOK ISLANDS

ANZ AUSTRALIA AND NEW ZEALAND BANKING GROUP, LTD.

P.O. Box 907, Avarua
Rarotonga, Cook Islands
Telephone: 682-21750
Fax: 682-21760
Telex: 62038

FIRST REPUBLIC BANK, LTD.
One Harbor Road
Rarotonga, Cook Islands
Telephone: 68220514
Fax: 682-20667
Private stock company; commercial, merchant, and investment bank.

HONG KONG

AUSTRALIA AND NEW ZEALAND
BANKING GROUP, LTD.
One Exchange Square, 27th Floor
8 Connaught Place Central, Hong Kong
Telephone: 852-8437111
Fax: 852-5252475
Telex: 86019
Branch of bank in Melbourne, Victoria, Australia.

BANK OF AMERICA (ASIA), LTD.
17/F, Devon House, 979 Kings Road, Hong Kong
Telephone: 852-5972888
Fax: 852-5972500
Telex: 73471 BOFAAHK
Type of bank: Commercial. Ownership: BankAmerica Corporation–San Francisco, CA, US.

BANK OF CHINA
Bank of China Tower, 1 Garden Road Central
GPO Box 19, Hong Kong

Telephone: 852-826688
Fax: 852-8105963
Telex: 73772 BKCHI HX
Branch of bank in Beijing, China.
Services: Deposits, credit cards, general banking activities, international banking and finance activities.

THE BANK OF EAST ASIA, LTD.
10 Des Voeux Road Central
GPO Box 31, Hong Kong
Telephone: 852-8423200
Fax: 852-8459333
Telex: 73017 BEASI HX
Type of bank: Commercial bank; Joint Stock Company. Established: 1918. Member: The Hong Kong Association of Banks–Hong Kong.
Services: Worldwide banking services including investments, property development and management, asset management, corporate formation and management.

CHEKIANG FIRST BANK, LTD.
60 Gloucester Road, Wanchai and 1 Duddell Street, Central
GPO Box 691, Hong Kong
Telephone: 852-9222122
Fax: 852-8669133
Telex: 73686 HX FIRST
Type of bank: Commercial. Established: 1950. Member: Hong Kong Association of Banks. Hong Kong ownership: The Dai-Ichi Kangyo Bank, Ltd.–Tokyo, Japan (95%); Goodwood Investment, Inc. (5%).
Services: Comprehensive range of banking and related financial services, including trustee services.

CITICORP INTERNATIONAL, LTD.
36th Floor, Citicorp Court, 18 Whiefield Road, Causeway Bay

P.O. Box 74, Hong Kong
Telephone: 852-8078211
Fax: 852-8078322
Telex: HX 73243 FNCB
Type of bank: Merchant Bank and licensed deposit-taking company. Subsidiary of Citicorp International Group–Delaware, US. Member: Association of International Bond Dealers.

FIRST INTERSTATE BANK OF CALIFORNIA, LTD.
29th Floor, One Exchange Square
8 Connaught Place Central
P.O. Box 35
Telephone: 852-8443500
Fax: 852-8101113
Telex: 73052 FICAL HX
Established: 1973. Wholly owned subsidiary of First Interstate Bank of California–Los Angeles, CA, US.

HONG KONG AND SHANGHAI BANKING CORPORATION, LTD.
1 Queens Road
P.O. Box 64, Hong Kong
Telephone: 852-8221111
Fax: 852-8101112
Type of bank: Commercial. Established: 1865. Member: Hong Kong Association of Banks, Hong Kong; British Bankers Association–London, UK. Ownership: numerous shareholders, each with less than 1%.

THE HONG KONG CHINESE BANK, LTD.
Lippo Centre, 89 Queensway
P.O. Box 194, Hong Kong
Telephone: 852-8676833
Fax: 852-8459221
Telex: 73749 HONCH HX

Type of bank: Commercial. Established: 1954. Member: The Hong Kong Association of Banks–Hong Kong. Ownership: Worthen Holdings (H.K.), Ltd. (99.73%). Principal Correspondents: Tokyo Irving Trust Company Hong Kong; Hong Kong and Shanghai Banking Corporation.

KOOKMIN FINANCE ASIA, LTD. (H.K.)
Suites 309A-311, Jardine House
1 Connaught Place, Hong Kong
Telephone: 852-2530-3633
Fax: 852-2869-6650
Telex: 68015
Type of bank: Merchant Banking. A wholly-owned subsidiary of Kookmin Bank–Seoul, Korea. Managing Director: Hyung-Sa OH.
Services: Corporate banking, sydicated loans, lease financing, bond investment, bond trading, trade financing, project financing, money market operations.

MITSUI TRUST AND BANKING COMPNAY
9th Floor, Hong Kong Club Building
3A Chater Road Central, Hong Kong
Telephone: 852-5211121
Fax: 852-8459088
Telex: 82718 MTRBG HX
Local branch of bank in Tokyo, Japan.

ISLE OF MAN

BANK OF SCOTLAND (I.O.M.), LTD.
Bank of Scotland House
P.O. Box 19
Douglas, Isle of Man
Telephone: 44-1624-623074

Fax: 44-1624-625677
E-mail: bosiom@enterprise.net
World Wide Web Page: http://enterprise.net/bosiom/aboutbos.html
Local branch of Bank of Scotland; wholly-owned by Bank of Scotland.
Services: Private and business banking; checking, money market accounts and other investments.

BARCLAY'S BANK PLC (ISLE OF MAN), LTD.
P.O. Box 213
Douglas, Isle of Man IM99 1RH
Telephone: 44-1624-684444 (Personal); 44-1624-684343 (Premier)
Local branch of Barclay's Bank–London, UK. Contact: Malcolm Whetnall, Senior Account Manager, Premier International.
Services: Full range of services including offshore banking services, multi-currency banking, international payment service, letters of credit, cash management, trade and international services, checking. Ability to order checkbooks, statements, and other information via e-mail.

BARCLAY'S BANK PLC (ISLE OF MAN), LTD.
P.O. Box 9, Victoria Street
Douglas, Isle of Man
Telephone: 44-1624-682164
Local branch of Barclay's Bank–London, UK. Contact: Paul Swindale, Offshore Consultant.
Services: See description in previous listing.

CAYMANX TRUST COMPANY
34 Athol Street
Douglas, Isle of Man IM4 4NY
Telephone: 44-1624-672320
Fax: 44-1624-662192

World Wide Web Page: http://www.enterprise.net/caymanx/

Incorporated as a trust company; holds a full banking license issued by the Isle of Man Financial Supervision Commission. A wholly-owned subsidiary of Cayman National Corporation–Cayman Islands, British West Indies.

Services: Private banking, trusts, company formation and incorporation, investment management, credit cards.

NORTHERN BANK (I.O.M.), LTD.
P.O. Box 113, 49 Victoria Street
Douglas, Isle of Man IM99 1JN
Telephone: 44-1624-629106
Fax: 44-1624-627508
World Wide Web Page: http://www.northernbank.co.uk/iom.html

Member: National Australia Bank Group. Ownership: Northern Bank Group–Belfast, UK.

Services: Investment management services, trust and company services, loans, deposit accounts, checking accounts, expatriate services.

STANDARD CHARTERED BANK (I.O.M), LTD.
64 Athol Street
P.O. Box 43
Douglas, Isle of Man
Telephone: 44-624-623916
Fax: 44-624-623970
Telex: 628665 SCBIOM G

Commercial bank owned by Standard Chartered Bank–London, UK.

LIECHTENSTEIN

BANK IN LIECHTENSTEIN
Aktiengesellschaft Herrengasse 12
FL-9490 Vaduz

Fürstentum Liechtenstein
Telephone: 41-75-235-11-22
Fax: 41-75-235-15-22
Telex: 889222
Type of bank: Commercial and Merchant. Established: 1920. Member: Liechtenstein Bankers Association and Swiss Bankers Association. Ownership: Prince of Liechtenstein Foundation (99.7%). Management Chairman: Christian Norgren, President. General Manager: Dr. Egmond Frommelt.
Services: Domestic and international credit and lending services including mortgages, foreign exchange, money markets, securities dealings and administration, portfolio management, investment counseling.

CENTRUM BANK AG
9490 Vaduz, Liechtenstein
Telephone: 41-75-235-85-85
Fax: 41-75-235-86-86
Telex: 889203

LIECHTENSTEINISCHE LANDESBANK
Stadtle 44
P.O. Box 384
9490 Vaduz, Liechtenstein
Telephone: 41-75-236-88-11
Fax: 41-75-236-88-22
Telex: 889400
World Wide Web Page: http://www.bodan.net/llb/index.html
Universal Bank. Established: 1861; Member: Swiss Bankers Association, Liechtenstein Bankers Association. Ownership: Liechtenstein Government. Management Chairman: Andreas Vogt.
Services: Financial and custodial services, investment transactions, credit and lending, money markets and other investments, portfolio management.

NEUE BANK AG
9490 Vaduz, Liechtenstein
Telephone: 41-75-236-08-08
Fax: 41-75-232-92-60
Telex: 889444

VERWALTUNGS-UND PRIVAT-BANK AKTIENGESELLSCHAFT
P.O. Box 885
FL-9490 Vaduz, Liechtenstein
Telephone: 41-75-235-66-55
Fax: 41-75-235-65-00
Telex: 889200
Type of bank: Commercial and Merchant. Established: 1956. Member: Liechtenstein Bankers Association, Swiss Bankers Association, Association of Swiss Stock Exchanges. Ownership: More than 700 shareholders, mainly in Liechtenstein.
General Manager: Dr. H. Heinz Batliner
Services: Domestic and foreign lending, money market transactions, deposits, portfolio management, precious metals trading.

LUXEMBOURG

ABN-AMRO BANK
4 rue Jean Monnet
L-2180 Luxembourg-Kirchberg, Luxembourg
Telephone: 352-42-49-49-42
Fax: 352-42-49-49-498

BANQUE DE LUXEMBOURG
80 Place de la Gare
P.O. Box 2221
L-1022 Luxembourg City, Luxembourg

Telephone: 352-499241
Fax: 352-494820
Telex: 2449BLLUXLU
Type of bank: Private Stock. Established: 1937. Member: Association des Banques et Banquiers, Luxembourg. Ownership: Credit Industriel d'Alsace et de Lorraine, Deutsche Bank Compagnie Financiere, Deutsche Bk Saar AG.

BANQUE GENERALE DU LUXEMBOURG
14 Rue Aldringen/27 Avenue Monterey
L-2951 Luxembourg City, Luxembourg
Telephone: 352-47991
Fax: 352-4799-2579
Telex: 3401 bgl lu
Type of bank: Commercial. Established: 1919; Member: Association des Banques et Banquiers, Association des Banques et Banquiers Luxembourgeois, Luxembourg. Ownership: Generale Bank NV Brussels (44%); Luxembourg Public Ownership.
Services: Checking and savings accounts, foreign exchange and depository transactions, security dealings, portfolio management, lending, investment advice.

BANQUE INTERNATIONALE A LUXEMBOURG
2 Boulevard Royal
P.O. Box 2205
L-2953 Luxembourg City, Luxembourg
Telephone: 352-45901
Fax: 352-4590-2010
Telex: 36265 Bil lu
Type of bank: Commercial. Established: 1856; Member: Association des Banques et Banquiers Luxembourg, Associated Banks of Europe–Brussels, Belgium. Ownership: Groupe Bruxelle Lambert SA (20%), Pargesa SA (20%). Principal Correspondents: Boston–First National Bank of Boston; Brussels–BBL-BK Brussels

Lambert SA. Rated by Moody's (1995): bank deposit rating: Aa3/P-1; financial strength rating:B.

Services: Foreign exchange and money market transactions, portfolio management, precious metals trading, securities dealing, project and international trade financing, letters of credit, life insurance, loan syndication.

BANQUE PARIBAS (LUXEMBOURG) SA
IOA Boulevard Royal
P.O. Box 51
L-2010 Luxembourg City, Luxembourg
Telephone: 352-46461
Fax: 352-46464141
Telex: 2253

Type of bank: Commercial. Established: 1964; Member: Association des Banques et Banquiers, Luxembourg. Ownership: Groupe Paribas–Paris, France. Management Chairman: Georges Bettermann. Principal Correspondents: Brussels–Banque Paribas Belgium; New York–Manufacturers Hanover Trust Company.

Services: Checking and savings accounts, foreign exchange and deposit transactions, investment fund management, asset management, money market transactions, fiduciary representation.

CHASE MANHATTAN BANK LUXEMBOURG SA
47 Boulevard Royal
P.O. Box 240
L-2012 Luxembourg City, Luxembourg
Telephone: 352-4626851
Fax: 352-24590
Telex: 1233 LU

Type of bank: Joint Stock. Established: 1973; Member: Association des Banques et Banquiers, International Bankers Club, American Bankers Club–Luxembourg. Ownership: Chase Manhattan Overseas Corporation

(100%). Management Chairman: David Gibson-Moore. Principal Correspondents: Brussels–Chase Manhattan Bank.

INTERNATIONAL TRADE AND
INVESTMENT BANK S.A.
22-24 Boulevard Royal
P.O. Box 320
L-2013 Luxembourg City, Luxembourg
Telephone: 352-226004
Fax: 352-462829
Telex: 1350
Type of bank: Commercial. Established: 1973; Member: Association des Banques et Banquiers, Luxembourg. Ownership: Middle East Financial Group Holding S.A. (100%). Management Chairman: Khalid Salim bin Mahfooz.

KOOKMIN BANK LUXEMBOURG, S.A.
11A, Boulevard Prince Henri
L-1724 Luxembourg City, Luxembourg
Telephone: 352-466555
Fax: 352-466566
Telex: 60130
Type of bank: Merchant Banking. A wholly owned subsidiary of Kookmin Bank–Seoul, Korea. Managing Director: Soon-Ho KIM
Services: Corporate banking, sydicated loans, lease financing, bond investment, bond trading, trade financing, project financing, money market operations.

UNION BANK OF FINLAND INTERNATIONAL S.A.
189 Avenue de la Faiencerie
P.O. Box 569
L-2015 Luxembourg City, Luxembourg
Telephone: 352-4776111
Fax: 352-477611251

Telex: 1575 UBFIN LU

Type of bank: Merchant. Established: 1976; Member: Association des Banques et Banquiers, Luxembourg. Ownership: Union Bank of Finland, Ltd.–Helsinki, Finland (100%). Management Chairman: Kari Kangas. Director Chairman: Ahti Hirvonen.

PANAMA

ABN AMRO BANK, NV
Calle Manual Maria Lcasa (4)
Apoartado Postal 10147
Panama City, Panama
Telephone: 507-63-6200
Fax: 507-69-0526
Telex: 2644

Branch of bank in Amsterdam, Netherlands. Branch Manager: P.H. Scharringa. Head Office Chairman: R. Hazelhoff. International Department: J. J. Oyevaar, General Manager.

BANCO DE SANTA CRUZ DE LA SIERRA
(PANAMA) S.A.
Avda Samuel Lewis, Edif Torre Bco Union, 11th Floor
Apartado Postal 6-4416 (El Dorado)
Panama City, Panama
Telephone: 507-63-8477
Fax: 507-63-8404
Telex: 2613 BSCSAPG

Type of bank: Commercial. Established: 1980. Member: Panama Banking Association–Panama City. Ownership: Sociedad de Inversiones Santa Cruz de la Sierra, SA, Panama City; Banco de Santa Cruz de la Sierra, SA, Santa Cruz, Bolivia. President: Juan Manuel Parada. General Manager: Luis Saavedra B. Principal

Correspondents: Buenos Aires–Banco de la Provincia de Buenos Aires; New York–American Express; International–Chemical Bank, National Westminster Bank.

BANCO POPULAR DEL ECUADOR (PANAMA), SA
Calle 51 Bella Vista;
Apartado Postal 6-1061 (El Dorado)
Panama City, Panama
Telephone: 507-69-5587
Telex: 2872 BANPOPAN PG
Type of bank: Commercial. Established: 1981. MemberAssociation Bancaria de Panama–Panama City. Ownership: Banco Popular del Ecuador–Quito, Ecuador. Management Chairman: Francisco Rosales Ramos. General Manager: Incolas Landes. Principal Correspondents: New York–Chase Manhattan Bank, NA; Quito–Banco Popular del Ecuador.

BANK OF AMERICA NATIONAL TRUST AND SAVINGS ASSOCIATION
Edificio Bank of America, Calle 50 y Calle 53
Apartado Aero 7282 (5)
Panama City, Panama
Telephone: 507-69-5971
Fax: 507-69-3727
Telex: 2756 BNKAMER PG
Branch of bank in San Francisco, CA, US. Manager: Roberto Anguizola, Vice President.

BANK OF NOVA SCOTIA
Edif Bonanza, Calle Manuel Maria Icaza, Campo Alegre
Apartado Postal 7327 (5 R.P.)
Panama City, Panama
Telephone: 507-63-6255
Fax: 507-63-8636
Telex: 2073/3266

Branch of bank in Toronto, Ontario, Canada. Manager: M. J. Gonzalez-Delgado.

CHASE MANHATTAN BANK, N.A.
120 via Espana
Apartado Postal 9A-76
Panama City, Panama
Telephone: 507-63-6972
Fax: 507-63-4432
Branch of bank in New York City (Manhattan), NY, US. Manager: Luis H. Moreno, Jr.

FIRST NATIONAL BANK OF BOSTON
Edif Banco de Boston, Via Espana
Apartado Postal 5368 (5)
Panama City, Panama
Telephone: 507-64-2244
Fax: 507-64-7402
Telex: BOSBANK PG
Branch of bank in Boston, MA, US. Holding Company: Bank of Boston Corporation–Boston, MA, US. Branch Manager: Luiz Navarro. Head Office Chairman: Ira Stepanian, CEO. President: Charles K. Gifford.

UNION BANK OF SWITZERLAND (PANAMA), INC.
Edif UBS, Calles 50 y 56
Apartado Postal 6792 (5)
Panama City, Panama
Telephone: 507-63-9766
Fax: 507-63-8437
Telex: 2645 UBSPG
Type of bank: Commercial. Established: 1975. Member: Association Bancaria de Panama–Panama City. Ownership: Union Bank of Switzerland–Zurich, Switzerland. General Management: Werner P. Luthi. Principal Correspondents: Miami–Northern Trust International; New York–Irving Trust Company.

SINGAPORE

ABN AMRO BANK, NV
18 Church Street #03-01 OCBC Center South
Singapore City 0104 Singapore
Telephone: 65-5355511
Fax: 65-5323108
Telex: RS 24396
Merchant bank. Branch of bank in Amsterdam, Netherlands. Branch Managers: J. Slotema, H. J. Buss. Head Office Chairman: R. Hazelhoff. General Management: J. J. Oyevaar.

BANK OF NOVA SCOTIA
10 Colyer Quay, #15-01
Ocean Building
Singapore City 0104 Singapore
Telephone: 65-5358688
Fax: 65-5322240
Branch of bank in Toronto, Ontario, Canada. Branch Manager: A. Von Hahn. Head Office Chairman: C. E. Ritchie, CEO.

FIRST NATIONAL BANK OF BOSTON
20 Collyer Quay #16-00
P.O. Box 2900
Singapore City 9048 Singapore
Telephone: 65-2962366
Fax: 65-2960998
Telex: 23689 BOSTNBK
Branch of bank in Boston, MA, US. Holding Company: Bank of Boston Corporation–Boston, MA, US.

KOOKMIN BANK SINGAPORE, LTD.
6 Battery Road, Standard Chartered Bank Building
#17-03/04
Singapore City 0104 Singapore

Telephone: 65-227-3566
Fax: 65-227-9598
Type of bank: Merchant Banking. A wholly-owned subsidiary of Kookmin Bank–Seoul, Korea. Managing Director: Nam-Taek KIM.
Services: Corporate banking, syndicated loans, lease financing, bond investment, bond trading, trade financing, project financing, money market operations.

OVERSEA-CHINESE BANKING
CORPORATION, LTD.
65 Chulia Street, #08-00, OCBC Centre
P.O. Box 548
Singapore City 9010 Singapore
Telephone: 65-5357222
Fax: 65-5337955
Type of bank: Commercial. Established: 1932. Member: Association of Banks in Singapore. Management Chairman: Teo Cheng Guan, CEO. Directors: Choi Siew Hong. Principal Correspondents: London–Midland Bank PIC; New York–Chase Manhattan Bank; Tokyo–The Fuji Bank Ltd., Mitsubishi Bank, Sanwa Bank, Ltd.

OVERSEAS UNION BANK, LTD.
1 Raffles Place, OUB Center
Singapore City 0104 Singapore
Telephone: 65-5338686
Fax: 65-5332293
Type of bank: Commercial. Established: 1947. Member: Association of Banks in Singapore. Principal Correspondents: Hong Kong–Hong Kong and Shanghai Banking Corporation; Tokyo–Dai-Ichi Kangyo Bank, Ltd.

TAT LEE BANK, LTD.
63 Market Street, Tat Lee Bank Building
P.O. Box 5099, Robinson Road Post Office
Singapore City 0104 Singapore

Telephone: 65-5339292
Fax: 65-5331043
Type of bank: Commercial. Established: 1973. Member: Association of Banks in Singapore. Ownership: Publicly owned. Management Chairman: Goh Tjoei Kok. Principal Correspondents: Hong Kong–Standard Chartered Bank; Tokyo–Baiwa Bank, Ltd.

SWITZERLAND

ABN AMRO BANK (SUISSE)
12 Quai General-Guisan
P.O. Box 3026
CH-1211/3 Geneva, Switzerland
Telephone: 41-22-311-66-44
Fax: 41-22-311-72-09
Ownership: ABN AMRO Bank NV–Amsterdam, Netherlands

BANCO BILBAO VIZCAYA (SCHWEIZ) AG
Todistrasse 60, P.O. Box 1024
CH-8039 Zurich, Switzerland
Telephone: 41-1-202-65-00
Fax: 41-1-201-30-08
Type of Bank: Commercial and Investment. Established: 1984. Ownership: Banco Bilbao, Spain (100%). Management Chairman: Emilo De Ybarra.

BANK HOFMANN AG ZURICH
Talstrasse 27
CH-8001 Zurich, Switzerland
Telephone: 41-1-217-51-11
Fax: 41-1-211-73-68
Telex: 813485
Type of Bank: Commercial and Stock Exchange. Established: 1897. Member: Swiss Bankers' Association–Basel; Zurich Stock Exchange–Zurich. Ownership:

Leu Holding AG–Zug, Switzerland (100%). Principal Correspondents: London–Barclays Bank PIC; New York–Chase Manhattan Bank, Citibank, Credit Suisse, Irving Trust Company, Morgan Guaranty Trust Company.

CHASE MANHATTAN BANK (SWITZERLAND) SA
63 Rue du Rhone
P.O. Box 257
CH-1211/3 Geneva, Switzerland
Telephone: 41-22-35-35-55
Fax: 41-22-36-24-30
Telex: 28121
Type of Bank: Commercial. Established: 1969. Member: Swiss Bankers' Association–Basel; Association of Foreign Banks in Switzerland–Zurich. Holding Company: Chase Manhattan Overseas Banking Corporation. Management Chairman: Robert D. Hunter. General Manager: William M. Rowan.

CITIBANK, N.A.
16 Quai General Guisan
P.O. Box 162
CH-1204 Geneva, Switzerland
Telephone: 41-22-20-55-11
Fax: 41-22-28-85-17
Telex: 823920
Branch of bank in New York City (Manhattan), NY, US.

HABIB BANK AG ZURICH
Bergstrasse 21
P.O. Box 4931
CH-8022 Zurich, Switzerland
Telephone: 41-1-252-43-30
Fax: 41-1-252-43-75
Telex: 815151 HBZZ CH
Type of Bank: Commercial. Established: 1967. Member: Swiss Bankers' Association–Basel; Association of For-

eign Banks in Switzerland–Zurich. Management Chairman: Richard Schait. General Management: Hyder B. Habib. Principal Correspondents: Amsterdam, London–Habib Bank AG Zurich.

KREDIETBANK (SUISSE) S.A.
7 Blvd. Georges-Favon
P.O. Box 334
CH-121/1 Geneva, Switzerland
Telephone: 41-22-311-63-22
Fax: 41-22-311-54-43
Telex: 427303
Type of Bank: Commercial. Established: 1970. Member: Swiss Bankers' Association–Basel; Association of Foreign Banks in Switzerland–Zurich. Ownership: Kredietbank S.A. Luxembourgeoise, Luxembourg. Management Chairman: Jean L. Blondel.

ZURCHER KANTONAL BANK
Bahnhofstrasse 9
P.O. Box 4039
CH-8010 Zurich, Switzerland
Telephone: 41-1-220-11-11
Fax: 41-1-221-15-25
Telex: 812140
Type of Bank: State-owned Universal Bank. Established: 1869. Member: Swiss Bankers' Association, Association of Assis Cantonal Banks. Ownership: Canton of Zurich (100%).

VANUATU

EUROPEAN BANK, LTD.
International Building, Kumul Highway
P.O. Box 301
Port Vila, Vanuatu

Telephone: 678-24106
Fax: 678-23405
Telex: 7711022
Type of Bank: State-owned Universal Bank. Established: 1869. Member: Swiss Bankers' Association, Association of Assis Cantonal Banks. Ownership: Canton of Zurich (100%).

POWER OF ATTORNEY

I/We the undersigned (please print) ______________________________

residing at ____

____

hereby grant ______________________ (hereinafter called "the Bank") full powers with a view to represent me/us validly within the limitations of the following provisions:

1. The Bank is authorized to dispose, on behalf of the principal(s), of the securities and assets whatsoever of the undersigned principal(s), lodged with the bank, insofar as these deposits and assets may be increased or reduced as a result of purchases, sales or conversions of securities, and for this purpose any possible subscription rights may be exercised or sold at best.
2. The Bank is furthermore authorized, in a general manner, to do everything it will deem necessary or appropriate for the management of the assets lodged with the Bank.
3. However, the Bank is not authorized to carry out, in any way whatsoever, any withdrawals of all or part of the funds and securities deposited or to pledge the assets and securities in question; nor is it empowered to order bonuses, except when these are destined for taking over securities of an equivalent amount.
4. The principal(s) expressly approve(s), and they/he do(es) so in advance, all acts of management or abstentions of the Bank and recognize(s) that the bank does not assume any responsibility whatsoever for the consequences of the transactions which the Bank, acting in good faith, will have made or will have abstained from making. In addition, the principal(s) undertake(s) to compensate the Bank for any expenses or damages it might have incurred on account of this power of attorney.
5. The power of attorney will remain valid until and unless revoked in writing.
6. It is expressly agreed that this power of attorney will not become void upon the death or loss of exercise of the civil rights of the principal(s), but will continue in full effect.
7. The parties agree that the constitution and validity of this power of attorney are governed by the laws of the jurisdiction in which the Bank is domiciled and that transactions carried out by virtue of said power of attorney will be judged in accordance with such laws. Any litigations between the parties will be brought before the competent courts of said jurisdiction. The Bank, however, is authorized to assert its claims at the legal domicile of the principal(s).

Signed at this place: ______________________________

And on this date: ______________________________

By the principal(s): ______________________________
(signature)

____
(signature)

Account No.: ______________________________

Application for Opening of Account

I/We request you to open an account with the following specifications (mark if applicable):

☐ Individual Account
☐ Joint Account
☐ Corporate Account

☐ Current Account
☐ Deposit Account
☐ Managed Portfolio, Type ___________

☐ In Swiss Francs (Sfr)
☐ In U.S. Dollars (U.S.$)
☐ In German Marks (DM)
☐ Other ___________

Personal Information (Please Print or Type):

Family Name(s)
or Company Name ___________________________

First Name(s) ___________________________

Street and No. ___________________________

City, State, Zip Code ___________________________

Country ___________________________

Nationality ___________________________

Occupation or Type of Business ___________________________

Date of Birth or
Company Formation ___________________________

Telephone No.: ___________ Telex No.: ___________

Correspondence Is to Be:
☐ Retained at the bank and forwarded only on special request
☐ Forwarded regularly to the following address (if different from above): ______

____

Initial Deposit in the Amount of
☐ Is Enclosed ☐ Will Be Mailed Separately
☐ Will Be Wire Transferred Through (Bank Name): ___________

Place: ___________ ___________
(Signature)

Date: ___________ ___________
(Signature)

Department of the Treasury
TD F 90-22.1 10/92
SUPERSEDES ALL PREVIOUS EDITIONS

REPORT OF FOREIGN BANK AND FINANCIAL ACCOUNTS

For the calendar year 19

Do not file this form with your Federal Tax Return

Form Approved: OMB No. 1505-0063
Expiration Date: 9/95

This form should be used to report financial interest in or signature authority or other authority over one or more bank accounts, securities accounts, or other financial accounts in foreign countries as required by Department of the Treasury Regulations (31 CFR 103). You are not required to file a report if the aggregate value of the accounts did not exceed $10,000. Check all appropriate boxes. SEE INSTRUCTIONS ON BACK FOR DEFINITIONS. File this form with Dept. of the Treasury, P.O. Box 32621, Detroit, MI 48232.

1. Name (Last, First, Middle)

2. Social security number or employer identification number if other than individual

3. Name in item 1 refers to
☐ Individual
☐ Partnership
☐ Corporation
☐ Fiduciary

4. Address (Street, City, State, Country, ZIP)

5. ☐ I had signature authority over one or more foreign accounts, but had no 'financial interest' in such accounts (see Instruction J.) Indicate for these accounts:

(a) Name and social security number or taxpayer identification number of each owner ______

(b) Address of each owner ______

(Do not complete item 9 for these accounts)

6. ☐ I had a 'financial interest' in one or more foreign accounts owned by a domestic corporation, partnership or trust which is required to file TD F 90-22.1 (See Instruction L). Indicate for these accounts.

(a) Name and taxpayer identification number of each such corporation, partnership or trust ______

(b) Address of each such corporation, partnership or trust ______

(Do not complete item 9 for these accounts)

7. ☐ I had a 'financial interest' in one or more foreign accounts, but the total maximum value of these accounts (see instruction I) did not exceed $10,000 at any time during the year. (If you checked this box, do not complete item 9).

8. ☐ I had a 'financial interest' in 25 or more foreign accounts. (If you checked this box, do not complete item 9.)

9. If you had a 'financial interest' in one or more but fewer than 25 foreign accounts which are required to be reported, and the total maximum value of the accounts exceeded $10,000 during the year (see instruction I), write the total number of those accounts in the box below: ☐
Complete items (a) through (f) below for one of the accounts and attach a separate TD F 90-22.1 for each of the others.
Items 1, 2, 3, 9, and 10 must be completed for each account.
Check here if this is an attachment. ☐

(a) Name in which account is maintained

(b) Name of bank or other person with whom account is maintained

(c) Number and other account designation, if any

(d) Address of office or branch where account is maintained

(e) Type of account. (If not certain of English name for the type of account, give the foreign language name and describe the nature of the account. Attach additional sheets if necessary.)

☐ Bank Account ☐ Securities Account ☐ Other (specify)

(f) Maximum value of account (see instruction I)

☐ Under $10,000 ☐ $10,000 to $50,000 ☐ $50,000 to $100,000 ☐ Over $100,000

10. Signature

11. Title (Not necessary if reporting a personal account)

12. Date

PRIVACY ACT NOTIFICATION

Pursuant to the requirements of Public Law 93-579, (Privacy Act of 1974), notice is hereby given that the authority to collect information on TD 90-22.1 in accordance with 5 U.S.C. 552(e)(3) is Public Law 91-508; 31 U.S.C. 1121; 5 U.S.C. 301, 31 CFR Part 103.

The principal purpose for collecting the information is to assure maintenance of reports and records where such reports or records have a high degree of usefulness in criminal, tax, or regulatory investigations or proceedings. The information collected may be provided to those officers and employees of any constituent unit of the Department of the Treasury who have a need for the records in the performance of their duties. The records may be referred to any other department or agency of the Federal Government upon the request of the head of such department ore agency for use in a criminal, tax, or regulatory investigation of proceeding.

Disclosure of the information is mandatory. Civil and criminal penalties, including under certain circumstances a fine of not more than $500,000 and imprisonment of not more than five years, are provided for failure to file a report, supply information, and for filing a false or fraudulent report.

Disclosure of the social security number is mandatory. The authority to collect this number is 31 CFR 103. The social security number will be used as a means to identify the individual who files the report.

STF FED7869F

INSTRUCTIONS

A. Who Must File a Report Each - United States person who has a financial interest in or signature authority or other authority over bank, securities, or other financial accounts in a foreign country, which exceeds $10,000 in aggregate value at any time during the calendar year, must report that relationship each calendar year by filing TD F 90-22.1 with the Department of the Treasury on or before June 30, of the succeeding year.

An officer or employee of a commercial bank which is subject to the supervision of the Comptroller of the Currency, the Board of Governors of the Federal Reserve System, or the Federal Deposit Insurance Corporation need not report that he has signature or other authority over a foreign bank, securities or other financial account maintained by the bank unless he has a personal financial interest in the account.

In addition, an officer or employee of a domestic corporation whose securities are listed upon national securities exchanges or which has assets exceeding $1 million and 500 or more shareholders of record need not file such a report concerning his signature authority over a foreign financial account of the corporation, if he has no personal financial interest in the account and has been advised in writing by the chief financial officer of the corporation that the corporation has filed a current report which includes that account.

B. United States Person - The term 'United States person' means (1) a citizen or resident of the United States, (2) a domestic partnership, (3) a domestic corporation, or (4) a domestic estate or trust.

C. When and Where to File - This report shall be filed on or before June 30 each calendar year with the Department of the Treasury, Post Office Box 32621, Detroit, MI 48232, or it may be hand carried to any local office of the Internal Revenue Service for forwarding to the Department of the Treasury, Detroit, MI.

D. Account in a Foreign Country - A 'foreign country' includes all geographical areas located outside the United States, Guam, Puerto Rico, and the Virgin Islands.

Report any account maintained with a bank (except a military banking facility as defined in instruction E) or broker or dealer in securities that is located in a foreign country, even if it is a part of a United States bank or other institution. Do not report any account maintained with a branch, agency, or other office of a foreign bank of other institution that is located in the United States, Guam, Puerto Rico, and the Virgin Islands.

E. Military Banking Facility - Do not consider as an account in a foreign country, an account in an institution known as a 'United States military banking facility' (or 'United States military finance facility') operated by a United States financial institution designated by the United States Government to serve U.S. Government installations abroad, even if the United States military banking facility is located in a foreign country.

F. Bank, Financial Account - The term 'bank account' means a savings, demand, checking, deposit, loan or any other account maintained with a financial institution or other person engaged in the business of banking. It includes certificates of deposit.

The term 'securities account' means an account maintained with a financial institution or other person who buys, sells, holds, or trades stock or other securities for the benefit of another.

The term 'other financial account' means any other account maintained with a financial institution or other person who accepts deposits, exchanges or transmits funds, or acts as a broker or dealer for future transactions in any commodity on (or subject to the rules of) a commodity exchange or association.

G. Financial Interest - A financial interest in a bank, securities, or other financial account in a foreign country means an interest described in either of the following two paragraphs:

(1) A United States person has a financial interest in each account for which such person is the owner of records or has legal title, whether the account is maintained for his or her own benefit or for the benefit of others including non-United States persons. If an account is maintained in the name of two persons jointly, or if several persons each own a partial interest in an account, each of those United States persons has a financial interest in that account.

(2) A United States person has a financial interest in each bank, securities, or other financial account in a foreign country for which the owner of record or holder of legal title is: (a) a person acting as an agent, nominee, attorney, or in some other capacity on behalf of the U.S. person; (b) a corporation in which the United States person owns directly or indirectly more than 50 percent of the total value of shares of stock; (c) a partnership in which the United States person owns an interest in more than 50 percent of the profits (distributive share of income); or (d) a trust in which the United States person either has a present beneficial interest in more than 50 percent of the assets or from which such person receives more than 50 percent of the current income.

H. Signature or Other Authority Over an Account -

Signature Authority - A person has signature authority over an account if such person can control the disposition of money or other property in it by delivery of a document containing his or here signature (or his or her signature and that of one or more other persons) to the bank or other person with whom the account is maintained.

Other authority exists in a person who can exercise comparable power over an account by direct communication to the bank or other person with whom the account is maintained, either orally or by some other means.

I. Account Valuation - For items 7, 9, and Instruction A, the maximum value of an account is the largest amount of currency and non-monetary assets that appear on any quarterly or more frequent account statement issued for the applicable year. If periodic account statements are not so issued, the maximum account asset value is the largest amount of currency and non-monetary assets in the account at any time during the year. Convert foreign currency by using the official exchange rate at the end of the year. In valuing currency of a country that uses multiple exchange rates, use the rate which would apply if the currency in the account were converted into United States dollars at the close of the calendar year.

The value of stock, other securities or other non-monetary assets in an account reported on TD F 90-22.1 is the fair market value at the end of the calendar year, or if withdrawn from the account, at the time of the withdrawal.

For purposes of items 7, 9, and Instruction A, if you had a financial interest in more than one account, each account is to be valued separately in accordance with the foregoing two paragraphs.

If you had a financial interest in one or more but fewer than 25 accounts, and you are unable to determine whether the maximum value of these accounts exceeded $10,000 at any time during the year, check item 9 (do not check item 7) and complete Item 9 for each of these accounts.

J. United States Persons with Authority Over but No Interest in an Account - Except as provided in Instruction A and the following paragraph, you must state the name, address, and identifying number of each owner of an account over which you had authority, but if you check item 5 for more than one account of the same owner, you need identify the owner only once.

If you check item 5 for one or more accounts in which no United States person had a financial interest, you may state on the first line of this item, in lieu of supplying information about the owner, 'No U.S. person had any financial interest in the foreign accounts.' This statement must be based upon the actual belief of the person filing this form after he or she has taken reasonable measures to endure its correctness.

If you check item 5 for accounts owned by a domestic corporation and its domestic and/or foreign subsidiaries, you may treat them as one owner and write in the space provided, the name of the parent corporation, followed by 'and related entities,' and the identifying number and address of the parent corporation.

K. Consolidated Reporting - A corporation which owns directly or indirectly more than 50 percent interest in one or more other entities will be permitted to file a consolidated report on TD F 90-22.1, on behalf of itself and such other entities provided that a listing of them is made part of the consolidated report. Such reports should be signed by an authorized official of the parent corporation.

If the group of entities covered by a consolidated report has a financial interest in 25 or more foreign financial accounts, the reporting corporation need only note that fact on the form, it will, however, be required to provide detailed information concerning each account when so requested by the Secretary or his delegate.

L. Avoiding Duplicate Reporting - If you had financial interest (as defined in instruction G(2)(b), (c) or (d) in one or more accounts which are owned by a domestic corporation, partnership or trust which is required to file TD F 90-22.1 with respect to these accounts in lieu of completing item 9 for each account you may check item 6 and provide the required information.

M. Providing Additional Information - Any person who does not complete item 9, shall when requested by the Department of the Treasury provide the information called for in item 9.

N. Signature (Item 10) - This report must be signed by the person named in Item 1. If the report is being filed on behalf of a partnership, corporation, or fiduciary, it must be signed by an authorized individual.

O. Penalties - For criminal penalties for failure to file a report, supply information, and for filing a false or fraudulent report see 31 U.S.C. 5322(a), 31 U.S.C. 5322(b), and 18 U.S.C. 1001.

The estimated average burden associated with this collection of information is 10 minutes per respondent or recordkeeper depending on individual circumstances. Comments concerning the accurancy of this burden estimate and suggestions for reducing the burden should be directed to the Department of the Treasury, Office of Financial Enforcement, Room 5000 Treasury Annex Building, Washington DC 200220, and to the Office of Management and Budget, Paperwork Reduction Project (1505-0063), Washington DC 20503.

INDEX

How Much Is Your Business Worth?

A Step-by-Step Guide to Selling and Ensuring The Maximum Sale Value of Your Business

U.S. $29.95
Can. $40.95
ISBN: 0-7615-0432-X
hardcover / 320 pages

Frederick D. Lipman

Selling a business can be exciting and profitable, but it can also be slow, difficult, and loaded with pitfalls. In this comprehensive handbook to selling a business, corporate attorney Frederick D. Lipman shows you how to conduct the sale smoothly and profitably, from strategically positioning your company's assets to finalizing the perfect deal.

You'll learn how to:

- Establish the true value of your business
- Market your business discreetly and find a buyer
- Work with attorneys and investment bankers
- Minimize taxes on the sale proceeds
- And much more!

Going Public

Everything You Need to Know to Turn Private Enterprise into a Publicly Traded Company

U.S. $20.00
Can. $26.95
ISBN: 0-7615-0840-6
paperback / 400 pages

Frederick D. Lipman

This highly acclaimed, groundbreaking book details everything you need to successfully implement your initial public offering (IPO) and grow your business by founding a public company.

You'll learn how to:

- Learn the advantages and disadvantages of going public
- Develop a five-year advance plan
- Select the best underwriter for your company's needs
- Register and market your IPO
- Implement self-underwriting, "do-it-yourself," and SCOR offerings
- Qualify your stock for trading on stock and securities exchanges
- And many more specifics!

To order books, call 800-632-8676

Corporate Espionage

What It Is, Why It's Happening in Your Company, What You Must Do About It

Ira Winkler

U.S. $26.00
Can. $34.95
ISBN: 0-7615-0840-6
hardcover / 384 pages

Are your documents and your company vulnerable to prying eyes? In business, information can make the difference between success and failure.

Lose a trade secret to a competitor, and you lose the edge your product had. Lose a client list, and you lose the account. Lose too much, and you're out of business. Learn how to bulletproof your business from former National Security Agency expert Ira Winkler. If your company has any information of value, you can't afford to ignore the lessons in this fascinating book.

Last Chance Financial Planning Guide

It's Not Too Late to Plan for Your Retirement If You Start Now

Anthony E. Spare
with Paul Ciotti

U.S. $15.00
Can. $19.95
ISBN: 0-7615-0836-8
paperback / 240 pages

In this clear-eyed, upbeat book, financial advisor Tony Spare shows you how to ensure a worry-free retirement by investing in unloved, unappreciated "cheap" stocks. You'll learn how to cope with the coming Social Security shortfall, plan your retirement, build your portfolio, and ferret out those humble but high-returning stocks that conventional wisdom overlooks.

To order books, call 800-632-8676